ENDORSEMENTS

Are you suppressing youthfι _____ ιse you don't know how to reverse your sι

What if your internal biologic _____ ᴜack in a way that you could restore your ᴡ _____ ᴜ.ιιties to satisfy your sexual fantasies of adolescence?

Up until now, sexual dysfunction and loss of desire were considered irreversible consequences of normal aging. The problem is intensified by the misconception amongst the aged that great sex is reserved only for the young. The reality is that findings from hundreds of published scientific studies reveal that the age-related decline in sexual activity is largely reversible.

What makes this opportunity even more compelling is that the steps you follow to regain youthful sexual desire, performance, and gratification will simultaneously help to protect you against the most common degenerative diseases of aging, contributing to overall health.

For 29 consecutive years, the Life Extension Foundation has uncovered novel approaches to delay and often reverse the effects that aging inflicts on the human body. What had never been done before was assemble the numerous tidbits of medical data into a comprehensive program as has been done so thoroughly in the book *Ultimate Sexual Health & Performance* by John Abdo. This book is not just about fulfilling the sexual fantasies of our youth. It's about turning one's life around so that our physical and mental states are functioning in optimal fashions.

Life Extension Foundation

I would really recommend that people take advantage of John's book, which lists all of the viable options that offer them help and hope, to improve not only their sexual health, but their overall vitality and enjoyment in life.

Dr. Ann Marie Tommey
Ob-Gyn, Hormone Specialist, Sex Counselor

John's book is great because it addresses issues that are not mentioned in the media. People think that the easiest approach is to pop in a pill, and then they'll be okay. This is not true. If you really care about your health, and about (sexually) functioning properly, and about enjoying life, you have to look at the root cause of your abnormalities or dysfunction. I advocate putting life into your years, and John's book is in that vain of achieving this status in life.

Dr. Fouad I. Ghaly
Hormone Replacement Therapist, Genetic Engineer

Whoever gets a copy of John's book did the right thing; that's great, because there's a lot of information out there and a lot of it is erroneous. The colleagues and contributors that have supported this book are offering good, solid information. What I would say to all readers is to stay committed and use all this information to help you get back on track, and stay on track.

Dana Nelson
Hormone Specialist, Licensed Pharmacist

John's book and his Web site are outstanding resources for anybody seeking to improve their sexual health. Those who have lost their potency can benefit greatly from John's program. I highly recommend everybody get a copy of John's book and want to express that I'm honored to become a part of this program.

Dr. Joel Kaplan
Board-Certified Clinical Psychologist and Sexual Health Expert

Ultimate SEXUAL HEALTH & Performance™

John Abdo

Table of Contents

Please Read

- The information contained in this book is not intended to diagnose, treat, cure, or prevent any disease, condition, or illness. Therefore, it should not be construed as medical advice. If you have any concerns or questions about your health or sexuality, PLEASE check with a qualified licensed professional.

- All topics in this book are briefly explained and must be considered incomplete. More details are explained in the newsletters, audio seminars, and the Members' Section of the Web site. You can also refer to the various references provided at the back of this book.

- Some of the information provided in this book may become outdated at some point in time. Please refer to the Web site (membership section only) for all updates.

- This book does not give advice on the prevention or treatment of STDs; however, it is always suggested to practice safe and moral sex.

- The author of this book is not a doctor. Most of the information contained herein comes from reliable sources that are based on scientific evidence and can be substantiated. There are other materials that may be based on hearsay, public opinion, and/or, in the mind of the author, good ole common sense, and they should be regarded as nonmedical. Some fictional accounts are listed that may relate to some real-life scenarios.

- Although this book and its Web site contain graphic and explanatory materials that some people may regard as explicit in sexual nature, they are only intended to educate and promote healthy, ethical, lawful, and honorable sexual behavior and activities and to help with the expansion of the human population through our innate procreative forces.

Written by John Abdo

Charts and Illustrations Designed by John Abdo

www.SexHealthTV.com

Printed in Canada

Prologue

I'm going to reveal something to you. Something I swore I'd never share with anybody. You may be familiar with me from television commercials that promote the exercise DVDs and fitness equipment I've invented over the years. Health and fitness have been my life.

I'm a man on a mission, wanting to live a healthy, enjoyable, fulfilling, and productive life. I've had my successes, and it's fair to say that life has dealt me a few bad hands. Some of the challenges I've had to contend with have been the result of my own doings, and I've accepted full responsibility for them. Others, like the passing of my father, were completely out of my control.

As a kid, I wanted to be somebody. Not just anybody — somebody! I found a passion for sports, and I pursued the Olympic dream. I took what the neighborhood street bullies called a scrawny body and turned it into an elite performing machine. Much of it I did myself — hard (consistent) workouts in sweaty, stinky gyms; gobbling handfuls of horse pills loaded with dozens of funny-sounding substances; and melting a glacier of ice over the years to reduce the inflammation of my aches and pains. (But don't blame me for global warming!)

I'm an A-type. I guess you can say, *I'm never content*. Although I rose to national caliber, I wasn't satisfied — the Olympic dream was only in the sights of my (mental) telescope. I wanted more, and I wanted it fast. But I screwed up ....

The use of anabolic steroids nearly ruined my life, yet they never threatened to end my life. Oh, no, it was much worse than that. Instead, they made life far more challenging and (consistently) humiliating. The side effects I suffered from are written about in this book (and they're also one of the reasons why I reference athletes so much).

We've all heard the expression, "You don't know what you have until you lose it." Well, <u>I lost it.</u>

Desperately seeking motivation, I ordered several of Napoleon Hill's self-help success books and motivational cassettes from the Nightingale-Conant Corporation in Niles, Illinois. I was struck with surprise when, in one of the books, I read: "Out of man's greatest pain often develops his greatest reward!" There was also a similar line that caught my attention: "Adversity is man's greatest virtue."

When I first read those quotations I instantly asked myself, "How can he be right about that?" But Napoleon was a lot more successful than me, so I regarded his wisdom seriously, keeping his declarations close to my heart as I painstakingly sought after the part of me that was unexpectedly stripped away.

That was just shy of my twentieth birthday; I was still a teen. For over 35 years now, I've passionately (desperately) searched for the answers that would rescue the part of me that had suddenly vanished. The side effects I experienced from steroid use are referred to in urology as *hypogonadism,* or the shutting down of the gonads. In a man, those are his testicles and everything that makes the family jewels, *the gems*. My body stopped making its own testosterone. I was getting weak and the body fat started packing on. And my *little* buddy — do I really have to tell you his (anatomical) name? — totally rebelled against all of my requests, especially when I was in the company of a beautiful female.

Although it's a lot more complicated than what I just described, hypogonadism and its innumerable manifestations, like erectile dysfunction (ED), can occur in all types of men, no matter what their age, race, occupation, or lifestyle; it's not just happening to the dim-witted athletes who are using steroids.

Like Marco Polo, Lewis and Clark, Christopher Columbus, and Herodotus, my journey was long and littered with obstructions, fierce opposition, and lengthy setbacks. It was confusing and painfully arduous, often met with grave disappointment. But I had to keep on keeping on. I listened to Napoleon and dozens of other motivators who helped me keep my (*big*) head on straight. What I was looking for was as mystifying to me as were the treasures sought by those other expeditions. It wasn't that the information I was seeking for the treatment of male sexual disorders was buried in the tangles of medical literature, but it was merely out of sight. Astonishingly, it didn't exist at all. Conventional medical sciences didn't have all the information on how the male penis functions. How odd is that? Since the beginning of man, dating back to about seven million years, every person who has ever lived since is the result of somebody else's *little* buddy. You'd at least figure there would be a lot of documented materials and discussions about that. But I was taken aback when the vault was virtually empty.

Driven by a powerful upwelling passion, like my deceased comrades listed above, I had faith that upon the next horizon I would discover the answer. *Some* answer. At least a smidgen of a clue. But the years swept by, one right after the other, as I (mentally) carved notches into my brain like an inmate sitting on death row who counts down the days he's allowed to remain alive.

Eventually I came to my senses. I was searching for answers in the wrong places as the medical resources I was relying upon didn't know — or seem to want to know — what I was tugging them on their sleeves about. With what felt like the onset of *hemohidrosis* (perspiring blood), I returned to the scene of the crime; I went back to the athletes. Surprisingly, many of them had worse problems than what I was experiencing, but none (and I mean none) said a damn thing about it.

All of us had lost it, crushing our egos as a consequence. These were my trusted teammates who strongly supported one another during training and competition. But now we were divided, isolated, all alone; every man (or kid) for himself. We somehow knew — *sensed* is a better word — what we all were hiding. But God forbid, you don't (can't) tell anybody about that. You have to shove that skeleton deep inside your closet and hope you have the strength to keep that squeaky door bolted shut.

Obsessed with the same frustrations, needing to repossess their real identities, and unable to secure outside (professional) help, the athletes took it upon themselves to conduct their own research and experimentation. Their mission was aimed at battling their own sexual side effects by designing restoration methods that identified the causes of their hormonal disturbances and sexual disorders. From there, they addressed the remedies and cures. This process lent new meaning to the term *trial and error.* Of course, there were a lot of screw-ups. But soon there was a fuzzy glimmer of hope … then it became more clear … until finally … they nailed it!

The information that was being released from underground labs was nothing less than extraordinary. I was overwhelmed when I heard that the community responsible for causing my misery in the first place was able to ID the causes for their own hypogonadism, erectile dysfunction, testicular atrophy, and a host of other side effects too long to explain here. (Don't worry, it'll all be explained in detail in the following pages.) Methods had now passed the experimental phase and were in full use, designed to restore hormonal integrity once it got knocked out of whack. Steroid-related damage does not reverse by cessation — it's not that simple. There are very specific principles that must be applied in reversing steroid-induced sexual disorders. Precise timing must be implemented, along with a lot of careful babysitting. As you will read, the same principles apply for the non-steroid users who are experiencing hormonal imbalances and sexual disorders.

After a couple of long decades of trial and error, the experimentation paid off. There are now plenty of medical institutions, along with a specialized assemblage of distinctive individual practitioners (many who have contributed to the materials you will soon read), that embraced what the athletes had started. In embracing this, they've expanded, modified, and perfected the field of sexual health restoration into a legitimate discipline.

Concurrent with my gluttonizing consumption of this new information, I spent long hours in libraries and book stores studying endocrinology, male anatomy, glandular hormone secretions, sexuality, and anything my eyes could stay open for. I packed in as much information as my mind could receive. I filled notebook after notebook with information, kept audio records, attended seminars and symposiums, enrolled in classes, and even spent a small fortune on books and tapes. The knowledge I was gaining was inching me toward my own physical (personal) recovery, but it also granted me an extraordinary professional advantage that contributed to my health and fitness profession … I eventually became a professor in fitness training, which earned me an induction into the National Fitness Hall of Fame. In 2001, I was voted as the #1 Male Fitness Spokesperson by the prestigious ERA; then in 2007, I was awarded with a Lifetime Achievement Award!

As the years progressed, and my fitness television business became successfully established, I found it much easier to meet and interview doctors, antiaging specialists, hormone replacement therapists, and sex counselors. I no longer had to solely rely on books, magazines, and sit-in lectures. I now knew — and had the complete attention of — the authors, scientists, and engineers behind many of these developments, giving me full access to their information and services, many of which are listed in this book, recorded on the audio seminars, and posted on my Web site.

Let me make it clear: I am not a doctor. Instead, I'm a uniquely educated person who spent over three decades digging through the trenches to find the remedies and cures for sexual disorders concurrent with learning how to establish and maintain ultimate overall health. These days, much of what we're seeing advertised on television addresses the *symptoms* of male sexual disorders and, as you'll read, that's not the prudent approach. This book gives you the direction to pinpoint the *causes* of your sexual health disorders. Then, as a bonus, it divulges an astonishingly long list of options that identify, treat, and even cures them.

I guarantee that you'll be helped by reading this book. If you're sexually okay now, then use this book to make yourself better — a lot better! Use it also to arm yourself against the (inevitable) age-related hormonal decline and its concurrent loss of sexual functionality that will occur in your advancing years.

Age 28. About ten years after *IT* happened to me. I'm a mess. My hormones are on vacation. I'm depressed, fat, fatigued and hypogonadal.	I'll be 54 this year, and I'm in my best shape ever. I always knew the human body could heal itself provided it's given the proper nutrients and restorative techniques. That guy standing next to me is a complete stranger.

If you already have ED; if you've lost that part of you that you cannot live without; if you desire to regain your true identity; if this condition has been eating away at you for some time now; let me say that you've come to the right place and you're in for an extremely pleasant surprise. There's no better time in history to have a sexual disorder, like ED, than now. We have the answers and the cures. All you have to do is flip through the following pages and make the commitment that you are going to become the best *you* that you can be!

As for me, I found what I lost. I'm back, or should I say ... *It's* back! I'm not just a modest degree better; I'm completely restored, 100%, back to being me again, and in full ownership of my true identity. My restoration came in steps. Initially I was motivated to remedy my physical issues, but eventually my senses took hold of me, directing my focus onto the psychological implications of my sexual disorders. Therefore, in my unique opinion, mental recovery is exceedingly more challenging and must be spotlighted for you to institute an absolute holistic (complete) recovery; otherwise your *little* head will control your *big* head. And that's not a healthy way to live.

This book will help you wallop the physiological and psychological causes of ED, and it will certainly help you restructure and redefine the word *impotent*. After you read this book, you'll put a space between the "m" and the "p" and add an apostrophe; you'll be spelling it this way: *I'm potent!* (Along with the exclamation point, of course!)

I know how important your identity is to you. And let me add, I know how important your *little* buddy is too. That's my purpose for writing this book. So ALL men can be achieving their own Ultimate Sexual Health and Performance™. I'm certain that no matter how great your pain has been or how much adversity you have had to endure, your greatest rewards are coming in the days ahead.

I dedicate this book to you!

John Abdo

Let the expedition begin...

Preface

NOW HERE'S A CONCEPT: *The status of one's sexual health, or lack thereof, is a direct indicator of their overall health.*

I was taken aback when that concept was first revealed to me, but as a health and fitness professional, I quickly made sense of it all. Not only did that avowal come out of left field, but in the minds of many, it was very controversial; at least from a mainstream perspective. But times have changed.

How it was...

A man asks his doctor for help with erection difficulties. His doctor responds, "It's all in your head. Get some rest and you'll be fine."

A woman wants to regain the desire she had for her husband now that the kids are off to college. The doctor replies, "At your age, you must be realistic. Your best days are behind you. Just accept your condition as a fact of aging; there's really nothing you can do about it."

People have been asking for (demanding) a boost in their sexual abilities and even for hormone replacement therapy. But many doctors have frowned upon all that, saying things like, "Why would you want to do that?" and "That's too risky."

Times have really changed!

An extraordinary group of doctors, scientists, antiaging specialists, and life-enhancement institutions have been proclaiming (mostly under the mainstream radar) that sexual performance is the result of a complex and sophisticated cascade of events that involves the brain, the heart, the nervous system, and the myriad of other structures in the body. When these biological components are healthy, sexual performance is not only possible; it's often regarded as a bonus — for both pleasure and procreative purposes.

To substantiate this, one needs to look at the findings of the many great contributors who support this concept, many of which are part of this book. The Life Extension Foundation is one of them. And there are numerous other institutions that have been dedicated to finding the products, foods, supplements, drugs, services, and treatments to improve the quality of living, prolong life span, and enhance (or restore) sexual performance.

In my mind, I'm using the word *sex* in a lighter context compared to its common meaning, as I've come to understand sexual health and performance from a much deeper perspective. As stated, it's really about overall *internal* health. The following pages will address various viewpoints that relate to sexual expression and help all men who are experiencing ED and other sexual inadequacies. I will reveal the disorders that are (disappointingly) afflicting millions of men and women worldwide. I will also cover approaches for obtaining overall health while, as stated, revealing an amazingly long list of remarkable products, techniques, and services that can prevent, treat, and even cure sexual disorders. Meanwhile, the enhancement of sexual performance will be your bonus!

A quick reference to my dictionary defines disorder as "…a medical condition involving a disturbance to the normal functioning of the mind or body."

Proving Sex

The desire to prove sexual prowess has been encoded into the psychophysiology of almost every creature on this planet, especially man. To use a more ancient description, all species endeavor to demonstrate who amongst them is the strongest for advancing their species — *the strongest shall survive.* The ones who are the most potent (virile) have the best chance for survival and are the preferred selection as a mate, and the most protective of their offspring. Lions roar; peacocks spread their feathers; elephants spread their ears and flaunt their tusks; elk, deer, caribou, and moose proudly display their racks of antlers; rhinos show off their horns. Through these actions, all of them are saying, "I'm better than the other guys."

Although the topic of sexuality has become wrapped in controversy and perversion, this is a book that goes deep into the origin of the sexual response, and deep into the organism of man, to reveal how we *really* perform sexually. It delves into how to recognize, understand, and cure sexual disorders, and how to develop ultimate overall health combined with sexual vitality.

Here's Another Concept

Mother Nature rewards us for performing sex … explained (more than once) later on.

Introduction

When I presented the idea of writing a book on, of all things, sexual health, I was curious as to what the response would be. Of course, I went to various professional associates, athletes, coaches, and many of the health and fitness clients I had worked with throughout the years. I had to look every one of them in the eye, as eyes tell it all. This eye contact was important for me. With it, I would be able to tell if they felt I was off my rocker or if I had something important and worthwhile to share with my potential readership. Fortunately, the latter proved true, and I want to thank all of those who have supported my development of this book and its Web site.

Crazy or brilliant, I was determined to make it happen either way — it was just a lot easier having the support. Nonetheless, it was an extremely challenging decision for me to write this book, and more importantly, to promote it on TV. I am taking my head out of the sand because I, too, fell into the culture conditioning that talking sex should remain *hush-hush*. But the information I have compiled in this book is miraculous, so I am standing up for all of us. I believe this book will make a positive change in your productivity, confidence, happiness, and pleasure for the rest of your life.

Before I begin, let me just lay it out there: Men are in big trouble, and according to statistics, over 90% of them aren't doing a damn thing about it. When trying to tabulate the exact figures, the statistics on erectile dysfunction and other sexual disorders overwhelm the display on my calculator, which basically means that there are tens of millions of men in danger. Now, many of you might think that this is a book only about erectile dysfunction, but there's much more to it than that.

Although it might be embarrassing and painful to lose the ability to get a hard-on, many of you might believe that ED won't kill you. But you're going to be surprised to discover that modern male sexual health research proves that belief wrong.

ED is bad news, not only for a man's penis, but also for his overall health. This book addresses *both*, while also sharing with you an amazingly long list of remedies and cures *that really do work!*

As of this writing, it is estimated that there are in excess of 30 million men in America alone — and another 150 million worldwide — who are experiencing ED and other sexual disorders. Surprisingly, and one of the main reasons why I was compelled to write this book, less than 10% of men seek help, while some doctors say it's closer to 5%. That means that 90% to 95% of men (or well over 25,000,000 men in America) are walking around with a cloud over their heads and limp penises tucked away in their shorts, confused and frustrated about what's happening to them, not knowing where or whom to turn to. Or maybe they're too stubborn or embarrassed or macho to get the help they need to boost and restore their lagging sexuality.

I started writing this book decades ago. As I was compiling all the information, I noticed the escalating statistics of men suffering from all sorts of disorders, including ED. During my research, I have visited hundreds of bookstores that display new works and also offer older books. On these visits, I was never able to find one book that specifically targeted the issue of male sexuality or, more specifically, ED. There were overflowing sections on *Women's Health*, complete with rows and rows of books. But try finding a dedicated section for men and all you'll find are *Exercise*, *Camping*, and *Sports*, along with an extensive display of adult magazines.

Frustrated by the lack of options, I knew I had to publish this book. And having plenty of chances to try out these techniques, I'm proud to say that *this stuff really works!*

I've traveled a long road to compile this treatise. Over the years, I've been listening to the complaints of many men (and also listening to the complaints of their women). I've even observed the ways in which the medical, pharmaceutical, and nutritional industries have been addressing male sexual health issues, especially erections. And let me toss in the fact that I'm not getting any younger myself. (I will also add, I enjoy sex immensely.)

Right now, I'm going on 54 and there's a voice in my head (the *little* one) that keeps reminding me to stay committed to this program. What keeps me so motivated and capable of maintaining my promise to myself is the information in this book. All the suggestions here *work*, and I'm eager to share them with you. Although I am aware that what's good for me might not be the best choice for someone else, the great news is that there's a myriad of options to chose from. All of these options range in functionality, benefits, costs, speed, accessibility, risk, and convenience, so you can take your pick(s) and find what works best for you! One thing's for sure, you'll enjoy the process.

The Opposite Sex

As I was conducting my research — interviewing both doctor and patient, reading report after report — I couldn't help but delve into those sections on *Women's Health*. I spent time learning about the sexual health concerns of the female because, to my astonishment, women are statistically proven to have more disorders than men.

My reaction was: *WOW. This is too important to ignore.*

So I made the commitment to include a special section in this book for women, the *better* half of the couple ship. Relationship experts declare that men will (and should) learn how to understand a woman's needs, while the reverse applies to women for understanding men. That said, the sections that pertain only to men can be of great benefit to women. And you guys, I encourage that you read about the ladies. (I discovered that many of the techniques that are good for men are also extremely effective for women.)

As a health and fitness professional, I began my career (in the midseventies) focusing on how to make the *outside* of the body look terrific. But as time went by, I shifted my focus on how to make the *inside* of the body *feel* terrific and become internally super healthy. My research led me to understand that our states of sexual ability; the desire in the brain; and the physical function of our glands, hormones (sometimes the word *endorphins* is used interchangeably), heart, nerves, circulatory vessels, genitals, and prostate are direct biomarkers for our overall health.

Historically, it has been (secretively) known that many men live in quiet desperation about their sexual disorders, hiding it as ferociously as a panicking criminal would hide his smoking gun. In the past, any male sexual disorder was called *impotence;* today, it has been reduced to a two-letter acronym: ED.

Are You Ready?

If you're a man — doesn't matter what age — this book is for you. And if you're a woman — doesn't matter what age — this book is also for you. Couples? Of course, it takes two to tango, whether you are just starting to date or preparing to celebrate your fiftieth wedding anniversary. This is a book you will gain great benefit from, no matter what stage of life you're in, no matter what age you are, and no matter what your lifestyle may be.

If you're in your 20s or 30s, you will read this book searching for information with a "What's in it for me?" attitude. You will find sections that pertain exactly to your needs at this stage of your life. Ten years later, when you're in your 30s or 40s, you will pick up this book again to search for information with that same "What's in it for me?" attitude ... and guess what? Since biological changes are inevitable with age, you will read things in this book that relate to where you're at (biologically/hormonally) in life — things you didn't see or pay attention to ten years earlier but somehow crept up on you. I started out the same way. I was seeking information for my own sexual health in my late teens and early twenties, and everything I was looking for came from that "What's in it for me?" attitude. I still rely on this information and all of the wonderful advances some 35 years later.

This book was not written for any specific age group. No matter what age or stage of life you're in, or will be in, you can read this book with that "What's in it for me?" attitude to learn specific information that will apply to any stage of your life. I wrote this book to span all ages and all times, and I really believe that it will be extremely useful throughout the different stages in your life.

As stated, my research, surprisingly, led me to discover that women actually have a higher percentage of sexual disorders in comparison to men. I've been in plenty of relationships myself (I'm heterosexual), and I don't ever think I've known (or sensed) that my partner had a sexual disorder; it now turns out that I was very naïve on female sexuality. I do remember that some of those partners (at certain times) did have difficulty getting in the mood. They struggled to feel an equal amount of pleasure (the sexual experience wasn't always mutual), or they struggled to achieve an orgasm as easily as I always did. In fact, one partner I was with for a long time never had an orgasm, and this made me feel somewhat inadequate.

40% of men report ED while 63% of women report arousal and orgasmic disorders.

"The Sexual Pharmacy," M. Laurence Lieberman, R.Ph.

I also had a relationship with a beautiful woman who often complained that she *wasn't in the mood*. I couldn't understand it. I was romantic (not bragging, just being honest), I took my time (not a wham-bam-thank-you-ma'am love and shove experience), and I made it a goal to pleasure her before I allowed myself to be pleased.

I've also learned that many women often say (or *feel*) that "it hurts" during intercourse. According to Dr. Ann Marie Tommey, M.D. and Ob-Gyn — as a woman ages, so does her vaginal lining. It thins out and becomes easily irritated, while other issues like fibroids and increasingly painful menstrual cycles add to the mix.

Many women find sex painful as a result of varying degrees of vaginal irritation that can be largely contributed to lack of vaginal lubrication. When I heard about this, and started studying it, I made a comparison between lack of vaginal lubrication in a female and erectile failure in a man. In fact, many women, no matter how much romance, arousal, and foreplay they experience, find intercourse to be a dissatisfying experience — something I thought was never possible. But men with ED are (basically) encountering identical experiences.

Again, with my own experiences, I didn't regard my partner as having a *disorder;* I just felt, or was forced into thinking, that relationships lose their fizzle over time. I figured that age was progressing faster for my partner than it was me, that relationships take on different dynamics during the committed phase than they did during the dating or courting phase, when the fireworks were always exploding in colorful displays of ecstatic pleasure.

Women who are experiencing any one of the many female sexual disorders often regard them as normal. Dr. Tommey believes that the *priming* a woman receives growing up (and through our modern culture) makes her accept (or tolerate) depleting levels of health and sexuality that she once enjoyed during her younger years. Women are brainwashed into believing that as they age, they concurrently (inevitably) become less of a female (on a sensuous level). They start believing that their loss of sexual arousal, desensitivity, discomfort, and inability for reproduction are normal and natural parts of the aging process that they must learn to accept. Okay, reproduction ceases with advanced age, but sexual pleasure can last well into a woman's golden years!

Men are different. We want to have sex forever, and age isn't going to stand in our way. Men, however, have an obvious mechanical requirement that makes intercourse possible. In order to penetrate a vagina, a man must *obtain* and *sustain* an erection that's stiff enough to enter into a woman. Erections are considered an anatomical mechanical phenomenon that was totally misunderstood up until very recently.

When the penis fails to become erect, intercourse is impossible. Although women certainly have their own complex cascade of disorders that challenge healthy sexuality (as I've briefly listed but will expound upon later in this book), they don't have the type of mechanical responsibility that men do. Therefore, women can still have intercourse when they're *not into it*. And I'm sure all of us guys have had intercourse with women who we knew *were really not into it*. But I can tell you that when a man *isn't into it*, obtaining an erection is difficult or impossible, while sustaining that erection can be the most challenging task he has ever had to deal with.

It's obvious that men have the (physical) responsibility of achieving an erection hard enough to make intercourse possible. But, surprisingly, according to many statistics, there are more impotent women than there are men; they are now being labeled as having female sexual dysfunction, or FSD.

As you continue to read, you'll find that I have interwoven female sexual needs throughout this entire book, while adding special sections toward the end. For these reasons, this is an extremely helpful book for women to read as well.

Something For Everyone

Whatever your situation may be, I want you to read this book with a great level of hope, faith, and confidence. The strategies and techniques in these pages really do work, no doubt.

Many (but not all) of these materials are completely substantiated and come from reliable, credible sources. The main reason why you may not have heard of many of these sex-healing and performance-boosting techniques (until now) is because many of their inventors, developers, endorsers, suppliers, and distributors do not budget for mainstream advertising. So unless you're like me, digging and prying and researching and tugging on a lot of sleeves, most of this stuff remains hidden.

This book will certainly introduce you to new methods, while defining the methods you already know about, but from unbiased, professional viewpoints. It will also give you insight into new technologies years before they actually appear on the local news or are mentioned in a health magazine.

Even though this book contains a vast amount of information, it's to be regarded as a work in progress. I need to establish this up front because the fields of endocrinology, urology, and male and female sexuality have finally established themselves as a serious medical curriculum, and they are growing faster than ever before. That said, the Members' Section of the Web site will be constantly updated with the latest reports and news. (New drugs, supplements, treatments, remedies, cures, doctor interviews, success stories, products, services, etc.). Some of the products and methods you will read about in this book may become outdated by a new advancement, miracle cure, or an innovative procedure. I will continue to interview many of the developers and spokespeople for these technologies and post them regularly on the site, sharing valuable information that will enable you to always have that "competitive edge" *in the bedroom!*

As stated, most of this information won't hit the mainstream until years later, so you will be among the first to learn all these amazing techniques, cures, and remedies. For instance, I discovered the natural product Velvet Antler — hormonal booster, restorative agent, overall body tonic, *adaptogen*, and sexual stimulator — back in the 1980s. But it was nearly 20 years later that Velvet Antler started to receive any attention here in the USA.

What's Got You Motivated?

Before we get into the thick of things, let me ask: *Why did you buy this book?*

You don't really have to give me an answer — that's too personal, at least at this stage of our relationship.

Actually, if you're a guy, no matter what age, I know why you bought this book. Some of you simply want to get more of what you're already getting — to show your wife or girlfriend(s) that you're the *best man* she has ever had. Even if she's not a long-term partner, you want her to remember you above all her other lovers. And I know that a ton of questions flood your mind whenever you meet somebody new. Questions like: *What kind of lovers has she had in the past? Who else is she sleeping with? Are her lovers better than me? Are they bigger than me? Can her other lovers outperform me?*

Let the games begin!

Ready, Fire, Aim: Slightly out of Sequence

Simply stated, the "score" is the first result. *Then* the competition begins. How great it is when you're in the game or, better yet, at the top of your game — and hers! So you're the guy who has *it* going. You're okay sexually. You get turned on easily. And your penis, well, he's okay too; maybe his nickname is *Champ*. But you wouldn't pass up a chance to make *him* better. Better than what you are capable of and certainly better than any guy your lover(s) have ever had before.

Then there are you other guys (like me) who lost *it* but who simply want to get *it* back. You used to be that guy I just described in the previous paragraph, but now you're somebody else — and not by choice. Something has happened, and it's completely out of your control. You can no longer satisfy yourself, which means that your chances of satisfying your sexual partner are slim to none. It also means that your ranking has plummeted to a much lower score, and you begin to believe *her other lovers* "really" are better than you. In fact, you've proven to be a sexual failure more than you care to count, and you sense that, in her mind, you're a replaceable commodity.

But it doesn't matter which kind of guy you are. If you want to take *normal* sexual activity and magnify it to the nth degree, or you are in desperate need of restoring your libido and bringing life back to an uncooperative penis, this book is filled with plenty of goodies that will put you back in the game.

Encoded in our cellular DNA is a gene that drives us to create. More specifically, to *pro-create*. When a man loses his sexuality and experiences ED, he basically loses his innate masculinity and his identity. Once that occurs, he must actively seek out the options that will help restore his sexuality. And he shouldn't be ashamed either because it's a common problem. There are multiple tens of millions of men, all paddling up the same stream in the same boat.

We're all here as a result of sex. Considering that every human being originates from an act generated from a cascade of events that result in making an actual person, it's always been surprising to me that we don't have formal education that's mandatory in our schools; that the making of human life is shrouded in so much controversy and perversion; that a *normal* act is so secretive; and that the pleasure of sex is used to entice our curiosities but, at the same time, is not permissible according to the mainstream mindset.

However, things are changing more and more each day. If there ever was a time to have ED, it's now; sorry, Pops! Until recently, men who had ED were told that their condition was all in their heads. Back in the day, getting the courage to confront and open up to a doctor (or anyone for that matter) about penile inadequacies was tough enough, let alone being told you have something loose inside your (*big*) head. Men were crawling out of their doctors' offices, feeling ridiculed and rejected. But today, especially with billions of dollars being made with pills and other male enhancement products and services, the incentives to broaden the understanding and treatments for a huge and expanding market are enormous — no pun intended — and, as stated, are growing at an unprecedented rate. I suggest we keep complaining because the more us guys grumble, whine, and open up about *our* needs, the more the pharmaceutical companies, health institutions, medical societies, nutritional suppliers, and capitalistic entrepreneurs will research, develop, and make available improved products and services we all need; for men <u>and</u> women. In business, this is called *consumer demand*. So since we're the actual consumers, let's keep *demanding* so we will continue to obtain better options and treatments that keep us men, *men!*

So What's It All About?

The sexual benefits you will gain from reading this book offer much more than penis-enhancing advice. It's actually about *total health*.

For most of you normal guys who just want to prove to your girlfriend(s) or wife that you're a terrific lover, health may not be a full consideration for you at this time in your life. But let me be as bold with you as I would be with any one of my Olympic athletes — *your health must always be taken into serious consideration.* As you progress in age, biological and psychological changes are inevitable. However, many of these (aging) changes and their undesirable effects are also preventable, and I will explain all that later on.

To emphasize this, at some point during my lectures, I often tell my audience that when I'm 90 years old, I want to look and feel great at that age. But the fact is, I can't make that decision when I'm 89. I need to make that commitment early in my life. It's like any wise investment that pays its most profitable dividends the longer it matures.

Like any great businessperson, entrepreneur, or planner, living a long, healthy, productive, and pleasure-filled life is about investing, and that investing must be in yourself. Many of those investment measures are explained in this book. But don't be led to believe that you have to wait to get results. The results from many of these suggestions are immediate, conveniently available, and pocket-change affordable.

So even if you're more concerned about your *little* head right now, that's okay. Why? Because properly taking care of your *little* head also means you will be taking care of your *big* head, all at the same time. Not only that, but it also means you will take care of your heart, nervous system, brain, hormones, metabolism and much more. (We'll delve into this later.)

You don't have to wonder any longer about whether or not you'll ever find *the* answer to your sexual problems; it's right here in this book, and you'll be amazed to learn about how many remedies — and even cures — exist. You'll also be pleased to know that there are plenty of new advances in development for future release.

If anything, this book will make you a more educated patient. Here's an analogy: Let's say your car breaks down and you don't have a clue as to what's wrong. In fact, you don't know anything about how your car operates in the first place. All you know is that something's wrong.

You manage to get your car to a mechanic — somebody you don't know — and he asks, "What's the problem?"

You reply, "I don't know, it's not running properly anymore."

If statistics fall in your disfavor, chances are that mechanic will install a heap of costly parts, with excessive labor fees attached, when, in fact, you probably only needed to have your spark plugs changed. Get the point? The more you know about your car when it has a problem, the more educated you are when you bring it in to see your mechanic. So now, when the mechanic asks, "What's the problem?" you can tell him, "My car needs a new set of spark plugs."

The same relates to your body. The more you know about what's going on, good or bad, the more you are equipped with valuable information that you can share with your doctor about what to (specifically) look for. Doctors respond to your symptoms, and those are expressed (largely) by what you say, or don't say, and how you articulate yourself. If you go to your doctor and say, "Something's wrong, Doc," he has got the extremely challenging and often risky task of finding your problem(s). (Part of the reason for high insurance costs.) This is the pressure that's placed on doctors today; it is also a pressure that has been placed on them historically. People simply don't know what's wrong with them. So doctors have become notorious for quickly prescribing drugs in response to their patients' complaints. Of course, the doctor won't replace your liver when you go in for a sprained knuckle, but my belief is that if a patient goes in to see their doctor and has a more educated understanding of their issues or, better yet, has pinpointed their problem, chances are much higher that an accurate and expedient treatment and recovery can ensue.

That said, the information in this book is not meant to replace the examination and guidance of a doctor. But what this book *will* do is enhance your understanding of the causes of your sexual problems, so you can better explain them and give your doctor the ability to prescribe a focused treatment and recovery plan, many of which are mentioned in this book. (I recommend that you show your doctor this book or, better yet, ask that they read it.)

What Qualifies Me?

I am not a doctor, but I am an award-winning professional in the health and fitness industry who was recently inducted into the National Fitness Hall of Fame. I've competed as an Olympic weightlifter and have been a coaching specialist in sports, fitness, and health since the age of 17. My services have reached over 80 countries around the world and I have trained athletes for the 1976, 1980, 1984, and 1988 Olympic Games. I have lectured to various medical and therapeutic professionals on exercise, health, and human performance.

Health and fitness are my *life*, personally and professionally. What you will read in this book goes beyond what many doctors know. The science of sexuality (surprisingly) is still in its infancy and, in my opinion, grossly ignored (or regarded less seriously than expected) by many medical schools. And what you will discover is that sexual problems are intimately linked to other internal health issues, which means that having a sagging erection could be, as Mark Newel, Ph.D., Director of Medical Research at the Medway Research Institute claims, a potential biomarker for an underlying and undetected series of potentially serious disorders, which include hypertension, diabetes, and even a cardiovascular catastrophe in the making.

In my teachings, I've always been quick at giving advice on health, performance, nutrition, and fitness. However, when it came to giving advice regarding sexuality, particularly, another guy's penis, I was at a loss for words, at least for verbally expressing them. The words were *in* my mind but I wouldn't (couldn't) verbalize what I was thinking. But as time went on, the curtain slowly raised. I became more and more comfortable addressing the issue of sexuality, especially the penis, testosterone, sperm count, and intercourse, among other things—words and topics so many men shudder to even think about voicing. When I learned that the performance of a man's penis is directly related to his hormones and often directly linked to the performance of his heart (thanks to Dr. Steven Lamm), I felt obligated to share this critical information. That way, all of you can avoid certain misfortunes, becoming much healthier and happier — and add many productive years to your lives. This is about our penises, but it's also about everything else that makes our lives vibrant, prolific, productive, successful, and healthy!

But in my mind, what qualifies me the most to write this book is the fact that a very long time ago, *I lost it* when sexual health sciences were clueless on the entire subject. But more importantly, *I repossessed it*, and the time and energy that's filled the gap between then and now has given me the understanding and confidence to develop this program. So, literally, I'm not merely this books' writer; I'm also its first success story. And let's face it, all you have to do is listen to the long list of endorsements and testimonials from renown sexual health experts, the prestigious Life Extension Foundation, and above all, the men and women who have actually read my book, and followed my recommendations. These approvals exemplify the extraordinary influence this information has on its readers turning sad people into super glad people. In my mind, these are definite reasons that qualify me to be this books' author. I hope you will be of the same opinion.

Read on!

Chapter 1

Sexual Energy: The Power Force of Life

Sexual energy is one of the most powerful of all the energies known to man. Removing it from its religious, emotional, and cultural elements, sex is what drives man, consciously and subconsciously. Sex, or the result thereof, down to its core, is our *procreation* mechanism; it's our innate driving force; it's what makes the human race *a race*. Our survival is solely dependent upon sex. We must reproduce, and sex is the only way that happens. How a man manages his sexual driving forces determines much of his direction in life and the experiences he encounters.

Our brains are equipped with a strong sexual impulse to ensure the survival of the species.

The Brain, History Channel, History.com

Napoleon Hill, the great motivator and success self-help guru, discusses in his spectacular book *Think and Grow Rich* the necessity for a man to channel his sexual energy properly in order to achieve success. When a man allows his sex drive to distract him from important goals in his life, his *little* head does the thinking for his *big* head and he lacks wisdom, or he certainly lacks control and prioritization of life's true necessities. However, when sexual energy is used correctly, man has the potential to rise to the top of his game. Napoleon refers to this as *sexual transmutation*.

Growing Up Male

Many female sexual (and/or reproductive) problems are, and have always been, considered normal. Women have had access to their own *female*-specific doctors ever since they started having menstrual cycles, and they were educated, to varying degrees, to expect (and accept) cessation of many of their youthful attributes after a certain age, their *mid life crisis*. For men, we've also been brainwashed with this *mid life crisis* BS; but when it came to our sexuality, it was a much different story.

When I was growing up, no doctor EVER asked me about my sexuality. Not once. In addition to the regular checkups that my parents — bless their hearts — escorted me into the doctor's office for, I also went in for tonsillitis, a radical strain of the flu and measles, cuts and bruises, and a torn medial meniscus in my knee from a muddy football practice; I even had to see a doctor because I got hit by a car while riding my bike as a kid. But no matter what the reason was, the words *sex, preference, penis, libido, intercourse, masturbation,* and *sperm* were never mentioned by my doctors, even though I was supposedly undergoing a "complete" examination. I did have my prostate checked in my 30's, but that was it. And even then, there was still no mention of those taboo words; the doctor merely glanced up toward the ceiling as I was kneeling on all fours butt-up on top of his examining table, and while wiggling his finger deep inside my butt-hole (scientifically known as the anus), he said to me, "I'm just probing for a potentially enlarged prostate." (If you want to view the video recording of my first rectal colonoscopy experience, please visit my Web site. I'm just kidding!)

Doctors were not interested in sex. They took my blood pressure; placed a stethoscope on my chest and back to listen to my heartbeat and respiration; tapped a little rubber hammer on my patellar tendon to test my knee-jerk response; pointed a flashlight into my eyes, ears, and nostrils; and flattened out my tongue with an oversized Popsicle stick to look down my throat. And all the while, my penis was kept tucked inside my shorts, silently thinking, *"I really am a private part."*

I realize that I'm not the only male patient that was (is) being sexually ignored. Growing up, my (male) friends never told me about the details of their doctor visits either, but if even the tiniest of sexual innuendos were ever presented, we would have definitely talked about it. But like our dads and uncles and grandpas, we kept a shroud over our *little* buddies, believing they were to always remain *private parts*.

With a society that refuses to confront the real issues of sex, now look at what has happened. As I stated before, there are tens of millions of men in the U.S. alone who have ED. That's a lot of depressing nights. To put this into perspective: That's more people than the total populations of New York, Los Angeles, and Chicago *combined*. Just think of all the broken egos and crushed emotions. The anxiety. The rates of depression. If sexual failure happens to a guy, it also happens to his partner. It's never a one-way street; however, the guy suffering from sexual disorders is not necessarily feeling this as a "we" thing. Instead, he believes it's a *"me"* thing, and it digs itself deep into the core of his consciousness.

What angers me is that most of these disorders are preventable on top of the fact that many doctors were, and many still are, completely ignorant or lacking the knowledge and skills to address any type of sexual disorder. The reason why we're all here in the first place is the result of a sexual act. There's no question that sexual health is of vital importance. Treating, better yet, *preventing*, our sexual problems should be a top priority among us all, as procreation is a top priority with other creatures on this planet, equal to eating; another *survival* code.

Millions of men today would be far more sexually active and healthier if the medical societies had only focused on men's health as they've done historically with women. But later is better than never, so let's support the advances of many of the current medical societies who are now recognizing sexual health as a serious curriculum they must study, apply, and evolve. I'm proud to say that this book is supported with such pioneering breakthroughs.

Guys Have It Easier

Disappointingly, many medical sciences once regarded that *all* a man has to do to fulfill his *male* responsibility to procreate is to ejaculate — a pretty easy thing to accomplish that, according to the Kinsey Report, takes only a few short minutes. Compare that to the nine months it takes for a female to carry a baby, along with the hours of labor, the burden placed onto her body, and the sacrifices she must make; it appears that man's involvement in procreation is a teeny piece of the pie. No wonder many women have expressed their differences with men on this issue. And so, the man, who only produces the sperm and plants the seed, was (is) not regarded significantly enough by many cultures, even the medical societies, to require high levels of medical attention, especially in comparison to women and all their needs and burdens and sacrifices in the procreation process. Many may consider this unfair, but it's logical, given the levels of understanding these conclusions were based on. But we now know better … at least *you and I* do.

According to J. Stephen Jones, M.D., author of *Overcoming Impotence*, of almost 3,000 pages in the 1970 edition of Campbell's *Urology* (the bible of urology), less than four pages were devoted to impotence. Jones proudly admits that as a testament to advancement in male sexual health, the most recent edition devotes well over 100 pages to impotence. (In my opinion, that's still insufficient.)

What It's Like Today

Even today, many doctors still don't know what actually *causes* ED. In response to the demand, they are largely moving in accordance to the influences from pharmaceutical companies who are marketing prescription erection pills, which are primarily addressing *symptoms* of erectile disorders. Many doctors who prescribe these pills don't attend semesters of education, sitting long hours in a classroom to learn the deep information behind the chemistry of these drugs, but read only a few pages of information regarding the (incomplete) science behind them. They place trust in the source and the pharmaceutical companies, quickly prescribing these drugs to their male patients who come into their offices asking for help with their ED. It's my opinion that if a man goes into a doctor's office and says, "Doc, something's wrong with my penis," and that doctor issues that man a prescription for an erection pill without a thorough examination, that's malpractice. Why? Because as you will read, penis problems can be significant warnings for potentially more devastating problems brewing up elsewhere inside the body — and even in the brain. Yesterday, many doctors didn't know this; today it's a completely different story. Get an exam; then the pills will be a bonus.

Many doctors issue prescriptions because they feel obligated to; they do it out of the "instant gratification" demands of their patients. Doctors are the real — or legitimate — drug dealers, literally. Adding things up, these (erection) pills are grossing in the multiple billions. I'm not against them, per se, nor am I against being incentivized to sell a product. What I am against is issuing prescriptions without a complete reason, or thorough examination, along with a monopoly in a specific drug category. There are so many other options out there for sexually ailing men. But with millions of dollars being spent to advertise and distribute erection pills, many men just don't have a clue as to all of the other solutions that do exist. To fan the flames, television, Internet and magazine ads, celebrity endorsements, and even your family doctors are presenting you with limited options. Just wait till you see the myriad of options presented later on in this book.

Additionally, and surprisingly, prescriptions for erection pills are being administered without concurrent advice on any psychological challenges. Men with ED also have varying degrees of confusion, anxiety, embarrassment, disappointment, depression, and even anger. These are psychological enemies that, if left unaddressed, will remain embedded in the subconscious mind and go on to negatively affect all areas of a man's life. (More on anxiety, specifically *performance anxiety*, later.)

SCENARIO: A male patient in his late 40s — let's call him Tom — schedules a visit to see his doctor. On his way to the clinic, and even while he's sitting in the waiting room, Tom silently and nervously rehearses what he's going to say to his doctor. Tom says one thing in his head, then goes on to imagine what the response from his doctor will be. He tries different ways of expressing himself, running through numerous questions and possible responses. As he sits there in the waiting room, Tom continues to feel uneasy. The rehearsing and positive self-talk isn't turning out to be so positive. He takes a few deep breaths; tries to calm himself down. He knows that it was his own decision to see his doctor — something he has been procrastinating for nearly two years. Tom can't chicken out now; he has to get the help he needs.

Tom is finally let into the doctor's office. He sits alone for a few remaining minutes, trying to build up his courage as he waits for the doctor to enter.

Like most doctors' offices, diplomas from what seem to be prestigious medical institutions adorn the walls, pumping trust into Tom's mind. This is somewhat soothing. These official certificates prove to Tom that his doctor is someone he can trust with his deepest, darkest secret — his faltering penis.

The doctor enters the room, and after some awkward pausing and clearing of his throat, Tom admits he's having difficulties with his sex life. He goes on to explain that his penis doesn't cooperate like it used to.

Without much examination or questioning, Tom's doctor responds, "That's normal. I see plenty of guys with that exact same problem. How many do you want?"

Tom is instantly relieved because he knows what the doctor is referring to. Tom is about to get a magical solution (prescription) for what he *believes* will be the remedy he desperately needs. (Belief is a powerful and influencing emotion.)

Tom finally lets out a sigh of relief and says, *"Well, Doc, as many as you can prescribe to me."*

The doctor scribbles onto a prescription pad and hands Tom the Rx without any hesitation. Then off Tom goes to the local pharmacy to purchase his *erection pills.*

Tom calls his wife Judy as he's rushing home with his magic potion tucked secretly into a white paper bag. Judy doesn't know where Tom was today, nor does she (completely) know that Tom has been having an erection problem. There have been many challenges with their sex life, but Judy attributes all that to how busy they've been lately. Between Tom's new business venture, taking care of their two growing-up-so-quickly kids, and looking after Judy's ailing mother, things have been a bit hectic. (A logical reason for the lack of romance, right?) But Tom knows the truth. All this time, he has felt guilty about his inter-mittent bouts of ED, yet his ego wouldn't allow him to admit it to his own wife.

But Tom finally has his relief plan ready to spring into action!

The erection pill prescription is certainly a boost to Tom's confidence — as it is to most first-timers. Determined, Tom decides to initiate some intimate action with Judy the second he gets home. They end up having their best night in nearly two years. The intimacy restores a lot of deeply buried emotions. It's quite a healing experience for Tom and Judy.

Too Good to Be True

However, as time goes by, Tom becomes dependent on his secret stash of little pills. Before he knows it, the romance with Judy has fizzled again … and so has his ability to achieve an erection. Sad to say, the pills stop working, as they do for a high percentage of men, according to some reports. Even when they do work, there's no sensation in Tom's penis. As he struggles to thrust in and out during intercourse, Judy thinks to herself, *Why can't he cum? Maybe I don't feel as good to him down there as I used to.* Judy puts pressure on herself now, which really exasperates the problem for this couple. When they don't think they're pleasing their men, most loving and caring women blame themselves and, worse yet, believe they are physically deteriorating.

Tom is like many men who seek short-term remedies that only address the *symptoms* of their ED, while ignoring the *causes*. Tom never made any changes in his thinking, eating, or the ways in which he dealt with stress. His (unhealthy) lifestyle was exactly the same after his script relief as it was prior.

Pills are great for the guy who *only* desires an erection. And for most guys, at least for the short term, an erection is all they're concerned about or satisfied with. But deep down, a man using a (synthetic) prescription drug to make his penis perform a *once natural* function, realizes he's no longer normal. Now he has that seed in his mind that prompts him to wonder when the inevitable will happen: complete cessation of erectile function. Others are totally oblivious to the underlying issues regarding the *cause(s)* of their erectile dysfunction. Many men neglect to dig to the very root of the issues at hand. And when you ignore the *cause*, the problem will only continue to get worse — 100% guaranteed.

60% of men find erection pills satisfying while 40% do not.

Mark Newell, Ph.D.

It's prudent to address both the *symptoms* and the *causes* and let the pills be the bonus. However, there should always be extra special attention paid to the *causes*, as I believe in prevention first, then remedy second. Pills do work, but they mostly address *symptoms*, which is not in the best long-term interest for a man's overall health (mentally or physically). Erection pills may create an erection in many — but not all — men; however, they offer little or no improvement, or are very inconsistent and unpredictable, with correcting emotional challenges, intimacy or libido, penile sensitivity, orgasmic display, and a speedier (natural) *refractory period**. These are fundamental ingredients for the complete fulfillment of pleasurable sex. In other words, pills don't get you *hot* and they don't get you *horny*.

---

* Refractory period is the time it takes a man to recover from one orgasm and then obtain another erection and have an additional orgasm. The refractory period varies broadly among men. Younger men can recover in 15 minutes (lucky dudes), and while middle-aged guys may take a full day or two, older men may have to wait a full business week. It's proper to note that some erection pills have an extended life. Depending on the dosage, Levitra claims 12 hours and a version of Cialis offers 36 hours, in comparison to Viagra at four hours. It's possible, then, that a man can achieve more than one erection during these periods; however, it's inconclusive that libido and semen volume will be replenished to the point of achieving a satisfying orgasm. (I welcome the makers of these drugs to provide that information, which I will gladly post on the Web site.)

Drawbacks to Prescription Erection Pills

1. Many side effects and risks

2. Meticulous (unnatural and clumsy) planning and timing for performing sex

3. Lack of spontaneity

4. May (temporarily) treat the *symptom* of an un-erect penis, but ignores the cause(s) of ED

5. Psychological implications of the sexual disorder are ignored

6. May not help performance anxiety

7. No positive, long-term changes in hormonal profiles

8. Some are rendered ineffective if taken around the consumption of food

9. It's a big secret for many men, as their lovers never know

10. If a lover does find this out, some may react offensively and say something like, "What? You can't get it up for me on your own?" Or, "You really need a drug to get turned on by me?"

11. Tolerance: the effects may wear off over time

12. Dependency: psychological addiction

13. Must get a prescription

14. Cost: Prescription erection pills cost a small fortune

15. Priapism: *An erection lasting more than four hours.* This is a serious medical condition that must be treated before the penis's vessels, tissues, and thin outer skin rupture or explode. Ironically though, every time I mention the word *priapism*, to men or women, they get a kick out of it. I truly believe the makers and marketers issue that warning because it benefits their sales. Most guys say, "Wow, having an erection for more than four hours? I can deal with that." Be careful not to OD

on erection pills! (Female priapism is called *clitorism*, or painful erection of the clitoris.)

Some Causes for Sexual Disorders, Including Impotence

✓ Smoking: #1 cause

✓ Heart medications

✓ High blood pressure medications

✓ Anti-ulcer medications, including Tagamet

✓ Environmental Estrogen: Xenoestrogens

✓ Eye drops

✓ Acne medications (probable reason why men are experiencing lower sperm counts at younger ages than historically recorded)

✓ Oral contraceptives (women)

"The Sexual Pharmacy,"
M. Laurence Lieberman, R.Ph.

Famous People with ED

✓ Bob Dole was the first high-profile person to admit he had ED; he later became a Viagra endorser.

✓ Famous NFL Super Bowl champion coach of the Chicago Bears, Iron Mike Ditka.

✓ Superstar NFL and MLB athlete, Deion "Prime Time" Sanders, admitted on his TV show that he was having challenges with his erections. His doctors prescribed pills. Deion also admitted to using Propecia* for his male-pattern baldness; this drug is

---

* Propecia — chemical name, *finasteride* — is a drug that is highly prescribed to treat male-pattern baldness, but it is also known to cause loss of libido, ED, and oligospermia (low sperm count).

known to knock down libido and sperm count. For Deion to appear on television and admit this challenge, in my opinion, took a lot of courage while, at the same time, it gives us men the confidence to admit our own challenges, seek professional help, and find the remedy. A much better scenario than holding your head in your hands, figuratively speaking. I applaud Deion for being a man's man.

✓ Jose Canseco was at one time the highest paid baseball pro, who once measured in at 6'4" and 250 pounds of chiseled rock-hard muscle. In the documentary *The Last Shot*, he admits to having no libido with zero sex drive, along with a testosterone level below that of a young female. Most likely, the cause was 20-plus years of continuous steroid use. (Love him or hate him, Jose is having a very tough time, probably an *impossible time*, at achieving an erection. He's not alone. His sexual dysfunctions are common with scores of steroid-using athletes and tens of millions of other men worldwide. To his credit, Jose had the courage to admit he has a problem and has sought professional help instead of isolating himself. I discuss a lot about steroid users later on.)

How Can Something So Natural Be So Taboo?

It's *in* men to possess and display their sexuality. In fact, it's our identity. This is how it goes in the animal kingdom, and we male humans are no different. The strongest shall survive — that is the basis for evolution on our planet. Admitting a fault or weakness can be self-destructive, especially in the midst of fierce competition. Animals sense the slightest sign of weakness in another animal and capitalize to feed, protect, and procreate. Men are no different. Men know when they're on top of their game, and they know when they're not. They're always wondering if their weaknesses are being seen (or sensed) by another human and fear being taken advantage of. In fact, competitions are often won by one man taking advantage of another man's apparent weakness(es).

So having any kind of sexual problem (or sexual weakness) is life threatening, and it's also chronically painful. A man's sexual health is his pride and joy. Money, love, and status also play huge roles in a man's confidence; but according to many experts, like world-renowned hormone specialist, Fouad I. Ghaly, M.D., a man's sexual health, or lack thereof, is what makes the man, *a* man.

As men, we hide our sexual problems because we're taught to. Most parents never discussed *it*. Most schools ignore *it*. All churches hide *it*. Ask the teacher or clergyman about *it* and you'll get a lecture on abstinence, unwanted pregnancy, the consequences of unprotected sex, and the irreversible side effects from sexually transmitted diseases. When educators try to convince us that sex is wrong, unsafe, unlawful, or dangerous, we know they're either completely lying or completely perverting/suppressing their own natural human desires and interests. Sex, as most of us know, is not only for procreation. Mother Nature gave us the anatomical equipment to experience extreme pleasure before, during, and after the sexual experience; and when it's consensual, there's nothing better. Thanks, Mom! (I promised I'd get to this.)

For most men, discussing sexual problems is unmanly, while it exposes a man's weaker and vulnerable feminine side — God forbid that ever happen. But if men had more openness, we'd be much better off as individuals and as social creatures. Admitting faults is one of the best ways to correct them; it's also a characteristic of success. In fact, the great Henry Ford knew he didn't have all the knowledge he needed to become one of the greatest businessmen in the world, someone who literally started the entire automobile industry. Mr. Ford often stated that he had to select a specialist, or expert, in every area of his business to do what he needed to get done but couldn't necessarily do it himself. Ford called this group of delegates his *Mastermind*, literally strengthening all of his weaknesses and serving as an extension of his own mind.

Admitting faults and weaknesses is critical for growth. Athletes are always working on their weaknesses, not only their strengths, which they share with their coaches and teammates directly and eagerly, voluntarily asking for help. They're always sporting that passion to improve. That way, together, they can design action plans to correct these weaknesses.

If you can face your weaknesses with strength, and muster up the *will* to overcome them, there's no question that <u>you will succeed.</u> It's all a matter of staying the course, of never giving up. If you continue on this journey, you will become equipped with the tools and the knowledge you need to get you through all your sexual challenges and live an incredible life!

We're just warming up. Let's keep going ...

Chapter 2

Sexual Disorders: Finding the Cure

Over the years, I've been fortunate enough to have all types of people, including Olympic athletes, seek my counsel and guidance for self-betterment and athletic performance enhancement. Over the decades, many men have tugged at my sleeves whispering questions into my ears about improving their sex lives. Needless to say, many of these guys were just so horny that their libidos were out of control and, according to today's definition, are *hypersexual*, even though they were getting more sex than most other guys. The other guys, however, were just the opposite. These were the ones experiencing a disappointing *loss* in libido; they experienced difficulty obtaining and maintaining a firm erection, which was not only unsatisfying and embarrassing to them, but also affected the relationship with their sexual partners.

Decreased orgasmic disorder (DOD). Yet another acronym. Many men can achieve an erection (especially with erection pills); however they experience no pleasure or sensitivity that can create an orgasm.

In 1975, shortly after *I lost it* and was desperately seeking help, answers, and people to communicate with about my problem, I placed a small classified ad in a track and field magazine. My objective was to solicit responses from athletes who were experiencing undesirable sexual side effects, particularly from anabolic steroids. The ad read something like this:

> *If you're suffering from the side effects of anabolic steroids, send me your story. I'm studying the negative effects of steroids and I might be able to help. Complete discretion will be maintained.*

This was a tiny, black-and-white, text-only ad that was wedged in between many other ads scattered on the back pages of the publication. I didn't expect much, but I had to start somewhere. Before I knew it, the letters came flooding into my undersized PO box. The stories were heart-wrenching; there were dozens of letters from male steroid users, along with some letters from girlfriends and wives, and even the parents of athletes, all expressing their devastation. Their most common complaints, specific to sexual disorders, were total loss of libido, inability to obtain an erection (even with self-stimulation), dramatic drops in semen volume and sperm count, and testicular shrinkage (atrophy). Other complaints pertained to aggressively dangerous mood swings (also known as *roid rage*), rapid hair loss, liver and kidney problems, fat gain (with concurrent loss in muscle size and power), lethargy, depression, severe acne, gynecomastia (*gyno*, female-like nipple enlargement in men), and prostate problems. My forehead was dripping bullets just reading these letters.

The Future is Now!

1975 was a long time ago. I knew what these guys were complaining about then, because I was a competitive athlete, and I used steroids myself, coming to deeply regret it. This is how this book began. I was introduced to *it* and many of *its* dreadful relatives, and I've been on a mission to defeat *it* ever since. I realized long ago that sexual dysfunctions were becoming an epidemic of pandemic proportions in the making — but closely shrouded in secrecy. I was driven to find solutions because I am the type of person that believes *anything's possible*. I knew the solutions existed, either in the present time or in the future. I was determined to find the answers and the solutions … or develop them myself. Either way, I knew they existed. Unfortunately for me, the answers and the solutions existed in the future, the very distant future. Fortunately for you, they exist now, today.

There's something very special about the passion and drive of athletes. Their win-at-all-costs attitude puts them at an advantage at achieving what they're striving for, and I was no different. I had faith enough to know that in spite of the side effects we were experiencing, we'd work it out. That's what athletes (and their coaches and trainers) do; they *work things out*. Performances were shooting up but penises began pointing down. Athletes have always been determined to boost hormonal fortification, through natural and unnatural (synthetic) means. And in these attempts, especially when using *synthetic* measures through the use of anabolic steroids, the body's own natural production (called *endogenous*) of these hormones slowed down, or ceased altogether. This caused stagnation in boosting athletic performances along with a concurrent stagnation (and even cessation) in sexual performances; conditions like ED and testicular atrophy were experienced. Performance and health are closely intertwined, as you will read about shortly! Health is measured by one's level of sexual ability. The penis then can be your best friend in more ways than you think.

This might seem to be an odd and unorthodox way of addressing ED and other sexual disorders but, nonetheless, many of the same approaches used to restore the athletes' hormonal profiles, and to elevate drooping penises from synthetic steroid abuse, are applicable for all types of men who are experiencing disorders for other reasons.

Back in the 70's, almost every athlete on my team, and the other competitive teams, was using these steroid drugs. It was the thing to do, a critical part of that subculture; it was accepted amongst ourselves — coaches and athletes alike — but never disclosed to the outside world.

One of the great things that has come out of all this steroid experimentation is that we (the athletes and coaches) discovered a fascinating array of products, formulas, and techniques that doctors didn't (and many still don't) have a clue about. First off, most doctors don't spend much time studying nutrition, especially *performance nutrition*. And in the world of competitive athletics, sports nutrition often included *performance-enhancing drugs*, or anabolic steroids, along with natural supplements that boost hormonal levels, increase energy, and speed recuperation.

When approached — and trust me, they were approached plenty of times — many sections of the medical community didn't want to get involved with athletes. Mostly because they didn't have a clue about this science. Athletes are healthy people wanting to become super healthy. Doctors are mostly educated about sick and unhealthy people. But many of these doctors, to their credit, didn't believe in the *off-label* prescribing of steroids to make a healthy athlete healthier, and they didn't know how to treat unhealthy athletes suffering from the side effects associated with steroid use.

At first, my goal, and that of the steroid-using athletes around me, was to improve performance. We didn't believe we could ever acquire negative effects; that was only for the *other* guy. We were athletes and our egos had us believing, *It can't ever happen to me.* But immunity was not on our side. Steroids weren't (as) illegal back then, and they certainly didn't have the stigma they have today. Our intentions were to become the best athletes we could be, to take all the risks, and to proudly, and patriotically, represent our country in international competitions, especially the Olympic Games. Let me remind you that I'm describing a part of my life that actually occurred between the ages of 17 and 21. At the time, I was a kid with a lot of desire and passion, willing to risk it all to make my parents, coaches, peers, and country proud of what I could accomplish. I wasn't alone; every other athlete was striving for the exact same goals. Even entertainers, who have their own playing fields to display their talents on, have been caught up in the *roid* game. Hogan, Stallone, Rourke, Penn, and even Arnold have all used performance-enhancing drugs to climb the career ladder for themselves. They, and others, have reached the top of their game, going on to earn millions of dollars, while becoming international heroes and setting examples for all of the wannabes.

Today is a much different story, as the government — IOC, DEA, FBI — and mass opinion are both vehemently against, and cracking down upon, steroid use. But the point I'm trying to make is that athletes of yesteryear were doing what everybody else was doing; we just had to suffer the consequences in the process. Steroid use today is no different — in fact, it's even worse. Worse because there are new, more potent drugs, and athletes are abusing these drugs in greater quantities.

We (athletes) needed answers, but nobody was providing them to us or even showing much interest. So we relied upon each other, and not all of us were exactly biophysicists, but we had to experiment somehow. Trial and error was the foundation of our existence. What a concept. We were the trailblazers, so gutsy that if the *error* part was manifested, then we knew we had the determination to slam on the breaks, turn in another direction, and head down another route. We not only spun our wheels, but we also covered a lot of distance zigging and zagging over the decades to undo our steroid-related side effects. Many of these athletes shifted from performance enhancement — the main reason for their steroid use in the first place — to (sexual) health restoration. And this is how the *benefits* I mentioned earlier began as the entire sports community, detached from the medical communities, were determined to find the answers themselves. Now, three and a half decades later, I have great discoveries to reveal to you. We paid the price, and you're being handed our medals of honor.

So why am I spending so much time on this here? As you will read later on, there are many causes for sexual disorders, not only self-inflicted ones from steroids or illegal drugs. I believe many of those causes can be addressed, treated, and cured with the exact same techniques discovered from the *erroring* athletes throughout all their decades of *trial*.

I'm also happy to say that many sections of the medical communities are now on board, giving sexual restorative sciences a lot of attention, while (whether they want to admit it or not) gaining much of their influence from the athletes. This means more and more options for all of us now and well into the distant future. Growing old is going to be much better now.

Finding the answers to undo the steroid-related damage inflicted upon the hormonal and sexual systems wasn't easy, especially as antiquated as it was over three decades ago. Choosing and understanding which drugs athletes could use to boost their performance and build strong muscular bodies was a relatively easy process; take a drug and if you're stronger, faster, and more muscular after one week, then the drug's working. Different drugs were used for different athletes, depending upon what they wanted to achieve. We found out that there were drugs for *this* and drugs for *that*, and the real fanatics would take them all, at dosages that grossly exceeded the suggested potencies, just to make sure they weren't missing out on any benefit.

No wonder why a lot of these guys ended up losing their balls, literally. The side effects started to escalate. The athletes had no choice but to develop their own underground labs to design drugs and treatments that would reverse steroid-related troubles.

Ironically, there were more guys (and gals) scrambling on this issue than you could ever count. Fortunately, some of these athletes were formal or wannabe scientists, chemists, and bio-geeks who had a knack for figuring out biomolecular sciences. They'd mix up a batch of some new molecular formulation in their self-constructed labs and make these drugs available to other athletes who were eager to try them. I guess you can call them sports junkies.

For many athletes, Dan Duchaine was a hero who was regarded as an underground superstar, becoming a genius at both steroid use and sexual recovery. Dan didn't look like an athlete, but he sure knew how to train them. Of course, much of what Dan was doing was illegal; he was actually imprisoned for making and selling drugs, but his understanding of this science paved the way for many of us today. Also, I'm sure that many doctors have either peeked into what Dan was doing, or replicated his protocols identically. Dan was that good at what he did — and way ahead of his time. Sadly, Dan has passed.

Chapter 3

Stressing over Sex

(The following section pertains to all men who are under physical and psychological stress. Please exchange the rigors of athletic training to any hard lifestyle.)

> "When we're younger, it was easy to get hard. However, as we age, it's hard to get hard."

I've spent most of my life dedicated to the fields of health, fitness, and sports performance, as both a competitive athlete and a coach. Over the years, I've seen some of the most impressive-looking bodies, feats of strength and endurance, and acts of human performance. Ironically, however, not all of these great-looking, elite-performing bodies were always healthy. I know of big musclemen who have large rock-hard biceps, extremely low levels of body fat, and the ability to bench press a ton of weight, yet despite all that, they're not healthy. I've also seen many endurance athletes — like marathoners and triathletes — who endured distances between 30 and 70 or more miles in their weekly training, yet they weren't healthy either. I also know of many fitness fanatics who work out hours per day at the gym, keeping up with high-impact aerobics in structured classes or cranking out long sessions in the weight room, and guess what? They aren't healthy either. The cover of their book, or the way they appear on the outside, doesn't always match what's going on on the inside.

Hard-training strength (*anaerobic*) athletes can deplete essential hormones, sap their adrenals, tear up huge amounts of muscle tissue, and wear down their nervous systems. Although weight (or resistance) training is one of the best natural testosterone boosters, at the end of the day, it's very draining, and that's the primary reason why so many rely upon steroids — to accelerate recuperation.

Anaerobic training is excellent, but it does have its tipping point between adequate and excessive. Like any physical and mental expenditure, the key to success is to implement proper recuperative measures or else these performers will be prone to overtraining. The symptoms of overtraining are frustrating and often dangerous. They include lethargy, fatigue, weight (fat) gain, loss of strength, energy depletion, disrupted sleep patterns and insomnia, hormonal imbalances, poor digestion and elimination, amenorrhea (loss of menstruation in females), loss of sexual arousal in both sexes, and, yes, Mr. ED. (Stay with me on this, as overtraining, also considered *burnout*, depletes sexual functionality for anybody, not just the athlete.) According to many experts, stress is stress, no matter what causes it. It can be sparked from an argument at work, being stuck in heavy traffic, missing a flight, overtraining in the gym or running track, enduring the rigors of hard (physical) labor, or worrying if you're going to be able to perform sexually this Friday night. It's all the same to the brain and body organs.

The body experiences an incredible amount of wear and tear to the internal systems when people are excessively (hyper) active. This wear on the body is often called *catabolism*, or the breaking down of the tissues, while overtraining literally means that you're going *over* the limit of your body's natural capacity to manage stress and adequately repair itself. During rigorous training (or any overload, mentally or physically), microscopic tissue trauma is being experienced far from what the eye can see, as the muscle proteins (actin, myosin, and myoglobin) that compose the muscle and nerve tissues are being torn apart, along with hormonal depletion. Without ample recovery between exercise sessions, the body slows, or even shuts down, many of its operations instigating symptoms such as fatigue, lethargy, insomnia, muscle weakness, and dysfunctions to the genitals in both sexes.

Endurance (*aerobic*) athletes, however, are not under a lot of stress from resistances (weights) per se, as their challenges pertain to the *length* of exertion, or the duration of their activity. Since the loads, or resistances, for aerobic performers are low in comparison, the corresponding breakdown of myoglobin isn't as high as it is with the anaerobic performers. Instead, due to the high demands of longer nonstop activity, the lungs and their respiratory system, and the heart and its cardiovascular system, are under greater demand to increase the circulation of oxygen-filled blood to the trillions of tissues throughout the body. The protein inside the blood is called *hemoglobin*, and aerobic performers deplete this protein in large quantities during their excessively long training sessions.

When hemoglobin levels decline, a condition known as *anemia* is experienced; many use the term *sports anemia*. When a person becomes anemic, they are weak. Their body becomes starved of oxygen and protein, as hemoglobin is the oxygen-carrying protein that floats inside the bloodstream fueling the tissues with energy.

In addition to depleting adequate supplies of oxygen and protein from their muscle tissues and blood, anaerobic or aerobic performers (or anybody who's overly stressed) will also deplete many of their vital hormones, as hormones are needed to fuel the exertion power for the activity in the first place; then hormones are needed to fully recover from the exertion afterwards. (The same vicious cycle happens to laypeople who work hard but do not control stress or get ample rest and sleep.) All this can — and will — lead to exhaustion that often manifests as ED in males, as well as the long list of other sexual disorders in females that also include low libido, vaginal dryness, genital desensitivity, and even amenorrhea (disruption or complete loss of menstruation). So when you read the bumper sticker, "Runners do *it* better," you really have to wonder what *it* is they're actually claiming to do better. (More on this later.)

Now, don't be misled: Exercise and physical fitness activity is definitely something that everybody should (and must) partake in. But it's very important not to become obsessed with working out, and you must recover properly between exercise sessions. (Please see my article called "PAR" listed on the Web site. PAR stands for Preparation, Application, and Recuperation, the essential three phases for success when exercising.) In fact, as you will read, exercise is a major component for sexual health but, as I've just expressed, there are far too many members of our population who overdo it, naturally or with the aid of drugs.

Sex-Youality: The Pleasure Of Life

Nobody (in their *right* mind) can deny that sex feels great. And if you engage in sex with someone you love on a regular basis, you'll be living an ecstatic and healthy life. Unfortunately, as we age, we experience a decline of sexual functioning. This decline is often related to the degradation of one's endocrine system, which reduces the amounts of hormones our glands produce and secrete. The endocrine system is fundamental for making all life possible, while stimulating the entire cycle of sexual arousal to the performance of the sex act itself.

Healthy people have developed a younger internal (biological) infrastructure — regardless of how old they are. Even though they are progressing in age, their *chronological* age (how many candles they place on their birthday cakes) doesn't match up with their *biological* age (the true health, or age, of all internal cells, tissues, and organs). Suffice it to say, the integrity of healthy people's internal systems is much younger than they are old, at least when mathematically measured in years or candles.

As a contributing editor for the Life Extension Foundation, I have attended many antiaging and life extension symposiums which attract scores of longevity enthusiasts and specialists from around the world. Their research has completely shredded apart the myth that *age is a factor*, proving that people in their 50s, 60s, 70s, 80s, 90s — and even past 100 — can do things that younger people have difficulty doing.

The fascinating fact about all this is that the people and institutions dedicated to these fields of human science have been uncovering the *missing links* in Mother Nature, and through laboratory experimentation, they have shown how to enhance and extend lifespan.

Many of the protocols they represent and endorse are proven to reset a person's age by altering the ratio of their *chronological-biological* (body) clock. For instance, let's look at a person who is 55 years old — this is their *chronological* age, or the number of years they've actually lived, and the number of candles they stick on their birthday cake. However, upon examination through various tests, mostly blood profiles, the 55-year-old can actually be 70 years old on a biological scale if that person has lived an unhealthy lifestyle. However, if you take that same person and put them on a specific antiaging program, with hormonal resetting techniques, it's entirely possible that person can reverse much of their self-inflicted damage and become 45 or even 40 years old biologically, at least as proven through proper blood profiling. Unfortunately, they'd still have to poke 55 candles on their birthday cake.

In many respects, the sciences of antiaging medicine, in my opinion, closely parallel those of post-steroid restoration. Steroid users unnaturally speed up their *biological* clocks with their constant forcing to outdo themselves day after day, hence the term *performance-enhancing drugs*. Everything (biologically) accelerates with steroid users in order to make them bigger, stronger, and faster, which ages them prematurely. Biomarkers clearly indicate that steroids deplete hormones and create unhealthy imbalances, making a person look and feel many years older than they *chronologically* are. So biological and hormonal restoration is critical for, let's say, a 30-year-old steroid abuser who has a biological assay of a man 25 years his elder, or is medically 55 years old. And the reverse is true for the elderly man who wishes to reverse his *biological* age to a younger year.

Do Runners Really *Do It* Better?

To prove a point, billboards and bumper stickers like the one I mentioned earlier that read *"Runners do it better"* are obviously referring to (or bragging about) the sexual capabilities of those who engage in exercise activities, particularly running.

But don't go out and start running marathons, thinking you're also going to win trophies for your bedroom performances. As I mentioned earlier, you can easily overdo it when it comes to physical labor and stress. Too much exercise actually depletes the body of sex-boosting hormones, making (sexual) performance much more difficult, if not impossible.

I've always believed that all exercise training intended for body augmentation or performance enhancement must be based on the objective of improving one's health as one is striving for self-betterment. As odd as it might sound, many striving athletes, fitness buffs, and weekend warriors, as stated, are simply not healthy, nor do they spend their time on healthy practices. Overtraining, compulsive obsessiveness, muscular-skeletal imbalances from improper techniques, poor mental and nutritional habits, sleep deprivation, uncontrollable habits of drugs, alcohol, and smoking, high levels of stress, and a slew of other detrimental practices often prevent fitness buffs and athletes from obtaining optimum levels of health, from achieving that desired *look* they are fervently striving for.

The Connection Between Sex And Health

By now, you know that this book doesn't *only* have to deal with sex, although sexual activities are the result of what you're reading about. Instead, as stated, it's about *health;* or, in this case, it's about how sexual health *is* connected to total health. Many believe, including me, that sexuality, or the expression thereof, *is* healthy. And when your body, mind, and soul are healthy, so is everything else, including your sexual capabilities. Men and women are easily aroused and in the mood. Men become erect, women become lubricated, and sex is enjoyable! In fact, it's orgasmic! To make all these actions possible, we need to focus on overall health; chiefly, we must factor in the hormones.

So let's delve deeper into the body's endocrine system. Without hormones, nothing happens; that includes arousal, erection (or vaginal lubrication for the ladies), sperm production, and orgasm. It goes even deeper still, as the brain controls the production of these hormones and, yes — it even controls your penis. Literally, there really is a connection between your *big* head and your *little* head. And when a man is healthy, both his heads harmoniously agree with one another. However, when that same man becomes (sexually) unhealthy, his *little* head can become very stubborn while his *big* head becomes confused, frustrated, angry, and depressed.

The inability to achieve and/or sustain an erection is now known to be a very predictable *symptom* that indicates something more dramatic or harmful is going on *inside* a person's body. It's like that little yellow light that flashes on your car's dashboard, signaling that something under the hood is depleted or not functioning properly. *Check engine* can mean *check heart, check hormones,* or ... *check everything!*

Circulation and Nourishment of the Penis

Circulation is the body's ability to circulate, deliver, or transport blood out from the heart and into the trillions of cells throughout the body; it is vital for supreme physical condition. Blood is *liquid tissue* that contains all of the microscopic building blocks that will ultimately arrive at and then *become* skin, hair, muscle, bone, nerve, hormone, and organ.

After we've swallowed our food, digestion begins its operations. Taking the *macro* bits of particles that enter our digestive system, there are specific enzymes that dismantle our food into smaller, or *micro*, bits. This dismantling requires time, energy, and biochemical fortitude; it is necessary to break up the larger (macro) chunks of food we've swallowed, and make them small enough to permeate (cross through) our intestinal lining to enter the circulatory system. (Our mouths are a lot wider than the entry points inside our intestines, so our bodies need the strength to manage this dismantling and distribution process.)

Comparable to a flexible tubular pathway, the intestines are composed of several segments that are all connected to one another to form a long wiggling canal that starts at the stomach and ends at the anus. The intestines are lined with millions of tiny passageways that only allow microscopic particles to pass through them.

ANALOGY: To understand this better, think about what would happen if you poked tiny punctures into a garden hose. A percentage of the water that's inside the hose will now be forced to squirt out. The intestines are similar in that the food inside the body is being pushed toward the anus (a process called *peristalsis*) as the digesting (microscopic) particles pass through those tiny intestinal passageways and enter into the body's circulatory (blood) system. Once the food particles make it into the bloodstream, they start traveling long distances to arrive at their final destinations, places like the brain, eyes, pituitary gland, heart, bones, muscles, genitals, and so on.

ANALOGY: Macro particles of food are like trying to push a bowling ball through a chain-link fence — impossible. The bowling ball is too big, while the openings in the fence are too small. However, if the bowling ball is pulverized into smaller, or microscopic, particles, it's like taking BBs or sand particles and pushing them through the chain-link fence. The links in the fence represent the passageways in the intestines, while the BB pellets and sand represent the (microscopically) digested food particles that have become small enough to transfer from inside the intestines into the bloodstream.

Digestion is not biased. Health or junk food — it doesn't matter. Our digestive systems will always attempt to dismantle larger food particles into microscopic ones to enter our bloodstream, ultimately nourishing our tissues or raising our levels of toxicity. Not all entry into the bloodstream then is made up of good materials. A variety of toxins, drugs, bacteria, parasites, and other dangerous microbial agents, which are microscopic in size, can easily enter the deepest cells inside our bodies. This list is extended to include all synthetic (junk) foods, alcohol, drugs, and the residue from cigarette and cigar smoke.

The foods we eat that do not become small enough in size to pass through the intestines are collected as residue, called *bolus*, and hopefully can be eliminated with bowel movements. When left undigested and un-eliminated, this residue will grow toxic inside the body, eventually leading to plenty of gastrointestinal disorders, blood poisoning, obesity, cancer, and other illnesses. Unassimilated foods (foods that have not entered into the bloodstream) will also rob your body of strength, as your digestive and assimilative metabolism is forced to switch to a *waste management* process that consumes huge amounts of valuable energy. So even though you have food *in* your body, that food is actually draining you of energy, not providing it. It's like having a fuel tank full of gasoline, but your car putters down the street because the fuel in the tank is not being effectively transported into the engine. You'd think, according to the scientific definition of *calories*, that somebody who consumes loads of food would have more energy than a person who's a lighter eater. Fact is, most obese people, who technically have huge amounts of energy *in* their bodies, often experience the secondary effects of *chronic fatigue.*

ANALOGY: Take a fresh apple, cut it open, and leave it on the countertop for 15–20 minutes. The fresh, living cells in the apple quickly start to decay as they discolor, or turn brown. Toss that apple in the garbage and close the lid. Within days, you'll see little flies swarming inside your garbage can. Give it a little more time and the apple rots, developing a foul odor. Maggots crawl all over it. Although the apple is healthy and nutritious, if it's not consumed in sufficient time, a good thing will turn toxic. The same occurrence happens inside our bodies when (health or junk) food is undigested, unassimilated, and entrapped in our intestinal tract, causing a multitude of gastrointestinal disorders and leading to many devastating diseases, including cancer.

The circulatory system is a vast and complicated network of veins, arteries, capillaries, and other tubular pathways that serve as, for lack of a better term, *the plumbing system* for our body. If placed end-to-end, this entire network would cover a distance that wraps around the entire planet 2.5 times (I'm not exaggerating) — and this is not taking into account our circuitry of nerves and the trillions of other cells in the body. (Visit the *Bodyworks* exhibit when it comes to your area, and you'll be amazed at what we biologically own. You'll have an opportunity to see just how complex and vast our bodies are. It's absolutely amazing!)

The engine for the circulatory system is the heart, which works as a muscular pump, forcing blood into and throughout the arterial system that, again, reaches the trillions of cells in the body. The stronger and healthier the heart is, the more forceful it can contract and the easier the blood flows. The cleaner and healthier the circulatory vessels are, the faster and easier blood can travel to its destinations.

Now back to sexual health! (I knew you were waiting for this as you might have figured I lost my train of thought and deviated from the main mission of this book.) Circulatory health is imperative for the delivery of vital hormones to various organs in the body, including the penis, or let me put it this way — the penis depends on this process of hormone-filled blood flow or else it won't get hard. In fact, the circulation of blood into the penis is the only way it can become hard or erect (without artificial mechanics, of course).

With age, and certainly with poor lifestyle habits, the interior linings of our circulatory vessels lose their elasticity; they become rigid, stiff, or hard. They also accumulate plaque and other toxic buildups, which creates a narrowing or constricting of the vascular walls, sometimes referred to as *vasoconstriction*, which leads to the deadly condition known as *arteriosclerosis*.

ANALOGY: It's like shutting down the summer cottage for a long, cold winter. When you return months later, and the water is turned back on again, rusty gunk pours out of the faucets, showerheads, and garden hose. As a result of nonuse and exposure to the elements, the garden hose's elastic characteristics also deteriorate, and it loses its flexibility to bend and move, narrowing the inner diameter and impeding efficient water flow.

Basically — and I'm still on an analogy here — the same thing happens to the human body when people aren't active, or when they flood their systems with foods and products that clog everything up. Maintaining periodic bouts of circulatory flushing activity, like with aerobic exercise, is important to overall health, and as you'll realize, the penis is a proud and happy recipient. And when done correctly, many runners can *do it better!*

I can hear some of you saying, "Come on, now. How does all this really help my penis?"

Well, unfortunately, we've all heard of *arteriosclerosis*. It's a deadly disease that destroys the body's circulatory system. One of the causes for this devastating disease is the lack of proper exercise. Lack of sufficient exercise has been shown to compromise the (healthy) elasticity of the circulatory vessels, impede transportation of adequate supplies of blood throughout the body, obstruct sufficient vessel-cleansing actions, and effectively remove (toxic) waste materials out of the body. Plain and simple, arteriosclerosis causes circulatory disturbances and heart attacks. What us guys need to know is that the circulatory vessels in the penis are incredibly tiny in comparison to the size of other vessels elsewhere in the body. Actually, the vessels in the penis are microscopically narrow, fragile, and dependent on blood flow to function properly and, yes, to achieve rock-hard erections. This means that circulatory blockages (of any degree) in the penis will compromise erection quality and duration. According to Dr. Steven Lamm, author of *The Hardness Factor* and regular guest on popular TV shows like *The View*, "...*the more blood you can get into your penis, the harder it becomes.*" And the only way blood gets into your penis is through its circulatory vessels.

A lot of people, *especially men*, are walking around clueless as to the developing (internal) circulatory blockages and other potential health disasters going on inside their own bodies. I say "especially men" because most men, according to statistics, are too stubborn to seek medical guidance. Or they don't commit to regular examinations, including annual, or better yet, semiannual blood tests, to ascertain hormonal profiles and overall (internal) health. In his practice as a prominent urologist, Dr. Laurence Levine, from Rush University Medical Center, has found that men are still uneasy about this subject and need to understand that the symptom of limper erections (or no erections) is often a warning sign of circulatory disruptions and even *heart problems* brewing inside.

> *Your penis is your best friend that warns you when something potentially damaging is brewing up inside your body.*
>
> Nick Delgado, Ph.D.

It's prudent then for all men to start with a minimum of a one-time-per-year checkup until the age of 35, while most doctors will suggest that men over 40 should come in more often — especially if they're having hardness or erection problems. Think of it this way: Three heads are better than one: your two and the doc's one. I am personally examined twice per year, sometimes more, and I gladly spend the money on blood work. (The discounts I obtain through the Life Extension Foundation help a great deal.) It's so rewarding when my blood tests come back and I know that I'm healthy, especially in comparison to my hypogonadal steroid days. I'd love for you to experience this state of health and sexual strength, but it takes some knowledge and effort, which I'll continue to explain.

Now, the point I'm making here is this: If you're not properly taking care of your body, the tiny blood vessels in your penis will lose their elasticity and build up plaque from toxic residue; they will become clogged far in advance of the damage that's occurring to your larger circulatory vessels. It's almost like that little tickle in the back of your throat, or an out-of-nowhere sneeze. Those little signs can indicate that a full-blown cold is coming on, and you can use those warnings to get to work on preventing the illness; or, if you do catch the cold, you can recover much quicker. As Dr. Mark Newell puts it: "Your penis can act like that canary in the coal mine."

As of this very moment, you might only be thinking about your penis, but according to current urologists, endocrinologists, and skilled physicians, you should be thinking about much more. (The *little* head does have some wisdom after all, so make sure you pay special attention to how your penis is feeling.) And since the circulatory vessels in the penis are much smaller than those going into and out of your heart, a thorough examination from a qualified medical authority can potentially prevent a heart attack or other debilitating disorders later on in life.

I need to be honest and realistic. You are in charge of YOU. You need to assume full responsibility for your health and do what's necessary to achieve your own ultimate sexual health.

The ability to have an erection is not the only thing that's important; quality, or firmness and hardness of the penis, is equally vital. According to many experts on male sexuality, the firmness or hardness of an erection determines the circulatory health of the penile vessels and everything leading up to them, including the heart. According to Dr. Lamm, age reduces the stiffness of a penis, while its rigidity when erect is now taken into consideration upon urological examinations by specialists who have been educated in this science. It stands to reason that the more blood that enters the penis, the harder it becomes. And blood flow is largely dependent on the size and *receptivity* of the receiving vessels. You have the blood, but the question is, can you get enough blood inside those microscopically narrow vessels of your penis to pump it up? That's the trick. And there are many ways to make that happen.

Guess their age.

Sex Is Healthy

Not only does your physical health impact your sex life, but it works the other way around too! Your sex life has a great impact on your physical health. Everything is active during sex — your brain, nervous system, muscles, heart, circulation, thermogenics (body heat), lungs and respiration, hormone production, perspiration, and more.

Here's what some experts have to say about the health benefits of sex:

- In an article entitled "Which Are the Health Benefits of the Sex/Orgasm?" Stefan Anitei (a science editor) wrote about sex and longevity. A 10-year research study performed on 1,000 middle-aged men in Belfast, Ireland, revealed that sex on a regular basis is not only healthy, but it also increases our life spans. Anitei goes on to say that men of similar age and health with the highest orgasm frequency displayed half of the death rate of men who did not have such frequent orgasms. Researchers believe this is due to the drop in stress induced by sex.

- According to a report from TIME Online, entitled "Sexual Healing," "… making love can boost the heart, relieve pain and help keep you healthy." The article is based on studies that have proven that "… arousal and an active sex life may lead to a longer life, better heart health, an improved immune system and even protection against certain cancers, not to mention lower rates of depression."

- According to Daniel Reid, author of *The Complete Book of Chinese Health & Healing*, Western societies have a lot to learn about the therapeutic benefits of sexual activity. Reid claims that a "… strong sexual drive has always been regarded as a fundamental sign of good health and flourishing vitality …." Reid further explains that "… properly practiced, sex can be one of the fastest, most effective, and most enjoyable ways to build up abundant supplies of potent hormone essence...."

- Sex triggers the release of a variety of healthy hormones, including pain-relieving *endorphins*. This is probably why many sexperts recommend sex for headaches and other physical discomforts.

- Sex releases a tremendous amount of tension and, once an orgasm is achieved, can make you sleepy. Guys are notorious for falling asleep immediately after they ejaculate. (I'm guilty of multiple convictions.) Many sexperts regard sex as a great tranquilizer, and I will attest to that.

- Sex requires a degree of physical effort, often burning as many calories as you would burn running 15 minutes on a treadmill. That would come out to about 200 calories. Who needs a health club membership?

Male Orgasm Studies

In the early 1950s, Doctor Alfred Kinsey started releasing his studies, which delved into the sex lives of men and women. Kinsey reported that sex reduces stress and that people who have frequent sex and orgasms are less violent and less hostile than those who don't. This information led Kinsey to conclude that sex and orgasms can calm a person down for the long term.

Moreover, later studies showed that frequent sex and orgasms translate into lower death rates for both men and women.

In addition, a study conducted in Melbourne, Australia, found that frequent ejaculation between the ages of 20 and 50 helps to dramatically decrease the risk of prostate cancer in men. According to these studies, men who ejaculate frequently are better candidates for avoiding many prostate-related problems. (There have been some studies noting that orgasm and/or ejaculation achieved through masturbation does not accomplish these same results. I agree — orgasm-producing masturbation does not provide the same health benefits as orgasm through sexual contact with another person. My reasoning is that there are various other hormones that are released during sexual exchange between two people, while the boost in self-esteem and emotional gratification is also a noteworthy contributor to overall health.)

Prostate Facts

✓ One out of every six American men will develop prostate cancer.

✓ In 2012, more than 240,000 men will be diagnosed with prostate cancer, while 33,000 men will die from the disease.

✓ Two million men and their families are battling prostate cancer, and three million more will join the battle in the next decade.

Prostate Cancer Foundation

Chapter 4

What Causes *It*?

When we were younger, *it* referred to our erection aptitudes and abilities to perform spontaneous sex. However, *it*, to a man with ED, has an entirely different definition. The most probable reason why you're reading this book is that your *little* head hasn't been obeying orders lately, and you're just getting more and more frustrated, depressed, and withdrawn.

Well, you're not alone. In fact, you have a lot of company. Tens of millions of other men are struggling with *it* too. *It* in urology is known as *impotence*. On TV, *it* is simply labeled as ED, or erectile dysfunction. *It*, to you and me, is any reference made to an uncooperative penis. Either you have *it* or you don't.

The Life and Times of *"It"*

- *It* starts out as one isolated incident.

- Eventually, *it* overstays its welcome and becomes a regular visitor.

- *It* is located in one spot in your life, but then *it* shows up in others.

- Starting as a conscious thought, *it* ultimately becomes programmed into your subconscious, the deeper and controlling section of your brain.

- When *it* is in the subconscious, *it* influences everything you think, say, and do.

- At first, *it* is some of the things you do, but as time goes by, *it* becomes all of the things you do.

- Every thought you have, *it* is there.

- Every place you go, *it* is there.

- *It* is there, and *it* is everywhere.

- *It* is constantly on (*in*) your mind, and *it* controls you.

- *It* does what it damn well pleases, in spite of your begging and pleading.

- On vacation, *it* stows itself away, and you pay all the expenses.

- *It* overtakes you. *It* is that strong.

- *It* starts out slow, but accelerates, eventually consuming a huge amount of your energy.

- You think endlessly about *it*, exert effort wrestling with *it*, spend huge amounts of your money to deal with *it*, are forced to avert any recognition so you can hide *it*, and go to bed at night dwelling on *it*.

- At first *it* was *it*, but eventually *it* becomes you. *It* "is" you. *It* becomes your new identity, much different than your true identity, and *it* is a miserable partner you can't divorce.

- You define yourself by *it*. *It* is who you are, but you don't admit *it* or know how to deal with *it*.

    And so *it* goes …

- THIS BOOK CHANGES *IT* FOR YOU. You will learn *it*, understand why and how *it* becomes *it*, how to re-relate to and/or redefine *it*, and how to teach *it* (or remind *it*) who's the real boss. The more you keep trying to define *it* on your own, isolating yourself from real help, the more *it* will eat away and devour you, cell by cell, until you totally throw in the towel while falling to your knees a broken man.

- Leave the defining up to the experts.

- It's time to put *it* behind you.

- Successful living is a life in which you feel confident, happy, secure, healthy, and productive; it is a life in which you are experiencing joy and pleasure. When a man has to deal with *it*, the nagging discomfort (and pain) never leaves him, no matter what he does or where he goes. At the office, *it's* there. At home, for sure, *it's* there too. Go to a party or social function, and guess who's there with you? *It's* always sitting on your shoulder, reminding you that *it* is in command and that *it* is the real boss now.

- The goal for every man with ED, or any sexual inadequacy, is to learn to control and live with *it*, but this book goes beyond that. I endeavor to show you how to BEAT *IT*.

In later sections, I will show you a myriad of options so that all of you can walk proud again. All men must be responsible for doing what's best for themselves. They must make themselves the best they can become; they must not only focus on their strengths, but they must also work to overcome their shortcomings. This book turns your weaknesses into strengths. Turns your fizzle back into the sizzle!

Up for the Occasion

We took *it* for granted as youngsters. Getting an erection was a no-brainer, always a sure thing — anywhere, anytime, anyplace, no matter what. The *big* head had it easy. Our penises popped up regularly, and frequently, and even stood up seemingly for no reason at all. And when those special moments were presented to us, our trusted *little* buddy often became so anxious that he couldn't make the experience last. (Translation: *premature ejaculation.*)

To understand ED, we must first look at what we're dealing with …

Types of ED

Primary: Impotence that relates to men who have never been able to obtain an erection and perform intercourse.

Secondary: Impotence relating to men who were once capable of achieving erections and performing successfully pleasurable intercourse, but somewhere along the way, they lost their erectile ability.

Vasculogenic: Impotence pertaining to sexual/erectile dysfunctions stemming from vascular or circulatory issues. This pertains to poor blood flow, or the inflow of blood to engorge the penis in order to *obtain* an erection, poor storage of blood, or the inability to entrap the blood once it's inside the penis to *sustain* an erection.

Neurogenic: Impotence relating to sexual/erectile dysfunctions stemming from nerve disorders or interruptions that begin in the brain and branch throughout the nervous pathway, including the entire spinal cord and all the way down into the penis. Because neurogenic impotence relates to the nerves, and since the brain is the headquarters of the nervous system, neurogenic impotence can also include the brain's lack of sexual functionality.

Psychogenic: This refers to the plethora of psychological causes for impotence. When the (thinking) mind is consumed with negative or fearful emotions, feelings, and beliefs (especially anxiety), normal sexual function is either impeded or completely blocked, as the mind's influence on brain chemistry stimulates the secretions of erection-killing hormones, while causing a disruption in blood circulation and nerve energy with concurrent vasoconstriction of the penile vessels.

No matter what type of ED a man has, he will experience varying degrees of *sexual disappointment*, a mental emotion that leads to a cascade of negative consequences. More on psychology later.

Some Common Causes for ED

- ✓ Smoking (#1 cause)
- ✓ Diabetes
- ✓ Obesity
- ✓ Stress
- ✓ High blood pressure: *hypertension*
- ✓ Drugs
- ✓ Age-related (our hormones and sexuality decline with age)
- ✓ Poor eating habits, especially consumption of excess sugar, toxic fats, and synthetic additives
- ✓ Poor lifestyle habits
- ✓ Alcohol (excessive use)
- ✓ Broken heart (sadness and loneliness)
- ✓ Fear or paranoia
- ✓ Anxiety: performance anxiety or fear of failure
- ✓ Fear of rejection
- ✓ Environmental toxins: hidden particles in our drinking water and food containers that destroy hormonal integrity, including *environmental estrogens* (or *xenoestrogens*), pesticides, plastics and many more.

Sugar, especially late at night, increases the production of insulin that often strains the pancreas gland, which correspondingly destroys the secretion of human growth hormone (HGH) from the pituitary gland. According to Dr. Robert Goldman, cofounder of the American Academy of Anti-Aging Medicine (A4M), people with depleting levels of HGH will age much faster because this is our youth hormone, vitally important for tissue repair and body maintenance. When the hormone HGH declines, ED has the opportunity to rear its ugly head.

On Larry King Live, May 27, 2008, Dr. Vinni Khurana, a neurosurgeon from Canberra Hospital, stated that "radiation from cell phones can cause infertility."

According to Dr. Joel Kaplan, diplomat with the American Board of Sexology and certified sex therapist, a major cause for (psychogenic) ED is sexual criticism and embarrassment:

All it takes is one condescending remark from a sexual partner, and even sexually capable men will suffer ED. When a woman makes critical remarks about her lover's penis, or his inability to please her, many men will experience the turtle effect as the penis withdraws into the body nullifying any chance of an erection. This is extremely damaging to a man's psyche, which, obviously, has a negatively profound physiologic impact. Psychological counseling is imperative to clear the man's mind and help him return to normal sexual functionality.

Different Reasons for Sexual Dysfunctions

✓ Religious guilt or ideals

✓ Death of a loved one

✓ Lost job/business

✓ Low confidence and self-esteem

✓ Financial insecurity

✓ Anabolic steroid side effects

✓ Post-traumatic stress syndrome (PTSS)

✓ Wearing condoms: Let's face it, most guys hate using them, especially since condoms desensitize the head of the penis.

✓ Fatigue

✓ Germophobia: fears of sexually transmitted diseases (STDs) like catching herpes or AIDS, catching colds, etc.

✓ Ritualistic disorders: These pertain to people who can only have sex under certain (unusual) conditions that can include, but are not limited to, having sex in the dark, under the sheets, only in the bedroom (that person's), in a certain position, after drinking alcohol, smoking marijuana, etc.

✓ Fetishes: These fixations typically pertain to the sexual attraction to objects or make-believe scenarios, and can include, but are not limited to, women's shoes, having sex in uniforms, smelling the odor of soiled underwear, leather clothing, bondage, and a person's body odor or sweat. People who have fetishes oftentimes cannot perform sexually unless their fetish conditions are met.

Weight Loss Pills

Many people strive to look good and keep their body weights low of fat. Some actually work at it, while others try popping pills and expect miracles to happen. Many of the weight-loss pills on the market do not (cannot) provide benefits on their own; they must be used in conjunction with exercise. It's like the analogy of the automobile where the fuel tank that's filled with gasoline is symbolic of the fat stored in your body. However, the gas is never burned inside the tank. The only place that gas is burned is inside the engine, or according to this analogy, inside the muscles — specifically inside the *mitochondria*, which are the microscopic fuel-burning organs located inside the tissues. But the gasoline has to have a delivery system that transports the fuel in the tank into the engine; in the car analogy, that's the fuel pump and fuel line. In the body, it's (basically) the circulatory system. Once the stored fat is broken down, it's then transported via the bloodstream to the muscles, then into the mitochondria, which is operated by the cardiovascular (heart-circulation) system. Exercise activity, with its heart-stimulating benefits, in many senses, serves as the fuel pump while the circulatory system serves as the fuel lines. If fat doesn't reach the *mitochondria*, it does NOT get burned. So popping pills, then watching Monday Night Football won't help you lose an ounce of fat. Plus …

The problem I've always had with weight-loss pills is so many people who are using these products simply aren't exercising properly (or at all); and they're certainly not eating the way they should be. In addition, many weight-loss pills are notorious for containing some very powerful central nervous system (CNS) stimulants that place enormous strain to the adrenal glands and vital hormones, dropping testosterone levels, which over time, eventually become depleted, leaving the individual feeling totally drained. Hence the start of that vicious cycle known as the *yo-yo*, or *rebound* effect. The reason why there's such a profound rebounding is because the body *supercompensates* for the hormonal depletion it has suffered from these powerful (depleting) weight-loss agents and begins to reaccumulate and hold onto stored fat stronger than ever before. In the midst of this battle, sexual ability wanes dramatically, especially in men who have to demonstrate the mechanical action of obtaining firm erections to become sexually satisfied.

Diabetes

Ranking high on the list of health disorders and no longer isolated to adults, diabetes is responsible for causing ED in men of all ages. This disease causes vascular damage that narrows the tiny vessels of the penis, preventing blood from entering into the *corpus cavernosum* — the receptive chambers inside the penis, and creating erections. Men inflicted with diabetes also suffer from neurological damage, which desensitizes the nerves of the penis, blocking sensation and pleasure.

Smoking: Ranked #1

Smoking is the #1 cause for erectile dysfunction, and the culprit for hundreds of thousands of deaths (and millions of other disorders) annually in the United States alone. (I'm too appalled to even try to comprehend this.) Erectile dysfunction as a result of smoking is a double jinx, because smoking reduces the elasticity of the arteries, constricting (or limiting) essential blood flow that is responsible for sending blood, oxygen, and nutrients into the penile tissues. In addition to the circulatory vessels (veins and arteries), large organs like the heart (with its vast cardiovascular system) and the lungs (with their respiratory system) are also being destroyed. Since the penis's vessels are so tiny in comparison to the vessels located in the heart and lungs, they are often the first to show signs of damage — potential signs of *arteriosclerosis* — making erectile dysfunction a symptom signaling that more dangerous health consequences are brewing up internally.

According to J. Stephen Jones, M.D., author of Overcoming Impotence, "…even the healthiest penis cannot escape the damaging effects of smoking." Dr. Jones continues, "Erectile dysfunction, at least for the time-being, may not be life-threatening, but if the reason is from smoking, then other life-threatening diseases may be developing, like heart attack, stroke, all sorts of cancers and others."

The tobacco industry is completely aware of how fatal their product is for *all* its consumers. As stated, in addition to loss of sexual ability in both men and women, smoking kills nearly one-half million people each year in the United States alone — and millions of others worldwide. But don't just think that if you smoke, you die suddenly. It's not that quick. Instead, those who suffer from smoking-related disorders experience an agonizingly slow and painful persistence for years … then … it's lights out. So if you smoke, and you don't die this year, then stand in line, because your number will be called before you expect it to be. Especially before your kids and other loved ones expect it.

Let your erectile dysfunction tell you to quit smoking before your heart does. Smoking kills more people each year than deaths from AIDS, automobile accidents, murders, suicides, drug overdoses, and fires; COMBINED. Doctors suggest that quitting smoking can extend your life up to *10 extra years*. That's more time for your kids, grand-kids, fishing, golf, and, of course, *sex!* (Hey, I just had a flashback …. Remember that antismoking campaign posted on billboards that mocked the Marlboro Man with a *limp* cigarette hanging from his mouth? I haven't seen that guy for a long time. He didn't look that old but perhaps he died from the product he was endorsing.)

Okay, you're not a smoker, but you're around people who do smoke. Don't ignore the warnings: Second-hand smoke can (and does) deliver a deadly blow to your overall health. Let's say you don't smoke, but you were out playing cards with the guys, who were smoking all through the night. When you get home, it hits you like an avalanche. All of a sudden your head is pounding, you're on the verge of catching a cold, and — you guessed it — you're experiencing loss of erectile ability. Second-hand smoke is also linked to SIDS, or *sudden infant death syndrome*, so please don't expose your children to smoking. (It's a crime in many parts of this country to smoke in the presence of children, especially in closed environments like playgrounds and inside automobiles.)

Stress: The Silent Killer

According to Dr. Joe Dispenza, author of *Evolve Your Brain: The Science of Changing Your Mind* and featured guest in the popular docu-drama *What the Bleep Do We Know*, "75% to 90% of people who have been admitted to a health-care facility in the Western world are there because of stress-related disorders." Stress is not only responsible for hospitalizing millions of people; it's a proven killer. Regarding sexuality and erections, stress destroys the integrity of the tissues and cells that compose the genitals and penis; it is a major cause of ED and other sexual disorders.

The opposite occurs during stress of what's necessary to occur during erection. For the penis to become filled with blood, the tissues and vascular vessels must enlarge or *dilate*, also known as *vasodilation*.

However, stress constricts the tissues and prevents circulation, and when the constriction is to the vascular system, it's often referred to as *vasoconstriction*. It's like placing a tight strap around your upper arm, only to find your fingers quickly turning blue from lack of blood supply.

Stress is destructive to the penis and its ability to obtain erections, due to vasoconstriction. This literally means that the penis is being denied (or choked off from) nourishment and blood flow. But stress also has plenty of psychological culprits that are ignited with anger, anxiety, fear, low self-esteem, worry, depression, guilt, sadness, jealousy, fatigue, smoking, and junk food, to name a few. These reactions create a cascade of toxic chemicals that deny the body nourishment.

We're all aware that a high percentage of people with stress also have high blood pressure along with accelerated heart rates; that's known as *hypertension*. Hypertension, from one perspective, can be regarded as a natural defense mechanism we innately possess. Since hypertension causes vasoconstriction that literally slows, or even shuts down, the circulation of vital nutrients, including oxygen, the body compensates for this starvation by increasing the rate at which the heart beats in an attempt to pump adequate supplies of blood throughout the body. Unfortunately, during stressful situations the genetic coding of our DNA is not programmed to have sex (or make love), so the blood is sent to major muscles that are typically involved in fighting or flighting. (See "Cardio Economics" in Chapter 14.)

It's in the Water: Environmental Toxins & Estrogens

When you hear the saying, "It's in the water," take concern. Microscopic sperm-killing and erection-destroying chemicals have been found in many of the world's water supplies. Not only is this water harmful to man; it's also harmful to marine life. Many of these chemicals are known as *environmental estrogens*, also referred to as *xenoestrogens*, which are toxic estrogen-like compounds that exist in plastics, food wraps, bowls, canisters, and sandwich bags.

According to the National Center for Toxicological Research, an affiliate with the Food and Drug Administration, estrogens were found by microwaving plastic. Estrogens are linked to low sperm counts in men and to breast cancer in women.

A British report entitled *Male Fertility Fears over Pollution in Water Supply* goes into depth about how estrogen in rivers changes the sex of fish, posing potential risk to humans who consume these fish. In these findings, made by Geoffrey Lean and Richard Sadler, with a British research team headed by the Environment Agency, male fish exposed to estrogen were developing female characteristics, and in some stretches, they had become totally feminized. Researchers discovered that a powerful form of estrogen was being excreted into the urine of women who were taking contraceptive pills; this urine was being flushed into the sewage system, ultimately spilling into the rivers. When the water was cleaned up, unfortunately, the male fish remained sterile, so permanent damage was the result of overexposure to this type and level of estrogen.

In a documentary that aired on the National Geographic channel, entitled *Strange Days on Planet Earth*, hosted by Ed Norton, researchers revealed that many of our own waters are becoming a *plastic soup*, containing toxic elements that are destroying life. The levels of toxicity of many of these water supplies contain feminizing effects on men that destroy sperm and lower testosterone. Drinking unsafe water isn't the only concern; eating fish raised in estrogen-filled waters is also a culprit for the feminization of many men today.

Plastic products surround us. And all of them contain these estrogen-like toxins. Our sandwiches are wrapped in plastic bags, we store our food in plastic containers, our contact lenses are plastic, water and soda bottles are plastic ... the list goes on and on! Don't ignore this alert because the facts speak for themselves. And along with the ever-increasing rates of ED, men are registering lower sperm counts than ever before. Use of plastic products should be on the list of culprits for men experiencing ED — for women too!

The Hot Seat

According to Dr. Irwin Goldstein, prominent Boston urologist, bike riding can lead to impotence. Due to the positioning of the rider's entire torso and upper body weight on the seat, the vessels that enter the penis become compressed. Compression, even contusion from vibration and hitting bumps, can cause tissue rupture. Most riders, including me, experience penile numbness when sitting on their bicycle seats too long. I have the biggest, fattest seat you can find and, on top of that, I have a thick gel-loaded cover as well; even with all the precautions, my penis still gets numb after about 20 minutes on the bike. (Also refer to "Bike Riding" in Chapter 17.)

Is SOY Sexy?

In a study conducted at the Harvard School of Public Health in Boston, Massachusetts, by Jorge Chavarro and his colleagues, the researchers found that men who consumed soy-based products over a three-month period were found to have 40% less than typical sperm counts when compared to men who didn't eat such foods. Although touted as a great food, and a very controversial one at that, soy is very high in natural (phyto) estrogen and has been blamed for reducing testosterone levels in men.

According to some statistics (I haven't seen them all), Asian men, known to consume soy, have lower rates of prostate cancer when compared to American men. Personally, I believe this is due to the Asian's higher consumption of raw foods and fish, and lower levels of stress, while many American men are simply on a collision course when considering many of their (unhealthy) lifestyle habits, combined with the excessive (constant) stress Americans typically face. Soy has also been noted to prevent conversion of testosterone into the radical *dihydrotestosterone*, which is known to cause male-pattern baldness and *benign prostatic hyperplasia*. But many experts feel there are better ways to accomplish this, which may include using compounds like aromatizing agents and many natural products, like herbs, which you will read about later on.

Caffeine

We are living in the most caffeinated era ever. With coffee shops popping up everywhere, the draw is irresistible. Not just in coffee, caffeine is hidden in many products these days, and over-consumption of caffeine can cause excessive strain to the central nervous system while also draining the adrenals. This sets in motion a vicious cycle between energy surge and energy crash, placing that person under constant stress. As the person crashes they (obviously) feel tired and drained, so their typical reaction is to repeat that (vicious) cycle and drink up some more of that caffeinated drink (a sign of addiction or dependency, or what some experts label as *maladaptive behavior*). It's easy to see how ED is caused by some of the lifestyle habits I have exposed. But I'm far from finished …

The Spine's Role in Sexual Performance

Another anatomical factor that causes impotency, or ED, is spinal compression or vertebral deformity. Men who become overweight, out of shape, or weak; are traumatized in their back region by an accident; or have experienced an unnatural shift (swaying or compression) in their skeletal anatomy, especially the alignment of the vertebrae of their spinal column, can experience interruptions or a complete severance of proper nerve flow that feeds nerve energy into the pelvic and genital regions.

Spinal Column: The *spinal column* is composed of a tower of 24 bones, each called a *vertebra*, that are positioned one on top of the other. As a whole, the spinal column is also referred to as the *vertebral column*, and it's basically divided into three parts: 1) cervical, or upper spine, 2) thoracic, middle spine, and 3) lumbar, lower spine. The skull resides at the top, and the sacrum and pelvis sit at its foundation.

The *vertebrae* are relatively small bones that maintain their alignment to one another and are moved by our tendons, ligaments, and muscles. Because they are stacked on top of one another, assuming somewhat of a vertical-to-the-ground position, our vertebrae are very vulnerable to compression, shifting, swaying, and even collapse, much like those blocks you played with as a child, stacking them up on your parents' kitchen table. The main role of the vertebral column, in addition to giving our torso its structural support, is to house and protect the spinal cord.

The spinal cord is a rope-like tubular bundle of nerves that is long and thin. It is an extension of the central nervous system that originates in the brain. This cord is encased in and protected by the bony vertebral column. The main function of the spinal cord is transmission of nerve signals from the brain to all parts of the body. When the *spinal cord* is interfered with, becomes obstructed, or, worse yet, is severed, nerve energy ceases to flow, blocking brain-nerve signals that need to enter and influence the tissues and organs. Paralysis occurs when complete obstruction of the spinal cord, or one of its branching nerves, fails to make contact with the tissues. A slight tingling in your foot, for instance, may indicate that your lower spinal column is out of alignment, or that your spine is being overly compressed, placing extraordinary pressure onto the nerves that extend out of the spinal cord in that area and down into the muscles in your foot.

The same holds true for the nerves that supply the reproductive system, testicles, and your *little* buddy. Statistically, back imbalances, weaknesses, and injuries (especially to the lumbar region) are responsible for many irritating and painful ailments, including sexual disorders and ED. In fact, according to statistics, over 80% of our population complains about back pain. This lends an explanation as to why billions of dollars are spent annually to address back issues — everything ranging from a simple aspirin to invasive spinal surgery. Proper care of your body, especially your waistline and midsection, is not only important for sexual health, but it's also important for total health. Again, without proper nerve flow, erections are impossible.

The spinal cord is also responsible for orgasm as a *reflex* response explosively releases a huge amount of pent-up sexual energy, creating an *orgasm, peak,* or *climax*. It's like overfilling a balloon with air so that the balloon explodes. The same happens during orgasm as the spinal cord releases an enormous amount of constrained energy that has been building up during sexual stimulation.

Spinal-nerve-genital disruptions are also common in heavy weight-training bodybuilders, strength athletes, and to others who have suffered overloads to their torso and spinal regions, as the excessive pressure(s) have had a compressing and distorting effect to natural spinal alignment, creating interferences in nerve flow.

Having an orgasm is one of the most powerful human experiences.

Helen E. Fisher, Ph.D., author of *The Sex Contract*
The Brain, History Channel, History.com

Back to Basics

Can you touch your toes with your fingertips when leaning forward from a standing position while keeping your knees locked? If the answer is *NO*, can you at least touch your knees?

Is it easy for you to wash your feet when showering or bathing, then dry off your toes with a towel afterwards?

Can you lean over to pet little Fido, a Yorkshire Terrier, when he comes over for some attention?

These are normal and natural body motions that our skeletal and muscular systems have difficulty performing when the body lacks tissue integrity and flexibility or has excess amounts of body fat getting in the way of full and natural ranges of mobility. Simple care to your back's flexibility will not only improve nerve flow but also increase the circulation of blood. This enhances the integrity of the muscles, tendons, and ligaments, making them more flexible and stronger. (Exercise tips are provided on the Web site.)

Medications Believed to Cause ED (Partial List)

Accupril	Lotensin
Aldactone	Lopressor
Aldactazide	Maxzide
Aldomet	Minipress
Altace	Moduretic
Amytriptyline (Elavil)	Monopril
Catapress	Nitroglycerin
Capoten	Normodyne
Cimetidine (Tagamet)	Paxil
Corgard	Phenobarbital (barbiturates)
Cymbalta	Prozac
Digitalis	Sectral
Dilantin	Tenormin
Hydrochlorothiazide	Toprol
Inderal	Zestril
Ketoconazole	Zoloft

Categories of Drugs Believed to Cause ED (Partial List)

Anti-Baldness	Anti-Ulcer medications
Antidepressants	Blood pressure medications
Antihistamines	Cardiovascular drugs

Do Not Disturb

To experience the complete and most powerful effects of (endogenous) human growth hormone secretion, sleep must be uninterrupted. Before falling asleep, your pituitary gland has been eagerly readying itself to commence its operation, likened to a kid waiting in line for a toy store to open. The pituitary has been given its instructions: Repair DNA; regenerate hormones; accelerate digestion and remove waste; burn fat; repair muscle, nerve, and bone cells; renovate the heart and its vast cardiovascular network; oxygenate the respiratory system. The list is infinitely long.

As soon as you fall asleep — and when your brain reaches the stage of REM (rapid eye movement) — the pituitary begins operating full steam. Its operational power will remain that way for hours, unless you're suddenly awakened from a deep sleep. Once you're woken up, the pituitary, as wise as it is, believes it's time to return to activity. Human growth hormone secretion ceases as its *biological restoration operations* have been instructed to cease. Remember, the body has two basic phases, 1) energy exertion or activity and 2) energy replenishment or restoration.

Now, don't think: *Well, if I fall back to sleep then I'll reboot that pituitary-HGH operation.* Unfortunately, it doesn't always work that way. Instead, after disrupting a pituitary-HGH operation, you typically have to wait until the next night for the pituitary to secrete high levels of HGH. All too often this becomes a vicious cycle for those who are suffering from insomnia and sleep deprivation, now regarded as an epidemic that's directly causing many illnesses, including reproductive and sexual dysfunctions.

So before you go to bed, make sure you hang that Do Not Disturb sign on your bedroom door handle, so your pituitary gland is not bothered and you get the best recuperative-producing sleep possible.

Andropause — What Is It?

Andropause is one of the newer names in medical dictionaries pertaining to sexual and penile disorders in men. Unfortunately, it has taken a long time not only to come up with this name, but also to understand its definition, especially when you realize that medical sciences have been active with its female counterpart — *menopause* — for eons. Menopause is basically known as a woman's change of life. It's when her younger hormones and reproductive abilities drop off like a booster from a rocket ship as she enters the more advanced stages in her life. Since a percentage of women experience menopause in their 40s and 50s, this is referred to as a *midlife crisis*. (I guess doctors believed we're halfway toward completing our life spans at that point, hence *mid*.)

Men in Pause

As stated, statistics reveal that many men are (and have been) slowing down. I'm not referring to the speed at which they can physically run, and I'm not referring to their intellectual ability to quickly calculate a hand in blackjack. Rather, it's their overall health and, especially, their sexual abilities. Simply put, many men are slowing down, while millions of others are stuck in *pause* mode.

(*Andro* is short for *androgen*, referring to male hormones. *Pause* simply means a cessation.)

Men don't need a doctor telling them that they're low in sexual desire, and they don't need to undergo tests to prove they "can't get it up." Guys with ED already know that. Doctors are needed to ascertain hormonal deficiencies, then recommend strategic lifestyle modifications that will methodically "unpause" these men.

When men experience *andropause*, this, in their minds, is their version of the *midlife crisis*. And because most of us have been brainwashed into this *midlife crisis* thing, men and women alike often regard declines in their health and sexuality as the normal and inevitable *we-can't-do-anything-about-it* fact of aging. But this is no longer true. Maybe it was decades ago, when these sciences weren't very well understood, or even studied; but like everything else — computers, aviation, electronics, automotives, and most other technologies — the sciences that locate and remedy human sexual health disorders have also advanced. Unfortunately, a lot of this information is not yet widespread and available to the mainstream — unless, of course, you read this book.

Similar to menopause in women, andropause is a decline or imbalance of the male endocrine (or hormonal) system that mostly manifests itself as ED, or impotence. Statistics show that this is a serious and growing male health concern, made obvious by the escalating amount of erection pills being sold to desperate men. Andropause relentlessly decreases the quality of a man's life, oftentimes having a negative impact on his family and career.

Studying and treating male sexual disorders is not a new science for a select number of unconventional authorities and institutions. The pioneers, doctors, scientists, health advocates, and longevity specialists who have been developing various options to boost hormonal health and sexual functions, and to treat disorders, have simply focused more on R&D (research and development) than on allocating valuable monetary resources toward funding aggressive advertising campaigns. You now have access to an astonishing display of successfully proven products and treatments that address the *causes* and *symptoms* of sexual disorders.

Interestingly enough, key biomarkers to a healthy body and mind are, in fact, healthy degrees of sexual desire or libido and the ability to successfully achieve and sustain an erection for pleasurable intercourse. Also, the success of a man who's attempting to inseminate his wife is the result of a complete chain of hormonal secretions, functional testicles, a healthy prostate gland, vascular integrity of the penile tissues, and sperm-filled ejaculatory fluid. For pleasure or procreation (or both), sex is natural, healthy, and a necessity.

Some of the causes for ED and other male sexual disorders (that are independent of normal age-related hormonal declination) are brought about by psychological and behavioral factors, as well as lifestyle habits.

Dr. Fouad I. Ghaly, hormone specialist and anti-aging pioneer, states that "elevated estrogen levels in men will increase deposits of fatty tissue in a man's breast area, around the nipples, causing *gynecomastia.*" Ghaly continues, "…the prostate gland can also be damaged when a man's body has an unhealthy amount of estrogen."

ADAM: Yet Another Nickname for ED

This acronym stands for *androgen deficiency in aging males.* Age-related hormonal decline is a fact of life. Levels of all hormones start to drop with age. Longevity specialists who are also skilled in resetting declining hormones claim that after the age of 25, the decline begins. Depending on lifestyle and mindset, this decline continues until the day we pass. However, keeping an eye on your internal hormonal status is critical for maintaining "that youthful glow" as we continue to mature, making it possible to enjoy sex for much longer than normal.

Growing Up Male

As a teen (and even as a twenty-something-or-other), you could be shit-faced drunk, woken out of a deep sleep, and even pissed off at the entire world, but none of that would matter. Your *little* buddy would always rise to the occasion when opportunity knocked, sometimes rising for no reason at all. You could drive for hours, stay up all night, even subject yourself to the most uncomfortable — and often the most unhealthy — situations, and things would be just fine as your *one-eyed monster* would always be eager and willing to perform.

Young men typically have extremely high levels of libido, testosterone, and erectile ability. Their hormonal levels are so high that even if their levels are cut in half, they can still perform sexually and never know they're having a developing problem that will manifest into full-blown ED some time down the road.

Older men, however, have lower hormonal levels to begin with and can't afford the slightest drop. Since their sexual systems are far more sensitive, any dip in hormone power would probably put them completely out of the game. As men age, their sexual abilities typically won't respond when hormones dip to the lower end of normal — or below normal. So it's vitally important to do what it takes to elevate our hormones to at least the mid-level of normal, but preferably to the higher end of normal. Read on …

Chapter 5

Understanding the Penis

Male Parts: Penis, Testicles, and Prostate

As a generalized explanation, the penis is made up of three tube-like chambers that run parallel to each other, covering the length of the penis. One of those tubes, called the *urethra*, allows the exit of urine from the body and the release of semen during ejaculation. The other two

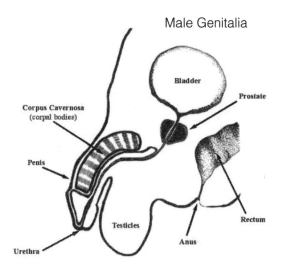

Male Genitalia

chambers, known as the *corpal bodies* (medical term, *corpus cavernosa*), are sponge-like tissues that capture blood, making the penis swell up and become erect. When blood is forced into the *corpal bodies*, these chambers expand in width and length, making a flaccid penis hard or erect. It's like pumping air into a balloon, except it's not the air that makes the penis firm and voluminous; it's blood.

Down below the penis, and hanging next to one another, are the *testicles*, also known as the *gonads* (in females, the gonads are the *ovaries*). This pair of sensitive ball-shaped organs has plenty of nick-names: *balls, nuts, rocks, family jewels, gems, kiwis, cahones, plums, package.* The testicles are located in a loose sac of skin, known as the *scrotum.* They produce testosterone through tiny "testosterone factories" located in testicular tissue, known as the *Leydig cells,* which are influenced by the pituitary gland way up on top of the body inside the brain. Testicles also play a role in sperm production along with the prostate gland, and they're influenced by other hormones, particularly luteinizing hormone (LH) and follicular stimulating hormone (FSH).

The testicles and prostate produce the sperm that creates new life, while the penis is the delivery system that injects sperm-filled semen into the female. A healthy prostate and testicles = healthy sperm. And, ironically, Mother Nature has done a great job of protecting a man's gonads. The reason why a man's testicles hang outside his body is for temperature control — yep, they're fussy critters that need their own air conditioning system. Since our testicles are persnickety, and they don't like when it's too hot or too cold, they must have their environment just right. It's actually a good thing, as the testicles are equipped with their own biological defense mechanism that allows them to adjust when temperatures don't meet their fancy; they act almost like a thermostat.

Heat destroys sperm. So I hate to break the bad news to you guys who like hot tubs, but every time you jump in, your nuts have a good chance of being roasted while your semen may become devoid of healthy (lively) sperm. Ironically, the inside temperature of your body is slightly hotter than what our testicles prefer, so as man evolved, the testicles came to be positioned on the outside of his body. This is such an odd place when you think about it. It's like seeing Michael Jackson hanging his baby off a hotel balcony many stories above the ground — it's risky and dangerous. (FYI: Sperm cells have their best chance for production and integrity at temperatures slightly under normal body temperature.)

Even the slightest bump to your testicles can drop you to your knees. But Mother Nature would rather do what's necessary to maintain the integrity and population of sperm (which is a procreative program that's innate in our cellular physiology and critical for the multiplication of our race) than have to worry about the pain that results from getting kicked between the legs. Like all good parents, Mother Nature probably hung our balls out to teach us men how to protect ourselves. Tough love, but it seems to be working. (Now you know the origin of the saying *one hung low*. But actually it's *two hung below*.)

However, despite all this, it's obvious that Mother Nature thought everything through. When the outside temperature cools to a point that our testicles cannot tolerate, a natural reflex-mechanism in the lower abdominal cavity pulls on the scrotum and raises up the testicles, which draw them near or even go inside the abdomen to keep them warm. The muscles responsible for this reflex action are called the *cremasteric* muscles. You'll know if your cremasteric muscles are working properly if you've ever taken a cold shower or gone out to shovel snow — and noticed your nuts have disappeared. Well, they haven't really disappeared; they've just snuggled up next to your internal fireplace. In reverse, when things start to warm up again, the cremasteric muscles relax and let your testicles hang back out.

Another defense mechanism Mother Nature gave us guys is a slight misalignment of our testicles. Yes, one ball hangs lower than the other. If you've ever suddenly crossed your legs together, you'd notice that one of your testicles deflects, or slides off the other one that's hanging slightly uneven. (Perhaps this is how the saying *pocket billiards* was inspired?) If (or when) your testicles ever crashed into one another, you'd become a candidate for voice-overs on the Chipmunks. (By the way, I'm sitting right now with my legs spread eagle.)

Sperm Count: Oligospermia

When healthy men ejaculate, they will emit over 20 million sperm cells per milliliter of fluid, or hundreds of million per orgasm. Men who emit *less* have a condition known as *oligospermia*, or low sperm count. As mentioned, sperm cells are very sensitive to temperature, especially heat. They are also sensitive to toxic chemicals like steroids, residue from smoking, excessive alcohol, junk foods, environmental estrogens, and many drugs. Men can improve the quality of their sperm and increase seminal volume by adhering to healthy lifestyle practices. This can also be done by using supplements like L-Arginine, Antler, vitamin C, zinc, and many of the other supplements listed in this book.

Ejaculation

Slang terminologies refer to ejaculation as the *load*, *jism*, or *cum*. Male porn actors are known to abstain from ejaculatory sex for days prior to a sex scene so that their prostate and testicles can build up higher volumes of seminal fluid and sperm; hence, a bigger *load*. The supplements listed in this book are often used by male porn actors to increase the volume of fluid that's ejaculated (expelled) during orgasm.

Shooting blanks: Men with oligospermia may, in fact, ejaculate normal volumes of seminal fluid, however their sperm count can be extremely low. This can be noticed by the amount of milky white-colored liquid of the ejaculate fluid. If the ejaculate is clear, absent of this white milky color, then sperm count may be very low. To give somewhat of a visual comparison, check to see if your seminal fluid resembles whole-fat milk, lowfat milk, or totally skimmed (nonfat) milk. As men age, they — and those who destroy their sperm with steroids, too many hot tub baths, smoking, and other unhealthy lifestyle habits — most likely shift in stages from the whiter whole-milk to the clearer nonfat milk.

For those men trying to father children, sperm count (not necessarily the seminal fluid) is the important thing to consider. Dr. Ann Marie

Tommey, Ob-gyn and couple's sexual health counselor, revealed to me during our interview that many women visit her to address the symptoms of depression that are generated from being unable to become impregnated. When Tommey requests the woman's husband come in for an examination of his own (which, not surprisingly, is often met with resistance), a percentage of the time she discovers that the husband has an extremely low sperm count while the wife's capability to become pregnant is perfectly normal. Once the husband is remedied of his *oligospermia*, babies are made.

To help you stop shooting blanks, sperm-count tests are easily and enjoyably available through a doctor's order. Just go into the clinic, close the door behind you, and sit in a room that's playing a porno on a TV monitor or read an adult magazine. You proceed to masturbate until orgasm, capturing your ejaculatory fluid in a little plastic cup. Then you leave the rest for the laboratory technicians. You're notified of your test results in a few days.

The Prostate's Role

As stated, the prostate produces seminal fluid (semen) and sperm but does not play any role in creating erections. That's not a reason to ignore this gland, because the more sperm you produce, the more your prostate and penis and testicles might (will) desire to discharge it.

I used to hear that an unhealthy prostate caused ED, but current understanding is that the (now outdated) treatments and surgical procedures of the past that addressed enlarged prostates were damaging the nerves that traveled into the penis, causing the erectile dysfunction. It was the treatment for the prostate condition, not the condition itself, that caused the ED. However, with advances in medical science, modern techniques for treating prostate enlargement have identified the location of these penile nerves, and skilled surgeons can target the prostate without nerve or circulatory damage. Today, men who undergo prostate surgery can get erections after recovery. (The same holds true for vasectomies of yesteryear, which have abruptly ended a man's sex life with outdated procedures.)

Hyperplasia

Enlargement, also referred to as *hyperplasia* or *hypertrophy*, of the prostate gland can cause irritating pressure onto the highly sensitive nerves that nourish the penis, causing urinary, erectile, and orgasmic difficulties. All men, especially after the age of 30, should obtain an annual prostate-specific antigen (PSA) blood exam. This test measures the chemical makeup of blood when the prostate is unhealthy. The fastest (and initial) way for your doctor to check your prostate, without drawing blood and/or going in for more extensive lab tests, is by manually inserting one of his fingers into your anus, and poking it into your rectum, to conduct a simple — but not necessarily *comfortable* — probing exam. Utilizing his index finger, the doc wiggles it as far up inside your anus as he can reach to feel the location, size, and texture of your prostate. Then, if the news is good, he'll shake your hand to congratulate you! (Just kidding about the handshake.)

Anatomy of an Erection

Obtaining and sustaining an erection is made possible through a complex chain of psycho-physiological processes that are under the control of the brain, hormones, nervous system, spinal column, circulation of blood, and the penis.

As a result of the *thought* of sex (fantasy, lust, desire, or libido), as well as a *physical* sexual sensation (touch), the hypothalamus gland, located in the brain, secretes gonadotrophin-releasing hormone (GnRH).

GnRH rushes out of the hypothalamus and speeds over to the pituitary gland, which is only a fraction of an inch away.

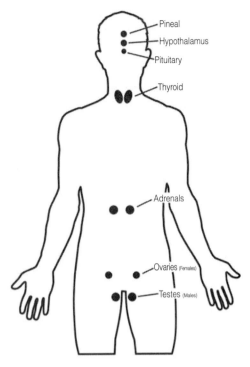

The pituitary gland responds to the GnRH signal by secreting two other hormones: luteinizing hormone (LH) and follicular stimulating hormone (FSH).

As LH and FSH rush out of the pituitary, they both travel all the way down to make contact with the gonads — testicles for men and ovaries for women.

When the pituitary gland produces LH and FSH from the GnRH, and when the gonads respond to LH and FSH, this is called a *positive feedback*. (Feedback literally means the glands are effectively communicating with each other through these hormonal/chemical messengers.)

However, if the pituitary fails to respond to GnRH, or the gonads fail to respond to LH and FSH, then this is called *negative feedback*, sometimes referred to as *down regulation*. This is a condition that all men with hypogonadism are all too well aware of, due to its disruption, shutting off, or complete disconnection of their glands and hormones; I often refer to this as the *brain-penis connection*. This same *negative feedback* occurs in men and women who are experiencing other types of declining sexual ability.

HPTA: The Sexual Response Axis

This entire cycle is referred to as the HPTA: hypothalamic-pituitary-testicular axis, or HPGA: hypothalamic-pituitary-gonadal axis (while *axis* is often replaced with the words *cycle, loop, system,* or *cascade*).

Sexual Hormonal Axis

Hypothalamus

Gonadtrophin Releasing Hormone

GnRH

Pituitary

Luteinizing Hormone

Follicular Stimulating Hormone

LH

FSH

Adrenals

Gonads

Testes - Males
Ovaries - Females

Sperm
Males

Testosterone
Males & Females

Erection
Male Penis
Female Clitoris

Once the gonads are stimulated, the genitals must be prepped for their tasks in performing the sexual act itself. This requires nerve flow that provides sensitivity and pleasure that ultimately builds up in the spinal column until it reaches its limit and explodes into orgasmic pleasure. The genitals must also receive a high volume influx of blood flow for erection of the penis to occur in men, and for vaginal lubrication and erection of the clitoris in women.

(The bigger the man's penis, the more blood needs to enter. Rumors about the notorious bank robber, John Herbert Dillinger, claimed he had a 22-inch penis. Legend has it that every time Dillinger got a hard-on, he fainted because his penis required so much blood that his brain was deprived. I couldn't find proof of this rumor, but I was first told this story when I was a young kid. Why it just popped into my mind as I'm writing this now, I don't know. Let's let the legend of Dillinger RIP so we can get back to normal-sized penises!)

In the penis, the dilation of the corpal bodies (primarily) makes room for the blood to enter. But to actually get the blood to flow inside the corpal bodies of the penis requires yet another component of this complex sexual system to spring into action, called *nitric oxide* (NO). (Let me inform all female readers that NO is imperative for your vaginal and clitoral health and sexual sensitivity. More on NO later.) NO helps bring blood flow into the genital region, while it is also instrumental in making what's probably the last key erection-producing ingredient, a chemical called *cyclic guanosine monophosphate* (cGMP).

CGMP is another key chemical ingredient needed for *obtaining* erections. It's also the key chemical that allows erections to be *sustained*. Without cGMP, a man cannot *achieve* an erection, and he cannot *sustain* it either.

Unfortunately, cGMP is destroyed by an enzyme the body naturally produces known as phosphodiesterase-V, or PDE-5. (V is a Roman numeral for the number 5.) PDE-5 binds and impedes cGMP. The trick is to block or inhibit PDE-5 so that NO and cGMP can perform their tasks for making and sustaining firm erections (for both men and women; penis and clitoris).

Viagra, Levitra, and Cialis are all erection pills that have been made popular by TV ads. All three drugs are PDE-5 inhibitors and very effective ones at that. So, again, when PDE-5 is blocked, and NO and cGMP are allowed to fulfill the vasodilation of the penis (and clitoris), erection occurs.

But before you run off and grab your lover, especially you guys, there's more to learn about erections.

Once blood gets inside your penis, that blood must stay in there long enough to *sustain* the erection to please you and, of course, your lover. But many men who are complaining about ED actually don't have a problem getting an erection; instead, it's *sustaining* the erection that causes their sexual frustration. Losing erections before ejaculation is a definite and reasonable definition for erectile dysfunction and impotency.

Lost erections can be blamed on the same culprit; PDE-5 is binding to or blocking the NO-cGMP cycle, which terminates the *vasodilatation* and now causes *vasoconstriction* (blockage, leakage, or removal of blood). It's like untying the knot that holds the air inside a balloon. The corpal bodies lose their girth and rigidity as the blood escapes. This is a likely reason why some men lose their erections — blood loss.

(Please note that there are other reasons for lost erections. Physically, there may be some kind of vascular rupture or leakage to the arteries of the penis or the corpal bodies, which also drains out blood from the penis. This is known as *venous insufficiency* or *venous leakage*. Erectile problems can also be psychological, as the man may suddenly feel uneasy, fearful, or have an embarrassing emotion that turns him, and his penis, off.)

Keep in mind, the current prescription erection pills available as of this writing are only effective at creating erections when accompanied with physical stimulation. Since these drugs work merely in the final stage of the erection-producing cycle (by blocking PDE-5), sexual thought alone typically won't be the cause of the erection. So even though your penis is hard and stiff, it's likely you won't be enjoying sex as much as you like, or were once (normally) accustomed to.

The Hormonal Cascade

Various terms are used to describe the sexual hormonal sequence by which hormones are produced, secreted, and delivered to the genitals in both men and women.

Here are the most common:

✓ Hypothalamus — Pituitary — Testicular — Axis (HPTA)

✓ Hypothalamus — Pituitary — Gonadal — Axis (HPGA)

✓ Hypothalamus — Pituitary — Adrenal/Testicular — Axis (also HPTA)

The amount of pleasure a man receives from sex relates to the function of his brain, hormones, central nervous system (spinal cord included), penile nerve flow, and his status of sexual health. Hormones are chemical agents that serve as *feedback* mechanisms that send *sensation* signals to the glands and tissues in the brain where pleasure is registered; the same works in reverse for pain. When the body is healthy, the body is highly sensitive, sexually speaking. Natural products like Antler, Tribulus, Epimedium, Yohimbine, and various other compounds are extremely useful in boosting sensitivity. (More on this later!)

Thyroid: In addition to the glands listed above, the thyroid gland also plays a significant role in our health, body weight, and sexuality. The thyroid is one of the largest endocrine glands in the body. It's located in the frontal neck region, in near proximity to the Adam's apple, the cartilage that protects this gland. The thyroid is responsible for turning the foods we eat into usable energy, while playing a major role in overall metabolism. The thyroid is also responsible for making proteins from amino acids and for producing other hormones. This gland is controlled by the pituitary and hypothalamus, both responsible for many essential body functions including mood, energy, strength, libido, and sexual function. The term *hypothyroidism* refers to a slow, hypoactive thyroid, while h*yperthyroidism* is a fast, hyperactive thyroid. Both conditions can wear out the integrity of the sexual system, causing ED and other disorders. Natural supplements like tyrosine, kelp, and iodine are known to be useful for thyroid health.

I Have an Erection! What's Next?

Okay, you went through a full cycle of *obtaining*, then *sustaining* an erection. During this process, semen and sperm have built up in the prostate. Sexual energy is stored in the spinal column (in both sexes), building up until that last stroke, twist, or thrust. And then it all lets loose like a volcanic eruption — an orgasm, a sexual climax.

As stated in an earlier section of this book, sex is healthy, especially for those who have frequent orgasms. Sex relieves stress, boosts immunity, conditions the glands and hormones (endocrine system), and is a natural tranquilizer. As also stated, Mother Nature rewards us for having sex — in more ways than one.

A natural tranquilizer? Yes, you're less stressed and should have much better chances of falling asleep after sex; guys might know this better than women, according to reports from Mars and Venus.

So when can you do it again? How long will you have to wait until you can get aroused again? Become erect again? Have another one of those volcanic orgasms again?

It all depends on the speed at which your HPTA cycle can repeat itself; it also depends on the speed at which NO and cGMP can be produced, the speed at which PDE-5 can be blocked, and how fast the testicles and prostate can manufacture seminal fluid and sperm. There's a lot going on there! It's known as the *refractory period*, the time between orgasms, and younger guys can recover in as little as 15 minutes, while older fellows can take 15 hours or longer. Proper care and use of the supplements listed in this book will definitely help all aspects of your sexual abilities and also increase your sexual frequency, speeding up your refractory periods.

Another gland that plays a role in erections is called the *pineal gland*, also located in the brain. The pineal gland produces a hormone called *melatonin*, encapsulated for purchase in health food stores to put you to sleep at night, or to prevent jet lag while crossing time zones. Melatonin-induced sleep can help to stimulate the release of human growth hormone (HGH) from the pituitary gland. HGH is known to be the chief hormone responsible for overall health and longevity. In fact, many antiaging and longevity advocates promote HGH as the *fountain of youth*, while using supplemental melatonin has become a staple practice.

Hard-Wired for Sex

We often take it for granted or are completely oblivious to the fact that Mother Nature is always eager to check the status of our sexual health every night when we're asleep. To monitor man's procreative abilities, a requirement for the future success of the human race, we have an internal system that produces erections while we're snoozing away (*nocturnal*, during sleep) and don't even know what's universally going on. For sure, you know exactly what I'm talking about. It's that hard-on you wake up with (or used to wake up with) for no apparent reason. Also known as the *morning erection*, it causes healthy men to pole-vault out of bed after they've awakened, while having to wait until their penises become flaccid enough to allow urination.

Our hormonal physiology operates like your computer that is set to automatic save, automatic sleep, or automatic backup. This nocturnal hormonal monitoring mechanism is inspecting (amongst an array of other things) our glands, hormones, and the circulation of blood and nerve flow into the penile vessels that make procreation possible. Typically, if a man is experiencing nocturnal erections but experiences erectile dysfunction with a partner, it's often concluded that psychological factors are the culprits for his lack of erection ability.

There are a variety of techniques for determining if Mom is checking up on us. We can use these techniques to verify that our systems and penises are primed for sex. The more sophisticated tests are conducted in professional sleep labs; however, there is a test you can perform in your own bedroom. (See "Going Postal" below!)

When You Can Pole-Vault out of Bed but Can't Jump Back into the Sack

There's another possible explanation for men who do experience nocturnal erections and are physiologically okay — but are still experiencing erection difficulties.

Since hormones, particularly testosterone, cycle throughout the day, week, and month (yes, men have cycles too), it's possible that when a man's in need of an erection for intercourse, his testosterone and other libido-yielding erection-producing hormones can suddenly plummet below performance levels. In these situations, timing your sexual activity can be tricky, as some guys peak in the morning, while others are night-time lovers. This drop in sexual ability can also be caused by having too much to drink, performance anxiety, fear of failure, or a plethora of other reasons. Keep track of the days, and the specific times of those days, that you feel you have the most sexual vigor; then plan your sexual schedule around those periods. You might have to start taking your wife or girl-friend on breakfast dates if after-dinner sex is challenging you.

Going Postal

To conduct their own nocturnal erection monitoring, many men perform the popular *stamp test*. Yes, the same kind of stamps you lick when you send an *I miss you* letter to your mother. This is a very simple self-exam that's easily performed at home, a hotel, or wherever you decide to sleep. Simply wrap a strip of postage stamps (the ones that are perforated together) around your (flaccid) penis before going to bed.

If, after awakening, you find that the stamps have split apart, *then guess what?* You may have had the erection fairy visit you in the middle of the night, and you achieved an erection. In fact, it's possible you had more than one erection, but there's no way to know for sure. Based on the broken stamps, you're physically fine; unless, of course, you split them apart by tossing and turning or inadvertently grabbing your penis. If the stamps didn't break apart, then you need to consult with a qualified authority.

Nocturnal (self) monitoring isn't always accurate since hormonal production runs in cycles. I believe this test has some validity, but more importantly, it can be useful for helping you become a more educated patient when you do see your doctor. Try this test several nights in succession then average out the results. If you're not splitting the stamps, then in you go, and say, "Hey, Doc, I'm not breaking apart the stamps at night." Now, with that information, your doctor has a far better understanding that can speed the remedies for curing your problems. (I forgot to mention the cost of the *stamp test*, if that's a concern. You'll need to invest between two and three bucks in postage, depending on the current postal rates and the thickness of your penis. Nonetheless, paying the U.S. Postal Service is much cheaper than the tests conducted in a lab.)

Sleep-Lab Penis Functioning Exams

There are professional sleep-lab testing facilities that are far more sophisticated at nocturnal erection testing than your postage stamp test conducted in your own bedroom. And let me say, professional sleep-lab testing facilities don't use postage stamps. (Did I really need to say that?) These examinations are the preferred *nocturnal penile tumescence* (NPT) tests. Tumescence is a term used to define a penis that is filled with blood, or a penis that is swollen and erect. Most of a man's nocturnal erections happen during a deep stage of sleep known as the REM period — *rapid eye movement*. Men can have up to five nocturnal erections every night, a number that decreases with age.

In the lab, you would need to stay overnight and be monitored with such technology as electroencephalography (EEG), electrooculography, and electromyography (EMG); and let's not forget that hidden video camera (possibly). Due to the hormonal cycles all men experience, and in order to make the results of the examinations more accurate, a course of two or three nights might be suggested.

Laboratory Penis Functioning Tests

Duplex Ultrasonography: According to many urologists, this is the most accurate test that measures blood flow going into and out of the penis. An erection-producing drug is injected into the penis for internal observation as ultrasound technology measures the response of the arteries and the rate at which blood flows into the penis.

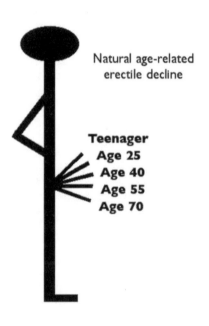

Natural age-related erectile decline

Teenager
Age 25
Age 40
Age 55
Age 70

Penile Arteriography: A dye is injected into the penis for external observation. The dye colors the blood vessels, allowing the clinician to actually see, through the thin skin of the penis, where and how the blood is flowing in. That way, the clinician can determine whether or not that blood flow is becoming trapped anywhere. This test also measures outflow, which is very useful for diagnosing any venous leakages and can direct the doctor to treating patients who are able to achieve but then prematurely lose their erections.

Dynamic Infusion Corpora Cavernosometry (DICC): Funny-sounding acronym, and perfect for testing your ... well, it sounds exactly like the part of your body that it's actually designed to diagnose. DICC measures both penile blood flow and the rigidity (strength or firmness) of the penis. The more blood that can become trapped inside the penis usually means the harder it gets. This is something men lose with age — their penile firmness, rigidity, or hardness. Another way of explaining this test is that it measures penile blood pressure.

Digital Inflection Rigidometer (DIR): Measures the strength of erections. The device is used by pressing it against the penis to make it bend, which then measures the strength, or determines the bending point of the penis. The company Fastsize is about to release a revolutionary patented device called the EQM (erection quality monitor) that has been tested and endorsed by highly credentialed urologists and medical doctors. The EQM is a home penis-monitoring device.

The Solo Test

Another obvious way a man can tell if his penis is physically capable of achieving an erection is through self-stimulation, or masturbation. This can be a useful method in assisting a stubborn penis in cooperating prior to intercourse, as a firm erection (need I say) is necessary. However, erection and ejaculation are two separate things, the latter relating to sensation and pleasure. So achieving an erection does not guarantee orgasm or ejaculation. (Refer to page 127, "Stepping into the Ring," i.e., constriction rings or *cockrings*.)

A possible clue that indicates a psychological cause for ED is when men are capable of achieving erections on their own, like in masturbation or through nocturnal erections; however, when the opportunity presents itself to achieve an erection with a partner, results are embarrassingly ravaging.

Psychological Evaluation

Psychological conditions such as performance anxiety and a host of mental health disorders (including depression and fear) can cause erectile dysfunction. Therefore, your doctor may recommend an interview with a psychologist that focuses on any psychiatric symptoms you may be experiencing.

I will always suggest that any man suffering from any disorder, especially those that pertain to his penis, obtain professional psychological help. I cannot emphasize this enough — the brain (and mind) plays a huge part in sexuality. When the penis is cooperative, the brain and mind have it easy; everything is in harmony — and the HPTA is a smooth running machine. But when sexuality is disrupted, the brain and its mind cease production of its once healthy hormones, while concurrently secreting different, sex-destroying hormones.

When you visit your doctor for sexual challenges, don't forget to explain how you're feeling "and" thinking. Don't just walk in and ask, "Hey, Doc, got anything to help me get erections again?" It's better to say, "Doc, I can't get this off my mind. It's consuming my time and draining me of my energy. Everywhere I go, it's affecting my thinking, and it's not confined to just between my legs anymore. How can you help me get over this and clear my mind?"

Up until the last five or six years, there had been no testing to confirm *psychogenic* impotence. But doctors now understand that stress, anger, guilt, depression, many religious beliefs, fear, anxiety, low self-esteem, and other negative emotions disrupt biological harmony and can disrupt — even destroy — sexual ability.

Psychological Tests: Questions to Ask Yourself

Add any other questions to the below list that you need to ask yourself regarding your challenges, and be honest with the answers …

How often do I think about sex?

How often did I think about sex?

How often do I actually have sex?

Am I satisfied, sexually?

Am I always confident I'll be able to sexually perform?

How often do I get erections?

Am I getting morning erections?

Am I comfortable talking about sex?

Am I holding in any sexual frustrations?

Is my penis sensitive enough to enjoy sex and have satisfying orgasms?

Am I still attracted to my mate? (If in a committed relationship)

Do I experience powerful libido and arousal; do I have desire?

Do I feel uneasy in sexual situations?

Can I achieve an erection when I need to?

Are my erections as firm as they need to be?

When I'm standing and have an erection, does it point up, straight, or down?

Can I maintain an erection long enough to please my partner and myself?

Does sex feel good?

How do I honestly feel about the way I look, especially when I'm naked?

Am I under a lot of stress?

Am I afraid to have sex?

Do I get angry easily?

Am I holding in any grudges?

Do I ejaculate the volume I used to?

What time of the day (or night) do I feel I'm at my sexual peak?

Do I sleep well?

Is my blood pressure within a normal, healthy range?

Has my upbringing, my environment, or my religion confused me about sex?

Am I overweight?

Do I tire easily?

Do I drink excessively?

Do I smoke?

Do I use drugs?

Do I get physical examinations regularly?

Did my father, uncles, or granddad have sexual issues?

How is sex regarded amongst my family and peers? In my religion?

Do I drink water or beverages from plastic bottles?

Do I microwave my food in plastic containers or wraps?

Do I have an insecure feeling about my status in life?

Do I complain over money?

Do I eat healthy foods?

Do I maintain a strong and positive attitude?

Do I have a relationship with a doctor who's skilled in sexual health sciences?

Have I had a complete physical examination this year?

Have I had a complete hormonal blood profiling conducted this year?

When was the last time I had a prostate exam?

Have I sought professional counsel for any of my emotional challenges?

Can I achieve an erection and ejaculate through self-stimulation but have difficulty with a partner?

Have I grown tolerant of and/or dependent on prescription erection pills?

Am I a junk food junkie?

Do I eat sugar in excess, especially late at night?

Has my body become fatter over the last year?

Am I losing my hair?

Have I lost energy and drive for life over the last year?

Do I embrace or avoid (avert) sexual situations?

Do I make up excuses for averting sexual opportunities just to justify my decision?

Am I taking anabolic steroids?

What changes will I make right now knowing the information from this book?

Clinical Tests

The following is a partial list of blood exams. Your doctor will request which ones you'll need and how frequently you'll need to be reexamined. (Please refer to the nationwide network of blood testing procedures offered through the Life Extension Foundation. In addition to outstanding blood profiling services, they offer the best money-saving discounts along with free phone consultations from a team of experts once your exams are completed.)

✓ Complete blood chemistry (CBC)

✓ Cholesterol

- LDL are "bad"; must lower into normal/healthy ranges
- HDL are "good"; exercise is one of the best means of boosting this, along with proper eating. This can reduce your risks of ED and heart disease.

✓ Triglycerides

✓ C-reactive protein (cardiac)

✓ Homocysteine

✓ DHEA: dehydroepiandrosterone sulfate

✓ Testosterone (total and free)

✓ Thyroid stimulating hormone (TSH)

✓ LH: luteinizing hormone

✓ PSA (prostate-specific antigen)

✓ Estradiol

✓ Somatomedin C (IGF-1)

OPTIONS FOR TREATING *IT!*

Early experimentation from virility and erection enthusiasts led to all sorts of bizarre experiments and concoctions like eating the testicles of animals or the infamous (and deadly) Spanish fly; injecting liquefied testicular tissue into one's own testicles (ouch); inserting hot metal rods into the urethra to cause some type of sexual stimulation (double ouch); and surgically implanting objects into the penis (like tree branches, bamboo, animal bones, antlers and horns, cartilage, and others). Needless to say, man's desire to prove his manhood, and/or please his lady, has historically been fueled by fierce ambition — and a lot of screw-ups along the way. But I'm secure in saying that all the barbaric experimentation conducted throughout history has led us to the current state of male sexual enhancement; and although it's nothing less than incredible, it is still very much considered an infant science that is advancing daily.

Chapter 6

Male Enhancement Products

Will they really make my penis bigger?

Unless you've been living on planet Zircon (wherever that is?), you're certainly aware of all those *male enhancement* formulas advertised on TV, e-mailed to your junk in-box from Internet hawkers, and posted at the back of men's magazines, each claiming to outdo the other when it comes to enlarging (or elongating) your penis. I don't know about you, but I'm the type of guy who assumes a *you're guilty until proven innocent* attitude when it comes to these types of advertising ploys (especially when directed to the penis). I need substantial proof that what's being promised actually works.

Although I factor it in, I'm not exclusively interested in reading the *scientific testing* from these hawkers because, to be quite honest, many of these formulas and gadgets don't have complete, effective, or accurate testing procedures; and by now we all know that most of these tests are commissioned by the *makers* of these products, more often concluding in biased results. Instead, I rely heavily (but not exclusively) on human trial, or user opinion. That said, the ultimate test is the old-fashioned *use-to-benefit* ratio. One example is the popular muscle-enhancing supplement *creatine* that was being written about in muscle magazines decades ago. The claims were outrageous, to say the least, beyond normal comprehension in regard to building muscle size, strength, and stamina: *Use it and benefit greatly, surpassing any results you've ever naturally obtained before — and without any negative side effects.*

Those ads drove scores of muscle-enhancing fanatics to place their orders, while making the producers super rich. But I gave it time, sitting back and shifting to a *wait-n-see* attitude. And as I waited with my arms crossed over my chest (figuratively speaking), sure enough, public opinion was extremely positive. I was convinced that this supplement had merit and was securing itself as a staple product that did, in fact, deliver on its promises. It's just like what happened with Viagra; word-of-mouth recognition has superseded any of the claims and laboratory results, selling more pills than the inventors could ever imagine.

That said, many of the products seen in ads for those male enhancement formulas, and that are being purchased on a regular (repeat) basis, do have varying degrees of merit for boosting sexual health. However, to claim that they actually enlarge, thicken, or elongate a man's penis is seriously doubted by many experts, as there's no scientific proof. (I welcome the makers and the users of these compounds to disprove the skeptics and provide substantiation that I'll gladly post their results on the Web site.)

What's impressive to me is that many of the developers of these formulas have, in fact, located some of those secret ingredients that I too have discovered. These are ingredients that come from natural resources and are known to benefit the body sexually for both men and women. As a result, these formulas are readily available off-the-shelf (OTS), on television, and on the Internet, providing for unprecedented easy access to sexual enhancing products.

Now don't regard OTS formulas lightly, especially if you're one of those who believe that drugs are the only way to go. Many of these natural products are extremely potent, while many (most) have no side effects other than good ones, unlike pharmaceuticals. In fact, many of these compounds are documented to possess a variety of health-promoting sex-boosting properties and have been around for literally hundreds, even thousands, of years, while most members of our modern mainstream societies are clueless about their existence.

A quick diversion here but I assure you that I'm staying on track: We've all heard about those mysterious and very old, yet divinely wise, medicine men from primitive jungle villages. Due to their extraordinarily intimate connections to Mother Nature, and perhaps a bundle of creativity, these miracle people have a gift for developing a myriad of remedies that originated from natural resources, e.g., animal parts, bark, leaf, plant, seed, stems, stalk, root, water, soil, and rock. These natural resources are used to treat a variety of disorders, as jungle people also get headaches, stomachaches, cuts, bruises, and broken bones. Some of the men are unable to inseminate their wives or cannot achieve an erection, and the women experience menstrual problems or are unable to become impregnated.

Some of the male enhancement formulas being sold today actually contain one or a combination of the items from the medicine man's basket of magic potions. The trick, however, to avoid buying snake oil is to check that the source of these items is a valid supplier. Also, make sure that the potency per pill is at a level that actually benefits your body while offering a fair cost-per-dosage ratio (if pricing is a concern for you).

Claims regarding the penis-enlarging benefits from using these male enhancement formulas can be misleading. Many of the ingredients are, in fact, useful for helping to boost libido, along with having a corresponding ability to create and sustain erections. So for the guy with ED who hasn't had a quality erection for some time, any results in the area between his legs may (understandably) make him feel like he really is bigger. This is generally due to the fact that he's seeing an erection he hasn't seen in some time. So the better (and more frequent) the erection, the more chances the penis expands to its maximum (normal) erect size, which is satisfying enough for most guys who, as macho as they are, believe they've earned new bragging rights and start to claim, "Of course, my penis is bigger. In fact, it's the biggest it has ever been!" Oh really? Your *little* buddy might be better, but he sure is not any bigger. (Sit tight! I'm getting ready to reveal the real male enhancement products!)

Penis Enlargement Devices: The Real Male Enhancement Products

Vacuum Erection Device (VED)

Also known as a *penis pump*, VEDs have been around for a very long time. In 1917, a doctor named Lederer was granted a patent on a specialized cylinder he developed that was to be placed over a flaccid penis. When the cylinder's outer edge was firmly pressed against the pubis area encircling the base of the penis, a seal was formed to prevent any leaking of air, in or out. Lederer fastened a pump to the opposite end of the cylinder, then withdrew the remaining air. With the penis still inside the chamber, Lederer witnessed his penis enlarging, just like it would during a normal erection. This was due to the vacuum's (suction) effect of drawing the blood into the corpal bodies of the penis. (I wonder if the examiners at the U.S. Patent and Trademark Office actually tried this product before issuing the patent, or if they just took Lederer's word for it?) Today, there are a variety of penis vacuum devices available, which range in quality, comfort of design, ease of use, price, and effectiveness.

To maintain an erection once the VED is removed, a *constriction ring* is often wrapped around the base of the penis to trap the blood and prevent leakage. VEDs are amazingly safe when used correctly. Once a man learns how to prevent his testicles from getting sucked up into the cylinder, it's smooth sailing from there. So a word of caution, and you'll thank me for this one — hold your testicles when pumping the air out from that cylinder, because you'll quickly discover how fast one of your balls, or both, can be sucked up. One mishap, or slip of a nut, is enough to make you an expert. (Hate to brag, but I'm an expert!)

The only drawback to a VED is spontaneity. Also, obese men may have difficulties with a VED, as their large extending bellies make affixing and monitoring the device difficult. To ensure that things run smoothly, their partners can assist them with this process and make it a part of their lovemaking experience.

Many credible urologists recommend VEDs as a penis-exercising device, just like the penile traction devices mentioned next. *Use it or lose it.* According to world-renowned pioneer in penile enlargement, Dr. Joel Kaplan, VEDs are terrific for exercising the elastic characteristics of the penile tissues and vascular vessels that provide a healthy stimulation of nourishing blood flow into the corpal bodies. In addition to the health benefits, Dr. Kaplan is truly convinced that VEDs will also make your penis bigger — a true male enhancement tool. The repetitive vacuuming (or suctioning) has a dramatic widening and lengthening effect on the elastic-like penile tissues and, according to Kaplan, adds over one inch of girth and up to three inches in length after consistent use. There are many legitimate versions available, some better than others. It's best to seek a model that's clinically tested and doctor-approved. I recommend the FDA-approved models that have been invented and patented by Dr. Kaplan. Some insurance plans will cover part or all of the costs for these devices.

Penile Traction

There are also many devices that clamp onto and stretch the penile tissues; these are called *penile traction devices*. They resemble little stretch-racks for your penis. Actually, these devices aren't new, nor are they harmful when obtained from a qualified source. Many versions of penile extension devices have been used for hundreds of years; many are man-made concoctions originally intended for one thing — to stretch or elongate the penis beyond its normal length.

Ironically, these devices sell extremely well. The FS Extender, made by Fastsize, LLC, is a medical-grade penis extension device with medically documented proof that those who are using it realize significant increases in the size of their penises. This product is tested and approved by Laurence A. Levine, M.D., and supported by Baylor College of Medicine's Urology Department. Findings reveal, "The Extender has been proven to add girth and length to the penis and it will help you regain or maintain penile length." The study goes on to state, "[The Extender] is also the only medical-grade device with a physician-approved treatment protocol."

I watched a video testimonial from a man who explained the penis-enlarging benefits he received from the FS Extender. I found the interview to be sincere, and it was interesting to hear about how big this man's penis became in a relatively short time of use. I also enjoyed hearing the satisfaction from his wife, who joined him for the interview.

According to Dr. Fouad Ghaly, in addition to increasing penis size, penile traction devices offer plenty of other benefits most guys may not be aware of. Under healthy conditions, the tissues and circulatory vessels of the penis possess elasticity, expanding and contracting to allow blood flow, which results in tissue expansion. Over time, men with ED experience declines in the elasticity of penile vessels and tissues that can lead to long-term consequences. However, using a penile traction device (and also a VED) will exercise the elastic characteristics of the small yet sensitive cells of the vessels and tissues, assisting in restoration of normal functioning. Remember the garden hose analogy? After a long winter of disuse, it can become brittle and subject to rupture; there was also a corresponding build-up of gunk on its inner linings that clogged everything up. A comparison can be made with an uncooperative penis. Dr. Ghaly, along with many other medical professionals, recommend penile traction devices as a treatment for *Peyronie's Disease*, an unusual and unhealthy curvature in the penis. (More on *Peyronie's Disease* later.)

Penis size can be a major part of a man's self-image, and if a larger penis creates a healthier self-image, then that is reason enough to justify a surgical procedure or use of a medically approved enlarging device.

Mark Newel, Ph.D.

Penile Elongation Surgery (Penile Augmentation)

There are several surgical procedures that help to elongate the penis. These procedures, however, don't actually make the penis longer. Urologists claim that at least one-third of the penis's length is actually tucked inside the body under the pubic bone in the lower abdominal region. As you can imagine, the larger a guy's belly becomes, the less of his penis will actually be exposed to the outside world. This surgical procedure releases the ligaments that hold much of that one-third portion of the penis that's located inside the body, lengthening it to the outside. (This procedure is requested entirely for cosmetic purposes.)

Penis of the Future

As of this writing, I was recently made aware of a new technology for penile health and functioning that was displayed at the American Urology Association (AUA) convention. This product has been developed, tested, and approved by a team of urologists. It is called the Enhancer and is another breakthrough product from the Fastsize group. This state-of-the-art high-tech modality utilizes the power of multiple frequency LED light technology, which pulsates through the thin outer skin of the penis, dilating the penile blood vessels and increasing the flow of nitric oxide (NO) that is directly responsible for triggering an influx of blood into the expanding tissues of the corpal bodies to *obtain* an erection. The process remains effective by trapping that blood from escaping the penis to *maintain* the erection. What's even more impressive: the Enhancer is also expected to be used as a preventative measure against future circulatory problems in the penis.

The Enhancer fits in the palm of your hand and has an opening chamber where the penis is inserted. The makers of this device claim the same erection-enhancing results as those experienced from traditional treatments that include oral drugs, injections, and suppositories, except with the Enhancer, there are no side effects. (refer to Web site)

Erection Pills

Hovering around $2 billion annually (probably more by now), Viagra has become the modern-day action hero for men with ED and those who enthusiastically desire to augment their natural abilities. Though Viagra works for many men, some believe it serves as a Band-Aid to cover up a much deeper wound and is certainly not the cure that will solve the ED problem for good.

Let's take a moment to consider all the erection pill competitors. These include pills like Cialis and Levitra, along with a few newcomers. When we add things up, we're faced with huge numbers. In 2007 alone: Viagra came in at $1.73 billion, Cialis at $1.06 billion. Levitra is (only) grossing hundreds of millions, not billions (2004 sales estimate, Forbes.com). Not only is that a huge amount of money, but that's also a huge number of erections. And it's obvious that a lot of guys are looking for something to aid them in an act that was once natural and spontaneous. Even though a percentage of these figures are from men who just want to boost normal performance, the higher percentage is from men who cannot sexually perform unaided; so these drugs have a high chance of developing into a dependency.

Viagra (Sildenafil)

This drug was discovered by a Pfizer scientist by accident. Pfizer was testing sildenafil (chemical name for Viagra) for hypertension and angina to dilate vessels in or near the heart. However, test subjects noticed firm erections shortly after taking this drug, and those erections lasted for hours without any sexual stimulation. What a way to flunk a test!

Sildenafil is an effective inhibitor of PDE-5, an enzyme that's responsible for degradation of cGMP in the corpal bodies of the penis. Put another way, using sildenafil leads to increased levels of NO and cGMP in the corpal bodies, which makes for better erections as blood flows and becomes entrapped inside the penis. (Sildenafil and other erection pills are also known to be effective at stimulating the clitoris in many women.) The action of this drug does not (always) work on its own, as sexual (physical) stimulation is required to ignite its erection-producing action. So if you pop a sildenafil pill and are slouching on your sofa watching a football game, chances are you won't get an erection...unless you're attracted to the cheerleaders.

Viagra was the first PDE-5 inhibitor on the market, receiving FDA approval in March of 1998.

Levitra (Vardenafil)

This drug also belongs to the PDE-5 inhibitors for erectile dysfunction. Some studies indicate that Levitra may be more potent than Viagra; however, on a molecular level, vardenafil differs from sildenafil in its structure. Compared to sildenafil, vardenafil can create an erection in a relatively short period of time and it also works longer.

Cialis (Tadalafil)

Cialis is a drug for those weekend warriors because it was designed to last up to 36 hours or longer; that's why its nickname is the *weekend pill.* In fact, some data suggests Cialis can last for up to 100 hours. In addition to its long duration, which makes it possible to have spontaneous sex, another advantage for using this drug is that it's not affected by food. Viagra and Levitra, on the other hand, are inhibited to varying degrees by all types of food. This means that if you're out on a dinner date, you'll have to wait until that meal clears your stomach before you pop that little sex pill. And the higher the fat that's in your meal — stay away from the prime rib — the more time you'll just have to wait to get your *little* buddy to stand up and take action. So if you're on the drive back to your apartment and your lady happens to start coming on to you in the front seat of your car, chances are she'll take the fact that your pants aren't getting tighter to mean you're not in the mood. Cialis, however, won't cause this problem!

As I was completing this manuscript the makers of Cialis released a new version that is intended for daily use. The ads claim that this medication is to be used on an everyday basis so men *can be ready for sex at anytime.* Obviously, the makers of this drug are responding to the importance of spontaneity. Sounds a lot like a ploy designed to prime addiction and dependency. (Be sure to exercise caution when considering a drug that should be used *daily.*)

PDE-5 (phosphodiesterase-V) is an enzyme produced in the body that blocks erection-producing hormones. The popular prescription erection pills are inhibitors (or blocking agents) of PDE-5, or derivatives of this categorization of drugs. When PDE-5 is present during sexual arousal, a man's penis (and also a women's clitoris) cannot become engorged with blood and get erect. However, two chemicals make possible this influx of blood into the genitals: 1) nitric oxide (NO) and 2) cyclic guanosine monophosphate (cGMP). By blocking PDE-5, the inhibitors allow the chemicals NO and cGMP to perform their tasks in creating erections. PDE-5-inhibiting drugs are very effective at creating erections. However, as good as they sound, these drugs are not free of negative side effects like dizziness, stuffy nose, nausea, headache, vision disturbances, and priapism.

Stepping into the Ring

Many men successfully remedy *venous insufficiency*, or the premature leakage of blood out of an erect penis, by using *constriction rings* (aka *cockrings*). Dating back to the Middle Ages, constriction rings are made out of any material that wraps around the penis. These are placed at the penis's base after an erection has been obtained; then the rings are fastened tight enough to trap blood from escaping and to maintain the erection for as long as the ring is left in place. (Use of constriction rings can be dangerous if left on for too long. If your *little* head all of a sudden becomes purple, chances are you're choking him to death. Check with a licensed sex therapist for proper applications.)

Erection Injection

Synthetic penile erection injections can be administered by inserting a needle (syringe) into the penis, then injecting drugs into the corpal bodies. These drugs are known to be extremely effective and very reliable for obtaining an erection. According to Nick Delgado, Ph.D., head of the Ultimate Medical Research Clinic in Newport Beach, California, a high percentage of men who have elected to use this form of erection therapy are very pleased after, of course, they get over the concern of poking needles into their penises.

Penile Injection Pioneer

In 1983, at the American Urology Association (AUA) convention, a doctor named G. S. Brindley was one of the scheduled speakers. As he was approaching the stage, Brindley hollered out something to the effect of, "I just injected my penis with a new drug I invented for impotence, and I'd like to show you the results."

Catching the audience completely off guard, Brindley unzipped his barn door, pulled down his pants, and proudly displayed an erect penis to the entire audience. (My kind of guy!) To prove what he was exhibiting was not an illusion, Brindley respectfully invited everybody in the audience to come up on stage to examine (to see *and* touch) his penis.

Now referred to as *intracorporeal pharmacology* (or the injecting of a chemical agent into the corpus cavernosa of the penis), Brindley's discovery changed urological science. Applied with a tiny needle, the drug enters the base of the penis, then acts as a vasodilator that allows blood to flow, creating an instant erection. I know many of you are cringing at the thought of sticking needles into your penis; however, to my surprise, many men who have exhausted other options are extremely satisfied with this method. Depending on the drug, or combination of drugs (as some doctors are compounding them), prices will vary. This option is not without risks, as some of the side effects are priapism, tissue and vascular rupture, and scarring.

Penile Injection Drugs (Partial Listing)

The following is a list of injectable erection drugs that require a prescription from a doctor. These drugs are vasodilators that are injected with a needle, directly into the shaft of the penis.

✓ Alprostadil (brand names: Caverject and Edex; also available in the form of suppositories that are inserted into the urethra)

✓ Apomorphine

✓ Forskolin

✓ Moxisylyte

✓ Papaverine hydrochloride (brand name: Pavadid).

✓ Prostaglandin E1

✓ Phentolamine mesylate (brand name: Regitine; also available in pill form)

(Some of these drugs may be outdated by the time you're actually reading this, so please ask your doctor for more information. Topical/transdermal or rub-on versions are also available.)

As stated, some doctors will mix two or more drugs together to compound a specialized formula. Erections usually last 30 minutes to one hour, so once injected, the clock starts ticking, and the window of opportunity is short. However, duration is often dependent on dosage and the health of the penis. Success rate is high at 85%.

Urethral Suppositories

Also referred to as MUSE — medicated urethral suppository for erection. The tube that leaves the bladder and ends at the tip of the penis is called the *urethra*. The urethra allows urine to discharge out from the body, and it's also the canal from which semen ejaculates. A suppository containing a drug named *alprostadil* is inserted into the opening of the urethra, at the tip of the penis, synthetically creating an erection. Alprostadil and other similar drugs are also available in injectable versions.

Penile Prosthesis — The Absolute Cure for ED

Also known as penile implants, these devices make erections possible without any psychological, hormonal, or even sexual stimulus. Due to a series of improvements in technology, there are a variety of safe and reliable penile implants available today. One of the more popular models utilizes a pump that's surgically implanted in your scrotum or lower abdomen. With a few short squeezes you quickly pump air into a rod (or two, depending on the model), that are surgically implanted into the corpal chambers, to make a flaccid penis erect. If there was ever a cure for ED, this is it. In addition to its high success rate, spontaneous sex is restored — just squeeze your testicles a few times and your *little* buddy perks right up. When you've pleased your partner (and yourself, of course), push the pump's concealed button or release valve, then down goes your *little* buddy to his resting place.

Prices for penile implants range based on the model, surgeon fees, and hospital fees. But expect to pay at least $6,000, while some of the better models can exceed $12,000. As with your eyes, don't cheap-out when it comes to your penis. Seek wise counsel (and not from your *little* head) to make certain you're making the correct decision about getting a surgical implant. This is an investment that's risky but, according to many doctors, offers the cure many men are seeking for their ED. And according to surveys, the satisfaction percentage is extremely high — above 90%.

Is an Implant for Me?

I've heard several perspectives regarding prosthetics. One guy will say, "The implant will mimic any erection you've ever had," while another will say, "The quality of your erections comes close but they're never exactly the same type of an erection that you had in your heightened virile days."

One fact to consider: Men who elect to have this surgery can never obtain a natural erection ever again, as the nerves that stimulate the erectile tissues of their penises are destroyed. Perhaps that will change one day — or perhaps it will change by the time this book is published. For the time being, if you have ED that's treatable through other means, then, according to Dr. Laurence Levine and Dr. Joel Kaplan, you should make use of the other options before considering a surgically implanted prosthesis. However, if all else has failed and you cannot obtain or sustain an erection with any of the other options, then a prosthesis may be the most logical choice.

Is It a Secret?

Some say penile implants are totally hidden. However, some models position the inflation-deflation valve next to one testicle, while others are positioned in the lower abdomen. So it's likely that your partner, who can't keep her hands off of you, might feel the valve, which may cause some embarrassment for you.

There are several kinds of prostheses available. Some consist of bendable rods, while others are composed of a hydraulic, inflatable mechanism. The plus side to these implants is the fact that they work at making a penis erect *every time* the mechanism is activated.

Regarding the surgery, the recovery is approximately six to eight weeks, which means *absolutely no sex*. After that, the guy is good to go. Infections are the highest concern, due to the microscopic bacteria that reside in the genital region. Mechanical failure, although becoming decreasingly prevalent, is another concern; but that has now become a rarity due to the aid of technological advances and skilled surgeons. Some insurance providers will cover most or all of the costs.

Of all the ED treatments, prosthetic implant devices have the best rating among users. That fact must be examined a bit cautiously, as these men are, most likely, in their *last resort* scenario and have probably failed to be satisfied with other treatments.

According to Dr. Joel Kaplan, most individuals regretted having undergone this surgery. He notes that "their biggest complaints included: results not being what they expected, pain, penis disfigurement, scarring, and no sizable gain."

Great promise, tough decision.

Meet William (a Man Faced with a Tough Decision)

William is not what many would consider an older fellow. He's in his mid-50s and in relatively good health. However, ever since he divorced his second wife, William has been experiencing fluctuations in his libido, along with varying degrees of erectile dysfunction. This has been going on for five years. Consumed with humiliation and frustration, William frantically begins looking for a solution to his problem.

One day an anonymous e-mail is sent to William. Typically, his junk mail protector automatically discards these e-mails, but somehow this letter gets through — and William reads it. The advertisement promotes a surgical procedure that implants a mechanical prosthesis into a man's abdomen, testicles, and penis. This prosthesis can be pumped, at will, to create an instant and spontaneous erection; then it deflates just as easily once intercourse is concluded. Unlike most e-mails, this one comes from what appears to be a legitimate source that had posted a medical seal claiming that over 90% of men who elect penile prosthesis surgery are satisfied with their results.

This is the inspiration William needs. He schedules an appointment. The doctor he meets with is educated in male sexual disorders and affiliated with a group of urologists who perform this exact same procedure. William is confident he's in the right hands.

After a complete examination, which includes a barrage of psychologically motivated questions and numerous physical tests, William's doctor informs him that he isn't a candidate for a penile prosthesis. This news takes a lot of wind out of William's sails, and his energy drops like a rock in water. The doctor proceeds to explain that other less invasive treatments could be more successful, less expensive, and less risky. He suggests that William try these options first for the next few months to determine whether or not he still feels the prosthesis is the way to go.

The doctor explains that penile prosthesis requires a lifetime commitment once a decision is made. These devices are expensive and, like all surgical procedures, carry several risks (although medical advancements have lowered those risks to single digits as opposed to the procedures conducted in the past). "Once the prosthesis is implanted, it's permanent." This is what the doctor explains, and this is what keeps ringing in William's (*big*) head.

Not completely getting what he came for, but somewhat relieved that he was given professional advice, William begins to make the changes the doctor recommended. This includes the use of several off-the-shelf herbal products that he needs to take a couple of times a day.

Other instructions include more fitness activity, careful watch over his rather poor eating habits, a positive outlook on life, and letting go of the bitterness he was carrying from his two divorces. William starts to apply the doctor's suggestions … and to his surprise … William starts to feel like William again. The first sign occurs when he wakes up one morning and discovers he has a stiff erection — a good sign for any guy. This boosts William's confidence, as a morning erection hasn't happened in a long time. He says to himself, "Heck, if I can get an erection while I'm sleeping, just imagine what I'll be able to do when I'm awake — and with a beautiful woman next to me!"

William becomes a new man, restored by making slight changes in his lifestyle and relieved he confided in a doctor to help him make the right decision.

Although I've seen reports that claim a 98% satisfaction rate with penile prosthesis, men should be like William and ask their doctors about all the other options first. They should undergo a complete series of examinations (psychological and physical) before obtaining a prosthesis.

Penile prostheses should be considered as the last option when all else has either failed or fallen short of satisfying the man. Ask your doctor a lot of questions. From what I've been able to gather, once an implant is inserted you will lose your natural ability to achieve an erection on your own, relying upon the mechanical implant for the rest of your life. Perhaps a new procedure will be developed in the future that makes both natural and prosthetic erections possible.

Finally, for many men, a prosthetic is the only and best option, a complete cure for their erectile dysfunction.

Testicular Augmentation

The health of the testicles is dependent on various hormones and nutrients. Many of the natural supplements listed in this book — like Antler, Tribulus, vitamin C, zinc, and others — are recommended to maintain testicular health. These supplements support the integrity of testicular tissue, but it remains questionable as to whether or not they will regrow cells once the testicles have atrophied. Men with testicular atrophy may then require more invasive approaches for restoring their testicular size. The compound *follicular stimulating hormone* (FSH), used concomitantly with human chorionic gonadotrophin (HCG), makes for a reliable injectable prescription medication that helps in restoring testicular size and function; Clomid is sometimes used for this purpose as well.

If supplements or drugs fail to satisfy the man and his doctor, then implants are available in various sizes. Testicular implants are made of a gel-like material (silicone) that's inserted into the scrotum next to the testicles. Problems exist as the implants can cause testicular irritation, while the surgeries are known to be risky. Many of these testicular implants are similar to the breast implants used for a woman — but much smaller, of course. Like all other areas in sexual health sciences, testicular implant surgery is bound to improve. Check with your doctor or urologist.

Another method for making the testicles more voluminous, according to Dr. Joel Kaplan, is to insert your testicles, along with your penis, into a VED and create suction. As noted, I became an expert when one of my own testicles accidentally got sucked up into a VED chamber, and that hurt like an SOB! Kaplan, however, is suggesting that you knowingly insert both testicles inside the VED, then remove the air from the chamber at your own discretion. This is still regarded as a practice that must be approached with caution. So I suggest you obtain proper instruction. (By the way, when people purchase one of Dr. Kaplan's FDA-approved and patented vacuum erection devices, they're granted free consultations from trained staff members — a valuable service that will save you the energy of screaming "SOB!")

Gynecomastia (also spelled *gynocomastia*): This is the unnatural enlargement of breast tissue (especially noticeable around the nipples) in men. It's even called *bitch tits* among athletes, and is the result of excessively high estrogen levels and low *free* testosterone. Use of (synthetic) anabolic steroids exogenously delivers more testosterone than the body knows what to do with. Radical hormones are created, which amounts to too much of a good thing. Gynecomastia is not confined to athletes. It is also seen in adulthood, particularly among older males, but it's starting to affect younger obese men. One statistic claims that 40% of adult men in the United States have some drooping or projecting flesh tissue in their chest. Men who seek medical attention for gynecomastia tend to do so for one of three reasons... 1) Many are concerned about developing breast cancer, 2) Others need a remedy for the pain and tenderness in their breasts, one of the possible symptoms of gynecomastia, and 3) Others are simply embarrassed that their chests look like younger girls.

After ruling out male breast cancer, a doctor will determine whether the man's enlarged breasts are caused by too much fatty tissue. "The more weight you gain, the more fat you get behind the breast," says Dr. Glenn D. Braunstein, an endocrinologist at Cedars-Sinai Medical Center. "Overweight men are doubly at risk for gynecomastia," says Braunstein, "because fat tissue produces enzymes that convert testosterone to estrogen."

With surgical procedures, which basically involve liposuction of the fatty breast tissue, gynecomastia may be slowed or stopped — but not reversed. An off-label therapy that lowers a man's estrogen levels with the drug *tamoxifen* (sold under the brand name *Nolvadex;* see glossary) has shown to be extremely effective for preventing and stopping "gyno." The face-label purpose of this category of drugs is treatment and preventive therapy for breast cancer in women. In a letter to the British Medical Journal, Dr. Hamed Khan of Nottingham City Hospital in England reported that up to 80% of gynecomastia patients respond well to *tamoxifen*, experiencing few side effects.

Annually, over 18,000 men in the U.S. undergo breast-reduction surgery. The procedures used today are far more sophisticated than before; surgeons now use smaller instruments and produce tinier incisions. "You don't maim the chest," says Dr. Rod Rohrich, a plastic surgeon at the University of Texas Southwestern Medical Center and president of the American Society of Plastic Surgeons.

A popular surgical procedure for eliminating gynecomastia is ultrasound-assisted liposuction. Surgeons use ultrasound to actually melt the fat away and to reduce the size of the excess breast tissue. The excess is removed (sucked out) with a liposuction device. Rohrich estimates that the procedure is adequate for up to 90% of patients; for the others, surgery similar to a mastectomy can eliminate excess skin and reshape the chest.

Typically, liposuction can be performed on an outpatient basis. As of this writing, breast reduction surgery for men is not covered by insurance and can cost between $3,500 and $6,000 (or more).

Say Yes to NO: Molecule of the Year

I have stated that blood is needed to engorge the penis to make erection possible. But *how* the blood is delivered into the penis is another part of the complex cascade. A chemical agent known as a *neurotransmitter* that we naturally produce in varying amounts is responsible for allowing the corpal bodies of the penis to become receptive for the influx of blood. This chemical agent is one I mentioned earlier; it has several different forms, and it's called *nitric oxide*, better known as NO.

Basically, NO is responsible for dilation of the penile vessels and tissues, making room for blood to enter. Named as the "Molecule of the Year" by *Science* magazine in 1992, NO has also become extremely popular with muscle-building athletes, and endurance performers. This is because NO offers benefits to other tissues of the body, not just the penis, with its *pumping-up* effects. During exercise, any extra surge of blood supply to the muscles will improve performance and speed recuperation. NO is the chemical agent that makes all of that possible.

NO Good

For athletes who have disrupted their erectile functioning through steroid abuse, NO can come in very handy now.

However, it seems that NO doesn't always work on its own. Instead, it requires a triggering mechanism to release adequate supplies in the body. For the athlete, that trigger is exercise. For a man wishing to achieve an erection, the trigger is sexual stimulation. In both instances, nerves are the messengers that pick up the sensation, signaling the body to produce NO and ultimately providing its tissue-dilating benefits.

Chapter 7

Anabolic Steroids and the Genitals

(Bear with me if you're not a steroid user. This science, to varying degrees, has significant influence for all men experiencing ED, hypogonadism, and other sexual dysfunctions.)

In spite of sophisticated agency drug testing, many athletes are skilled at beating drug tests at major events — even though it's obvious they are anything but natural competitors. The scientists who are supporting these athletes develop *designer drugs* that, basically, affect the body in the same way, improving appearance and performance; however, the molecular structure of these designer drugs are altered just enough to deem them undetectable through current testing procedures. All drug tests are preset to identify specific metabolites for drugs already known, or listed on the banned registry. New, or designer, drugs cannot be on that list *yet*, but they will ultimately end up on the list in the future, as the entire sporting community always shifts toward the new (undetectable) drugs. The International Olympic Committee (IOC) is now maintaining blood samples for up to eight years after each athlete is tested. So if an athlete comes up negative (or *clean*) today, they may actually lose their medals years into the future as more sophisticated procedures come about and are updated to locate metabolites previously not detected.

Careless steroid users, and even those who believe they're being conservative, often shut down their own endogenous hormonal system that's linked to the entire HPTA cascade. Some of the side effects they experience include testicular atrophy (or shrinkage), oligospermia (low sperm count), erectile dysfunction, and gynecomastia. Not being able to achieve an erection is depressing enough, but when the testicles shrink and a guy's ejaculate volume discharges an amount of seminal fluid that barely fills up a thimble, most guys opt out of taking showers in public and also begin to avert sexual opportunities; both are very demoralizing.

Although some of these side effects are reversible, unfortunately, some guys will never have complete restoration; they will never be able to go back to their pre-steroid status, especially if they ignore the proper knowledge and procedures like those mentioned in this book. Most of the sexual damage created from steroids will not reverse on its own. So if steroid abusers don't commence a restoration program and faithfully commit to a healthier lifestyle, their conditions will only get worse.

Negative side effects from illicit steroid use are
similar, and often identical, to those in men suffering
from hypogonadism and other sexual disorders.

Remember Lyle Alzado? Super stud NFL Pro-Bowler and Player of the Year who played with the Denver Broncos, Cleveland Browns, and Los Angeles Raiders? When we knew Lyle, we knew a behemoth of a man who stood over 6'3" and packed on close to 300 pounds of rock solid muscle. Lyle admitted to steroid use and pointed blame directly at these drugs for causing a spiraling sequence of traumatic health conditions that ultimately led to his death at the young age of 43.

Coming off Steroids: Restoring the Damage

(The following techniques are applicable for most men experiencing ED and hypogonadism.)

Many steroid users have, unfortunately, become keenly aware of the sex-altering hormone-depleting side effects of these synthetic (anabolic) hormones. (Refer to Jose Canseco in *The Last Shot.*)

The goal for correcting steroid-related damage, and helping to restore the sexual bio-functionality of hypogonadism, is to repair and reactivate the glands that have *down-regulated* (shut off) their natural or endogenous hormonal secretions due to the administration from exogenous sources of synthetic compounds. This is a psycho-physiological chain of events with the brain regulating all body functions, while the organs dance a fine balance between being subservient and independent.

The underground treatments developed and used in sports (that are widely successful but not yet fully recognized by modern medical sciences) include the use of three basic drugs — along with a lot of patience. The three chemicals are HCG, or human chorionic gonadotropin, an injectable agent; and Clomid and Femara, both oral agents that are available in tablets. These three agents are actually used to *trick* the sex-producing glands in the body into thinking it's time to come back from their vacation (cessation of endogenous production due to exogenous supplies). That way, they can start to produce their own natural hormones again. No one completely understands this science, which is probably why the medical institutions cannot endorse it. However, I can tell you from personal experience that this cycle works. As terrific as this sounds, the cycle needs to be supervised by a qualified doctor who is skilled in endocrinology. Blood tests are needed at first to establish current blood-hormonal profiles, then intermittently to determine how the body is responding to the drugs.

HPTA Restoration Drugs

HCG (Human Chorionic Gonadotropin): This may gross some of you out, but this drug is actually made from the urine of pregnant females. Hormones are excreted in our urine, and since pregnant females are experiencing a surge in lutienizing hormone, excessive amounts of this and other hormones are eliminated from their body during pregnancy. Due to its similarity to lutienizing hormone, HCG is used to trick the Leydig cells inside the testicles into producing testosterone again after they've become down-regulated. This drug also plays a role in restoring libido in addition to possessing possible fat-loss benefits. (Many esoteric weight-loss clinics are using this drug for that purpose!) Take caution however, as long-term use of HCG can cause even worse effects on the Leydig cells and create even more damage to the testicles, often permanently. So there really can be *too much of a good thing*, which is the reason why you need a doctor to monitor this therapy. And if you're using HCG to lose weight, in my opinion, there are much better (and safer) ways to lose fat. Be aware that numerous (if not all) black-market versions of this drug come from the urine of female animals; this is not what you want to inject into your body!

Clomid (Clomifene or Clomiphene): This drug acts as an inhibitor of receptors in the pituitary gland that monitor estrogen levels, tricking the gland into perceiving the levels of estrogen are lower than they actually are. Once the pituitary is convinced the estrogen levels are low, it releases gonadotrophin-releasing hormone (GnRH) from the hypothalamus, which then triggers the release of follicular stimulating hormone (FSH). FSH stimulates the gonads (testicles) to manufacture more sperm, a process often referred to as *spermatogenesis*. In addition to its testicular-spermatogenic stimulating effects, Clomid is useful as an aromatase inhibitor that blocks the feminizing effects of high estrogen levels in men, stopping gynecomastia. Clomid is known to kick-start failing testicles in both steroid users and men with hypogonadism, while jump-starting the body's own natural production of testosterone.

Obvious as it might appear, this drug is often referred to as a *post-steroid restorative agent* that is taken at the completion of a steroid cycle.

Femara is another drug that's used as an aromatase inhibitor, preventing the conversion of synthetic steroids into estrogens. As stated, steroids shut down the body's natural ability to produce its own testosterone, which leads to fat gain, decreases in muscle size and strength, loss of libido, erectile dysfunction, and abnormally low sperm counts. Femara, like Clomid and HCG, is used to address these negative side effects; however, most doctors won't prescribe any of these drugs. This is because they are considered off-label uses and many doctors do not want to risk entering into this area of science, which has not been studied much. (However, as I write this, those studies *are* advancing.)

HCG, Clomid, and Femara can also be used by those who are experiencing hypogonadism, along with corresponding ED. They are effective treatments for men who desire to jump-start their hormonal system, boost libido, improve erectile quality and frequency, and return to a more youthful level of sexual and overall health.

Although these drugs may work for many, they are not safe without a skilled doctor's supervision.

Hormonal Suppression and Homeostasis

(This section also pertains to men who are experiencing hypogonadism and ED; men who lead unhealthy lifestyles; men who are under the influence of certain drugs or alcohol; and men who experience stress, are smoking, and are depressed.)

Without a proper sexual restoration program, those experiencing the negative sexual effects of steroids will only find things worsening. This is because restoration of the hormones, erectile ability, sperm count, and HPTA rarely return to their full natural operation on their own. The body often goes into shock upon cessation of steroids, as it has become dependent on exogenous supplies of synthetic hormones, shutting its own (endogenous) productions off. From here, the body doesn't know how to turn itself back on again. The reason is because any hormone taken from an outside source will have a high tendency to shut down the glands that are naturally producing those hormones.

For instance, when anabolic steroids, which are synthetic chemicals, are taken, the Leydig cells in the testicles shut down in response to the pituitary gland sensing the presence of the exogenous source. The pituitary gland believes its responsibilities are completed — *so why produce more than what's necessary?* This is how the body reacts, which, as mentioned, is often referred to as the *negative feedback loop*, or *downregulation*, a biological programming mechanism that monitors the internal activities of the body to prevent drastic hormonal fluctuations and overloads. This is part of an innate system we all possess called *homeostasis* that, amongst other body operations, monitors the production of hormones in the body, similar to how the thermostat on your living room wall regulates temperature in your home. Set the thermostat to 70 degrees and it will click on and off to maintain the temperature in the room at that level; the same applies to the body's homeostatic system. Also, when an athlete abruptly quits steroid use, his/her body's own endocrine system, and its homeostatic monitoring, often goes into shock, slowing if not completely shutting down. When the body's own glandular production of hormones slows or stops, this is a very sluggish and painful process, because the steroid user has knocked their system completely out of kilter. It can take months for someone to recover — and only if they follow certain procedures. Let me remind you that these conditions also exist in men who have not used steroids. That's the reason why I feel obligated to spend so much time emphasizing these points, which may appear to be one-sided and only for steroid users, but it pertains to all men.

When these, or any, sexual disorders appear in men who haven't used steroids, it's easy to place blame on many lifestyle habits for destroying normal and healthy sexual homeostasis.

RESTORATION: Turning On What Has Been Turned Off!

When hormones are brought back into normal ranges, here's what you can expect to experience…

- Increase in libido and sexual desire

- Increase in erectile ability: quality, duration, and frequency

- Higher semen volume and sperm count

- More powerful orgasms

- Quicker refractory periods after orgasm

- Increase in muscle strength and energy, capability of lifting heavier loads, more endurance

- Increase in confidence: higher levels of self-esteem

- Stability in moods

- Better sleep

- Lower percentage of body fat (provided you are performing adequate exercise and applying healthy eating habits)

- Faster recovery from daily tasks and exercise

- Lower risk of heart disease and many other illnesses

- Lower risk of prostate issues
- Younger-looking face and body

Prohormones

Prohormones are precursors to hormones. This means that a prohormone either converts to or elevates natural levels of other hormones in the body, including testosterone.

Over the last two decades, prohormones have become extremely popular with athletes and other enthusiasts wishing to obtain the muscle-building, strength-enhancing benefits that anabolic steroids provide — but without any health and legal risks. (Little did they know at the time.) Prohormones can boost testosterone levels in the body, building muscularity and endurance, eventually boosting performance.

When they first hit the marketplace, prohormones were legal and easy to find. However, with scandals like the one that involved professional baseball player Mark McGuire and the series of governmental hearings that ensued, one of the most popular prohormones, androstenedione (andro), and many of the related compounds in its category, became illegal. A disappointing occurrence for many users.

Prohormones are known to be effective at elevating testosterone levels, boosting libido, and improving erectile function. But not all users are happy, as many have experienced side effects similar to those acquired from actual steroids, including loss of libido, acne, male pattern baldness, gynecomastia, adrenal insufficiency, hypertrophy to the prostate (BPH), and nervousness.

There are several versions of androstenedione that were once available. Here are two …

4-Androstenedione and 1-Androstenediol: These (androgenic) chemical compounds convert themselves into testosterone in the body. Although they exhibit anabolic properties, which is why so many athletes have relied on them, they easily aromatize, converting into estrogen and creating a host of feminizing effects in men. These chemicals are also known to increase the levels of dihydrotestosterone (DHT) in the body that have been known to cause male-pattern baldness, acne, prostate cancer, and testicular atrophy.

Anabolic/androgenic agents, even the OTC ones mentioned above, are extremely potent and can be very unhealthy, shutting down one's HPTA and eventually desensitizing healthy cellular receptors like the ones located in the Leydig cells of the testicles. Short bouts of these products require specific cycles of administration. If taken too long, these testosterone-boosting products can cause excessively high levels of estrogen, bringing about glandular confusion and hormonal imbalances. Even though many of these compounds have been available without a prescription, they are like other drugs; they send signals to the brain, telling your body that *it has enough*, so the body believes it doesn't have to make its own hormones.

Anti-estrogens (Anti-Aromatase, Aromatase Inhibitors): These are chemical compounds that are used to lower excessive estrogen. Some men have normal testosterone levels; however, they also have excessively high levels of estrogen. These compounds block estrogen production and create a higher level of free testosterone in the blood. As stated, excess estrogen can be linked to ED, oligospermia, gynocemastia, reduced muscle size and strength, and higher levels of body fat. These drugs are typically not prescribed for these purposes, so the prescriber has to issue them for their off-label uses. (Please note that there are plenty of potent and safe anti-estrogen compounds readily available *off-the-shelf.* Ones that are legal! More later.)

Excess Estrogen in Men

Excess estrogen in men can also be caused by a variety of other factors: high stress levels, poor eating, excess alcohol and sugar, worry, high levels of body fat, anxiety, environmental toxins, anger, and depression. High estrogen levels in males have a demasculinzing, or *feminizing*, effect, as estrogen is the dominating hormone in women. Men with higher estrogen levels will have higher levels of body fat, weaker muscles, lower libido, ED, and altered sexual interests.

Let's Meet Kevin: U.S. Male Man

Ambitious. Big dreams. An all-or-nothing attitude.

Kevin's parents would tell you that he was a good kid with lots of energy. Some of Kevin's teachers, however, would describe him as having ADD, while the other teachers labeled him ADHD. Being a hyper kid might not have pleased Kevin's teachers, but his little league football coaches were of a different opinion.

You could tell early on that Kevin was a great athlete in the making. He was always energetic, daring, competitive, and coordinated. He took direction well and was always improving, upping his game.

It has been years since Kevin played little league football. He still works out, and has improved, physically speaking. And that ambitious competitive drive hasn't slowed down. He's stronger than ever and has a terrific build. Surprisingly, despite all this, Kevin's not satisfied because he's an over-achiever … and he wants more. More muscles, more strength, more endurance, more masculinity, more girls. He feels he can really impress his peers and attract the ladies if he pushes his body to the absolute limit.

Since Kevin is no longer in school and cannot rely upon the institution's weight room, he looks for another facility to work out at. As he walks into a thoroughly equipped health club, he's amazed at the space, quantity of equipment, and number of members. It looks like the ideal place to accomplish his goals.

As Kevin is given a tour of the facility, he sees a couple of guys working out near the dumbbell rack. He stares at them incredulously.

These are the types of guys Kevin has only seen in muscle magazines, and now they're (literally) within arm's reach. These guys are huge. Bulging biceps, mountainous pecs, veins popping out everywhere, heavy weights being defied of gravity.

Although there are plenty of pretty and sexy girls in the gym, Kevin is oblivious to them. His burning focus is on bigger muscles; he has the blinders on.

Not long after he joins the club, Kevin builds up the courage to ask the musclemen some questions. *How did you guys get so big? What do you eat? How often do you train? What vitamins are you taking?*

The musclemen, to Kevin's surprise, are responsive, and they invite Kevin to join in as they train. They also spend a lot of time chatting in the locker room after their workouts.

Step into the Underground

Not long after Kevin begins training with his new muscle-clad workout buddies, he starts to sense something unfamiliar, unusual language and innuendos that don't add up to the common lingo. Finally, Kevin puts two and two together, and his naivety breaks. He has heard of steroids before but never thought he'd be training with them — at least not with guys who were under the *influence* of them. The transformation of Kevin begins.

Kevin's training partners let him in on their dark secret — they're on the *juice*, they use *the stuff.* Steroids! No wonder they looked so fantastic, so ... unnatural. And with all the working out Kevin was doing — certainly matching their efforts many times — he wasn't getting anywhere near the results they had achieved. Kevin had always chalked this up to genes. He had convinced himself that these guys' parents passed on better DNA to them.

After feeling a bit stupid for his ignorance, Kevin experienced a huge surge of renewed enthusiasm. He now knew the secret. He now knew how to make his hard training efforts even more effective. He immediately started using the steroids. And eventually *the stuff* did for Kevin what it did for all the musclemen he had been idolizing.

Within weeks, Kevin's muscles started growing *huge*. He was also lifting much more weight in every exercise and recovered much quicker between workouts. Every time Kevin stepped onto the scale or glanced into the mirror, he saw improvements in his muscle size and overall (external) appearance. Kevin was hooked. The *juice* was working!

Of course, Kevin and his training partners were not supervised by any doctor; they weren't using any scientific protocols. In fact, they knew nothing of (or completely ignored) the potential side effects behind anabolic androgenic steroids (AAS). For the next year, Kevin kept on growing. His body looked like a Michelangelo-carved marble sculpture. None of his friends or family could believe their eyes, nor could they believe their ears when Kevin would tell them, "It's all natural."

During the course of that year, Kevin competed in several physique competitions. He knew all of the other competitors were using *the stuff*, so he felt that what he was doing was fair. One day, when interviewed by a local reporter after a competition, Kevin denied all accusations of steroid use — for himself, his competitors, and the entire sport. Kevin became a liar.

When Dreams Turn into Nightmares

One evening, after coming home from the gym and looking buffed, Kevin joined up with his girlfriend Donna to have some "alone" time. Infatuated with his muscular body, Donna would often initiate sex with Kevin, and each time Kevin was "up" for the occasion, until ...

Until *it* happened. Kevin couldn't get an erection, which was pretty embarrassing for him. Both he and Donna blamed it on overtraining. They engaged in a back and forth bombardment of blaming Kevin's demanding workouts as the cause of his erectile failure. Kevin figured he was beating up his body a little too much, so he decided to slow down.

But the slowing down wouldn't help him. Because all Kevin planned was to cut back on the intensity of his workouts, using less weight on curls, bench presses, and squats. But he would do nothing to adjust (or terminate) his use of steroids.

The next day, filled with even more passionate arousal and believing a good night's rest was all Kevin needed to recharge his faltering libido from the day before, Donna pulled her muscleman back into the bedroom. After some kissing and touching — and more than enough time that was (normally) needed for Kevin to be ready to penetrate Donna — he could not get it up for that occasion either. Strike two. Kevin *wanted* to have sex but he *couldn't* have sex.

Not being the most emotionally stable person to begin with, Donna was upset with Kevin's inability to get an erection; she took it personally. She felt Kevin was either not attracted to her anymore, or Kevin had somebody else he was seeing that she didn't know about. Worries over Kevin's apparent waning interest swirled around Donna's mind like a swarm of killer bees.

Kevin's mind was also saturated with confusion. Confusion about not being able to achieve an erection, about how Donna must feel in regards to her (muscle) man not being able to get it up for her. This was the Opening Ceremonies to a steroid user's Mind Games. (Many of you guys with hypogonadism can relate to this more than you care to remember…or admit.)

In spite of the very obvious declining signs, Kevin continued using steroids. In fact, believing his erectile dysfunction was from a *lack* of hormones, he actually increased his dosages of steroids. As you can imagine, Kevin got much worse. Not only did his steroid-fueled muscles lose their size, but his testicles shriveled up as well. (This is technically known as *testicular atrophy*, something I've been mentioning throughout the book. It's an extremely common side effect of steroids and hypogonadism.)

Steroid users inevitably encounter varying levels of emotional shock as they've lost function of the one part of their bodies they've never actually had to exercise before — their penises. Losing the ability to obtain and sustain an erection is just a small part of a much deeper condition going on inside Kevin's body and brain. By now, you're well aware that there's a complex, sophisticated, and very sensitive cascade of events that makes penises erect; these intricate inner workings are also responsible for libido, the manufacturing of sperm, production of testosterone (and other sex-enhancing hormones), and ejaculation through orgasm.

An Unhappy Ending

Kevin and Donna split up. But Kevin is still not giving up on his dream to be as big as his training buddies. He has reluctantly accepted the fact that he can no longer get an erection. He has chosen bigger muscles over a hard penis, and he's pumping more drugs into his body than ever before. (This is a typical panic response for many steroid users.)

Kevin's penis is not the only organ giving him problems now. Shortly after Donna left, he started to lose his hair, a condition known as male-pattern baldness that is caused from a hormonal imbalance. Kevin's testicles used to be macho-sized kiwis, but now they're looking more like raisins. And it doesn't stop there.

Kevin always feels pressure in his rectum from an irritated and inflamed prostate. He regularly finds droplets of blood in his urine from renal (kidney) damage. His eyes are jaundiced from his injured liver. His testosterone has dropped to that of a young girl, while his estrogen has increased to that of an elderly, obese woman. As a result of Kevin's high levels of estrogen, his nipples have grown outward. Although he is obsessively careful about hiding his pecs, when changing in the locker room one day, another fellow caught a glimpse and whispered to a friend, "That guy's got bitch tits."

Kevin has lost all his muscle definition and is bloated. His joints ache constantly, and instead of struggling to leg-press 600 pounds for reps, he has a rough time taking out the garbage. And when he does take the garbage out he's complaining to himself the entire time how rotten he feels. Kevin's a mess. He's isolated himself from the world he once knew. He's a depressed and broken man.

How can something that makes you feel (and look) so good be so damaging? That's the question every steroid user asks themselves when they experience these side effects.

If you are a steroid user, you might know Kevin quite well. Or, at least, you'll be able to relate to Kevin in more than one way. I suggest you watch the documentary entitled *The Man Whose Arms Exploded;* it's all about the world of steroids. A former Mr. America winner, Steve Mihalik, is in that film. Voted as one of the most buffed bodybuilders in the world at one time, Steve resorted to anabolic steroids because he wasn't satisfied with just being Mr. America; he wanted more.

The steroids Steve was using were far less toxic than the drugs available today but, nonetheless, as a direct result of his steroid use, Steve suffered a massive heart attack. Desperate to clean up his life, Steve was on a mission to restore himself...until he later suffered a massive stroke.

Steve admits that steroids will make you look great on the outside; however, the inside is an entirely different story. The time bomb is ticking away and you'll never know when it's about to detonate.

As a growing athlete myself, I always admired Steve's physique and bodybuilding accomplishments. But now the admiration is for Steve's courageousness to appear in that documentary, because there are hundreds of thousands of steroid abusers (millions worldwide) who have crawled into a shell, disappearing from sight, leaving us without a clue as to what the long-term effects of steroids are. Steve Mihalik has broken the ice.

Cellular Receptivity

Ever wonder how one guy can down a 12-pack and (seem to) carry on a normal conversation while another guy drinks one beer and gets smashed? The science is complex, but it can be, basically, summarized by a couple of different terms like *tissue sensitivity* or *cellular receptivity*. To take it a step further, let me introduce you to a couple of wild and ambitious guys...

Let's meet Joe and Tim. These are two guys who hang out with one another constantly. They share identical ambitions for increasing muscle size and strength, are the same age and body weight, and have comparably equal strength. Their goals are the same: *Get big, get strong, get girls.*

Joe and Tim start working out together — same exercises, same routines, same foods, same supplements. Within one week, Joe increases his bench press from 300 to 325, while Tim's doesn't budge an ounce. Joe's biceps grow to 17" up from 15" in only 3 weeks, while Tim gets a measly quarter-inch gain. The pattern continues. Joe is the front-runner, and Tim lags behind. Both guys remain faithful to their regular evening workouts together; they even eat the same amount of food and pop all the same supplements.

So why is there a discrepancy between their results? *Receptivity.* Gym lingo would tell you that Joe's cells are more sensitive (or highly receptive) to receiving the anabolic (muscle-growing) trigger induced by the training and supplements, while Tim's cells are, compared to Joe's, more stubborn. Tim's cells have a quicker down-regulation, limiting the amount of nitrogen-rich protein and other energy-yielding nutrients that enter into his muscle cells. Joe's cells, on the other hand, are allowing more nourishment to enter into his tissues, as his cellular receptors are conditioned differently; this is often where genetics plays its favorites.

Both guys, internally speaking, may have similar hormonal profiles, but, as stated, Joe's tissues are simply responding better — and faster. This response is not limited to weight workouts and protein shakes. The same tissue-entering phenomenon occurs with food, alcohol (remember the 12-pack guy?), caffeine, cigarette smoke, drugs (especially steroids), and all ingestible items. Each person has an internal cellular monitoring system that possesses its own levels of sensitivity. So two people who are doing the same things — eating the same foods, taking the same drugs, or drinking the same beverages (12-packs or one can of beer) — will have different rates of digestion, cellular absorption, assimilation, metabolism, and, above all, different effects. This is one of the reasons why the Federal Trade Commission (FTC) requests that all advertisers of exercise and diet programs list, "Individual results will vary."

Knock Knock. Who's There?

ANALOGY: Cellular receptors are like doormen at a dance club who are trained (programmed) to allow entry to a certain number of people. When the club is filled, the doormen are commanded by the management (the brain and cellular receptors in this analogy) to cease entry until some later time, allowing entry of more people only when the club's management signals *there's room for more.*

Men with hypogonadism have obvious hormonal-cellular interferences that down-regulate the cells in the glands (hypothalamus, pituitary, gonads, and others), as well as inside all body tissues, including the penis. (Techniques to restore cellular receptivity are explained later.)

Chapter 8

Testosterone and Sexual Functionality

Testosterone Replacement

It wasn't that long ago that widespread medical consensus concluded that testosterone (obtained from exogenous sources) harmed the tissues of the prostate gland by enlarging it or creating a condition known as *benign prostatic hyperplasia* (BPH) that led to prostate cancer. (Sometimes the word *hypertrophy* is used in place of *hyperplasia;* they are synonymous.) This presumption, thankfully, has now been proven to be a myth, and is one of the primary reasons why so many men with low testosterone levels and consequential sexual disorders were denied testosterone replacement therapy by their doctors in the past.

Dr. Fouad Ghaly, an expert in hormones, believes that under the care of the right physician, testosterone replacement therapy can be extremely useful for correcting testosterone imbalances, returning an aging (and/or hypogonadic) man back to his more youthful sexual vitality. The challenge lies in the fact that testosterone needs to be regarded on two levels: *total* and *free. Total* means the actual amount of testosterone *in* a man's body. *Free* refers to the levels of testosterone that are bio-available, or usable to the body and its tissues. Specific blood testing can ascertain the difference between *total* and *free* very accurately.

Ghaly expounds upon the fact that "testosterone is a neuro-hormone, influencing nerves just as well as muscle, while we literally possess testosterone receptors throughout our entire body, including bone and even the brain." This means that testosterone has an ability to enter into and exert its powerful influences upon trillions of cells inside the body. That explains why boosting testosterone levels enables a person to feel terrific everywhere, in body *and* mind; it's not limited to just enhancing muscle strength or sexual vitality.

Some men with ED can have normal ranges of total testosterone, but their levels of free testosterone might be excessively low. Many specially skilled urologists are now prescribing testosterone replacement therapy to many of their male (and female) patients.

When total testosterone rises excessively high, and/or free testosterone is low, this indicates an obvious hormonal imbalance, and the body is prone to producing an abnormally high amount of dihydrotestosterone (DHT). The first thing to do is to determine whether or not there are any pre-existing problems with the prostate. (It might be time for your own finger-wiggling prostate exam from your doctor.) Since testosterone is an anabolic hormone, men with pre-existing prostate problems should avoid synthetic testosterone and even natural testosterone boosters like andro, as cancerous tissues may be propagated with testosterone's anabolic properties.

Anyone receiving testosterone replacement must understand that their body's own natural production will slow down, or even cease, when exogenous sources are applied. This feedback signal registers in the brain as "we have enough," so its own production proceeds to slow or even shut down, starting with the pituitary gland. Provided the user remains under the care of his physician, combined with regular blood profiles to determine hormone levels and to monitor dosing, most men (and women) are ecstatic with the results of using exogenous testosterone. Men can literally *turn back their biological clocks* and bring back their youthful energy and vigor while, of course, improving their sexual stamina.

A medical study found that testosterone may protect against prostate cancer.

Life Extension Foundation Magazine,
Collector's Edition, 2008

Testosterone Administration

Injection

Testosterone replacement is administered in several ways, with new delivery systems becoming available soon. The most popular application is by injection with a syringe that's poked into the upper quadrant of the gluteus (buttock) muscles, which are thick, deep tissues. Most patients are instructed as to how to withdraw the oil-based liquid testosterone preparation from the vial and into a syringe. They are then given specific instruction on self-injection; many men are doing this once they get over the concern of sticking a needle into themselves. If a patient doesn't want to self-administer an injection, they can simply visit their doctor's office each time they need an injection. They can do this weekly, every fourteen days, or monthly, depending on the kind of testosterone injected and/or the potency. The only downside to this is that you'll have to pay extra for the doctor's visit.

Patches

Another increasingly popular testosterone delivery system is transdermal administration (penetrating through the skin). Peel-and-stick patches, like Androderm® and Testoderm®, are placed directly onto the skin and left there for a period of time. A testosterone-saturated pad dispenses the hormone transdermally for a sustained duration that can go on for days. Some patches are placed directly onto the abdomen or even directly onto the scrotum.

Gels and Creams

Another convenient way to administer testosterone is with rub-on creams and gels, like AndroGel®. Simply dispense the amount of gel that has been prescribed into the palm of your hand, and pick your spot. You can rub it into one of your shoulders, your biceps, or your abdomen area, just as you would put on suntan lotion. However, there are risks to others that you must consider. When you're using gels and creams, the pores of your hands and fingers become saturated with the hormone and can be transferred to another person, especially if you insert your fingers into your partner's vagina. Ask your prescriber how to thoroughly clean your hands and how to protect your partner.

Testosterone patches and gels are very effective
and often prescribed for those who don't want to
(or can't) inject themselves; it's not easy
for many men to accurately, or confidently,
self-inject a needle into their buttocks.

Pills

Oral administration of testosterone has lost its popularity and is not recommended due to the high levels of toxicity on the intestines and liver.

Sublingual

Another form of testosterone is available for sublingual, or *under-the-tongue*, administration. This version is usually formulated by certain compounding pharmacies, like the HealthPlus Pharmacy, located in San Luis Obispo, California headed by Certified Compound Pharmacist Dana Nelson.

Pellets

Testosterone pellets are surgically implanted under the skin by your doctor. Their effects last for long periods, some for three to four months, while others can last as long as six months. Your doctor will perform periodic blood tests to make sure this medication is working correctly and not having adverse effects.

Testosterone Tidbits

- Low testosterone levels reduce lifespan.

- Testosterone replacement is used to prevent, even cure, diabetes.

- Testosterone replacement therapy was found to be more important for men with diabetes than oral diabetic medication, and for some, more important than insulin.

- Diabetic men have been shown to possess abnormally low testosterone levels.

- The importance of testosterone for diabetes is extremely useful to battle obesity.

- Most doctors do not understand, or properly define, "normal" levels of testosterone when it comes to blood profiles. For instance, depending on the source, a low *normal* level of total blood testosterone is 399 ng/dl (see below). However, when a guy is younger, and sexually pleased with himself, his total blood testosterone level could have ranged between 800 ng/dl to 1100 ng/dl; so a level of 399 ng/dl, although considered *normal*, is depriving him of the sexual energy he was once accustomed to.

- Ng/dl = nanograms per deciliter of blood.

- Normal range of *total* testosterone in blood is 399–1,000 ng/dl, according to Life Extension Foundation. Many conventional medical sources, unfortunately, use the range of 250–650 ng/dl as their low-normal to high-normal standards.

- Normal range for free testosterone is 20–25 pg/ml.

- Testosterone replacement should always be first applied through natural strategies such as exercise, proper eating, and specific supplementation. If a prescription is needed, for insurance and overall health boost, natural supplements should be a conjunctive practice.

Life Extension Foundation

What's Considered Normal?

Testosterone is surging in production when we're younger. Then, once we're in our 30s, it starts to decline. Of course, declines can accelerate, or come about at a much younger-than-normal age, with poor lifestyle habits and, as I've stated, from the use of steroids. Amongst a long list of responsibilities, testosterone plays a significant role in libido. Men claim that when they boost their testosterone with natural or prescription methods, they also, almost immediately, experience a boost in sexual desire.

Those of you who have healthy libidos might not understand the magnitude of this problem. You might be saying, and justifiably so, *I always have a strong desire for sex*. But, sadly, according to statistics, millions of men, and even more women, lose their libido, and that's an enormous problem. The hormones we rely upon, and often take for granted, make the psychological aspects of sex just as profound as the physical aspects. Without nitric oxide and blood supply, a man cannot achieve an erection. Without testosterone, dopamine, serotonin, lutienizing hormone, follicular stimulating hormone, and many others, a man can be seated in the front row at a gentlemen's club and be fixated on what he's going to be eating for breakfast the next morning.

Historically, doctors haven't understood *normal* when it relates to levels of the hormone testosterone. As stated, the tests that indicate the range, low to high, are inaccurate. Many doctors will not prescribe testosterone replacement treatment to a man who's within *normal* ranges (per se), even if their levels register at the rock-bottom of that *normal* range. (*Normal* for one doctor may be disfavorably different for another.)

For instance, as listed above by the Life Extension Foundation, 399 ng/dl is recognized as the low side of the *normal* range, while 1,000 ng/dl is considered high *normal*. However, according to my research, most conventional labs and physicians regard 250 ng/dl as the low *normal* level. So the man who goes into his doctor's office with a blood testosterone profile that measures 251 ng/dl, most likely might hear his doctor say, "You're fine, within the normal range. Just get some rest and you'll recover in no time." What the doctor is failing to take into consideration is that his ED-suffering patient may have once had a level of 750 ng/dl, so the current blood-test results indicate that the patient is nearly one-third the man he once was.

It's worth spending the time to locate the right doctor who's skilled in hormonal balancing and sexual health sciences. This doctor should also be associated with the right organizations, like the Life Extension Foundation, that are more realistic in determining low-normal and high-normal ranges for all hormones. That way, they can better diagnose and assist you with any of your hormonal abnormalities, sexual disorders, and other health concerns.

The science editors at the Life Extension Foundation
provided the following information from their
December 2008 publication under the title
"Vindication." This is an edited version to fit the
space requirements for this book, while the full
article, along with all its references, is posted
on the Members' Section of the Web site.

Vindication

When we [Life Extension Foundation] first recommended that aging men can restore their testosterone to youthful levels, a firestorm of criticism erupted.

The medical establishment proclaimed that by interfering with the natural decline in testosterone secretion, men risked all kinds of terrible fates. When *Life Extension* members asked their doctors for testosterone prescriptions, they ran into objections such as "I don't prescribe steroids," "Testosterone causes heart attacks," and "Testosterone causes prostate cancer."

We countered these criticisms with hundreds of scientific citations showing that testosterone deficiency is an underlying cause of age-related disease. We also demonstrated that none of the paranoid fears about natural testosterone had ever been substantiated.

To this day, a huge number of doctors view testosterone as if it were a *narcotic*. Other physicians admit they don't know *how* to prescribe testosterone to their patients. All of that is about to change.

Harvard Medical School

A new book authored by the "experts at Harvard Medical School" should bury, once and for all, the biased and ignorant misconceptions about natural testosterone restoration therapy.

Testosterone for Life is an exceptionally well written book that validates what we long ago published about the safety, testing, method of delivery, and multiple benefits of testosterone.

While this information has been widely circulated in the antiaging community, the fact that it has been so eloquently compiled by the "experts at Harvard Medical School" should forever dispel the myths that have misled mainstream doctors for decades.

Low Testosterone Increases Prostate Cancer Risk

Fear of prostate cancer is the leading reason why aging men have shied away from restoring their free testosterone to youthful ranges. To dispel this concern, *Life Extension* long ago analyzed every published study and found there to be no basis for asserting that testosterone causes prostate cancer.

Our observations from the thousands of blood tests we perform each year for our members confirm this. What we found is that men with low testosterone were <u>more likely</u> to contract prostate cancer.

What will come as a *bombshell* to the medical establishment are the scientific facts presented in a chapter of *Testosterone for Life* showing that men with low levels of testosterone have higher prostate cancer risks. This means that physicians who refused to prescribe testosterone to their aging male patients may have unwittingly contributed to today's prostate cancer epidemic.

A Generation Who Lost Their Quality of Life

Testosterone for Life discusses the many published studies showing that men with higher testosterone levels live longer and have lower rates of diabetes and heart attacks. While the book goes on to substantiate that enormous *quality of life improvements* are observed in men who are prescribed testosterone. These improvements include increased sexual desire, performance and fulfillment, along with marked enhancements in energy and sense of well-being.

Life Extension has dedicated many articles to the disease prevention potential of testosterone replacement therapy. One study, for example, showed mortality levels 75% higher in men with low testosterone compared to men with normal testosterone.

How to Safely Restore Youthful Testosterone Balance

Since most doctors still don't know how to properly prescribe testosterone, the staff at the Life Extension Foundation offers these guidelines:

1. Have your blood tested for free testosterone, estradiol, and PSA, along with complete blood counts and blood chemistries. (Refer to the Male Blood Test Panel.)

2. If your blood test results reveal free testosterone <u>below</u> 20–25 pg/ml, find a doctor with experience in prescribing natural testosterone cream.

3. To obtain natural testosterone cream at the <u>lowest</u> price, ask your doctor to write a prescription for compounded natural testosterone cream.

4. If your estradiol level is over 30 pg/ml, your doctor may also prescribe a very low-dose aromatase-inhibiting drug such as 0.5 mg of Arimidex® twice a week. This will usually bring estradiol into optimal range of 20–30 pg/ml.

5. Within 45 days, have your blood retested to verify proper testosterone dosing and to rule out prostate cancer. These blood tests also determine further administration.

pg/ml = picogram per milliliter

pg = picogram, one-trillionth of a gram

ml = milliliter, one-thousandth of a liter

(End "Vindication")

Chapter 9

Performance Anxiety: The Erection Enemy

The Brain's Role in Sexuality

The brain is considered to be the largest sexual organ. In addition to housing the pineal, hypothalamus, and pituitary glands, the brain's emotional centers ignite libido and can cause erection in the penis for a man; it can also cause vaginal lubrication and erection in the clitoris for a woman. All this can happen with a mere thought — and in the absence of any physical stimulation. Since thought is the chief mechanism for arousal, and contributes to sexual activity, sexy thoughts are also responsible for corresponding boosts in hormonal secretions. It's just like in wet dreams when a man ejaculates during sleep with no physical stimulation; just the thought or dream of something erotic is enough. Another example is a (healthy) guy who scans a *Playboy* centerfold and becomes erect without being touched.

Flipping through the pages of *Playboy*, watching pornographic movies, or fantasizing about your lover offer no physical sensation (unless you're touching yourself). But the sensual thoughts generate a series of reactions originating in the brain with a corresponding surge in sex hormones, resulting in an erection. As youngsters, most males could just think about their girlfriends and their pants would become instantly tighter. To achieve, restore, and maintain optimum sexual health from its cerebral origin, proper nourishment is imperative, as it feeds the brain's neurotransmitters and cerebral tissues and glands. Stress must also be controlled and a positive attitude must be maintained. *Thought* is a form of nourishing energy. It's an intangible force that influences the functioning brain, like in any type of arousal, waking or nocturnal. Thoughts are influenced by your emotional and intellectual self-language, memory and beliefs, and the words you use. (More on this later.)

Performance anxiety prevents erections even before they occur, or destroys them once the penis becomes hard. Men with this condition strike out even before they stand at the plate to swing their bats. The psychotic anticipation of sexual failure detours (or blocks) penile nerves, blood flow, and the upsurge of NO. This causes the *turtle effect*, or the withdrawing of the penis into the lower abdominal region.

Mind over Matter: Erection-Destroying Thoughts

When a man enters into a state of anxiety or fear, his brain quickly responds, protecting itself by searching for ways to ensure safety, security and defense, and — of course — victory over threat. Thoughts of fear cripple a man's ability to achieve an erection because fearful situations ignite a *fight or flight* response, preparing him to either put up his fists and duke it out or run as fast as he can to escape a dangerous confrontation. Fearful or fighting situations have never been overcome with a hard penis. Instead, the brain is preparing the body to actually put up a physical fight as adrenaline pours into the bloodstream, making the heart race to pump blood to the fighting tissues; the lungs huff and puff to provide the organs with a higher demand of oxygen; and the major muscles tense (the penis is not one of them) so they can contract as strongly and as explosively as possible to defend themselves in dire situations.

Fear of failure is another form of mental thought, often associated with performance anxiety (specifically in those dealing with sexual rejections and/or inadequacies). All this anxiety plays havoc on the brain and its neurochemistry. This havoc is transmitted from the brain and throughout the body, which ultimately guards the penis. When experiencing any form of fear, the brain reacts in extraordinarily similar ways as it would during an actual physical threat or real-life scary situation, like from an attacking animal or an armed robber.

The brain registers threat through the information it receives from memory, thought projection, sight, smell, hearing, touch, and fear. Here's an example: You're sitting on your balcony on a quiet, warm summer day, eyes closed and body relaxed. Without warning, a loud firecracker blows off in the backyard. You instantly react, jumping a few inches off your lounge chair. Your eyes pop wide open, as you look around frantically for the punk who lit the damn thing off. Your ears try to hone in on *where that blast came from*, as your heart races and you begin to huff and puff. All your body systems — eyes, nose, ears, brain, heart, muscles, lungs, and nerves — automatically kick into HIGH ALERT without you actually telling your body to do so. It's built into our systems to automatically react to threats, and that is deeply embedded into our subconscious programming and genetic codes. Sexual threats are triggered very similarly.

Mental stress, fear, anxiety, frustration, confusion, and anger produce erection-killing hormones like adrenaline (also called *epinephrine*) and cortisol. These negative emotions cause levels of free testosterone to drop, while estrogen levels are increased. As a result, a stiff penis becomes flaccid or erections become an impossibility altogether. Adrenaline is the hormone that signals the body, warning it of a potential threat and directing blood supply to major muscles, not including the genitals. (Cavemen were not horny when hunting dinosaurs.)

One anxious occurrence is sufficient enough to program the subconscious mind that failure is possible. It's like touching a hot stove for the first time — it's registered in memory forever and will resurface to various degrees of intensity every time a hot stove is merely imagined, and certainly when it's within close physical proximity.

When ED happens again and again, the brain continues to accumulate these failure "memories," which compound upon themselves time after time; it's like a garbage dump that has regular deposits and keeps filling up. Previous failures, which have nothing to do with today's (sexual) opportunities, embed themselves into the man's memory, moving deeper inside his subconscious mind. If these thoughts and memories are not managed correctly, the anxiety and fears will not only persist — *they will continue to deepen.* According to many experts, the subconscious part of the brain is the center that controls everything we do and everything we manifest in our lives.

Many men who have ED as a result of performance anxiety seek help from erection pills. These drugs are helpful for many of these men — and a real relief when their own ability has failed. But, unfortunately, a high percentage of these men are (eventually) met with failure (again) because their anxiety is so strong, or their subconscious programming is so dominant, that even the most reliable and potent erection pill can fail. The brain's power is so overwhelming an influence that it will override the power of the drug.

Sex Therapy: In all cases of sexual disorders, it's wise to seek counseling from impotence advisors who offer psychoanalysis for performance anxiety, stress control, and anger management.

Phobias That Can Contribute to, or Are the Cause of, Performance Anxiety (For Men and Women)

- Agoraphobia — Panic or anxiety around certain people, places, objects, or activities

- Androphobia — Fear of men
- Aphenphosmphobia — Fear of being touched
- Atychiphobia — Fear of failure
- Autophobia — Fear of being alone
- Bacteriophobia — Fear of bacteria
- Cacophobia — Fear of ugliness
- Catagelophobia — Fear of being ridiculed
- Caligynephobia — Fear of beautiful women: This causes many men a high degree of performance anxiety with just the thought of approaching a woman, talking to her, and — if they're lucky enough — becoming intimately involved with her. Also tied into fear of rejection, closely related to fear of failure. (Also see Venustraphobia.)
- Gynophobia — Fear of women
- Hemophobia — Fear of blood
- Lockiophobia — Fear of childbirth
- Obesophobia — Fear of gaining weight
- Pathophobia — Fear of disease
- Philophobia — Fear of love
- Venustraphobia — Fear of beautiful women (also see Caligynephobia)
- Verminophobia — Fear of germs

You can add to the above list ... fear of financial insecurity, fear of death, fear of guilt, fear of pregnancy, fear of violating religious vows, fear of rejection, jealousy ... the list goes on and on.

All men handle sexual disappointment differently. The most extreme case is to abstain from sex altogether to *avoid the pain*, as

Freud* puts it, from the fear of rejection. This is the fear a man with ED experiences that makes him believe he won't be able to perform sexually. The risk vs. reward factor forces these men to *opt-out* of pursuing sexual relationships or, in some cases, a one-night stand. This is referred to as SAD, or *sexual aversion disorder.* Instead, many resort to chronic masturbation, pornography, strip clubs, X-rated Web sites, and other solitary sexual activities. All of these are (in the man's mind) safe and protect him from failure, veering him clear of any kind of embarrassment.

Sexual disappointment can lead to many distorted beliefs compromising the body's vital constitution. Many men with ED justify their avoidance or withdrawal from sexual activity but deeply know they're just flat-out BS-ing themselves.

The hormonal driving force for sex is testosterone. Men who are experiencing sexual inadequacies may just have correspondingly low levels of testosterone. Actually more complicated than any other hormone, testosterone is the chief hormone that makes a man *a man.* Men with low levels of testosterone are known to be less aggressive than men with higher levels. Men with high levels of testosterone are often classified as A-types, always motivated and driven; they're also much braver when heading into, and dealing with, risks and challenges.

---

* The world-famous physician and psychoanalyst Sigmund Freud stated that everything we do is motivated by sex. Pretty gutsy statement considering he made it during the late 1800s and into the early 1900s. According to Freud, successful people are known to have high sex drives. The passion for sexual expression, and its release, is an extreme and often uncontrollable driving force that makes men strive to become even more successful and earn more money. After all, money does (in a man's mind) buy love … or, at least, the *sex* that they love. Freud also popularized the term *id*, which relates to the energy-force man possesses. This force drives libido and the constant longing to seek fulfillment of sexual desires. When man's id is not satisfied, the ego spins out of control and enters into varying states of neurosis. Freud's work, as you might guess, was considered controversial nonsense in his day. However, as sexuality has continued to evolve, so have Freud's unconventional theories.

Of two athletic competitors, tests have shown that men who win a competition have higher levels of testosterone than the men who lose. This could indicate that 1) the winners had higher testosterone levels to begin with or 2) winning, or its psychophysiological response, along with a corresponding sense of relief and joy, creates a surge of testosterone, while the losers become depressed and depleted. (This was taken from a TV show that aired on the National Geographic channel.) According to Dr. Nick Delgado, one study revealed that changes in testosterone levels were shown in those who merely sat in the stands as spectators of an athletic event. The winning team's fans had an upsurge while the losing team's fans showed a significant drop in testosterone. This study clearly indicates that the thought of winning or losing has noteworthy effects on hormones and body chemistry.

By now, you've read that the mind is an extremely multidimensional and complicated entity to manage, especially when challenges as sensitive as ED keep you frustrated and confused. When no noticeable clues are made evident as to the causes for sexual failure, the mind races, draining precious energy and strength from an already weakened hypogonadal man. The good news in all this is that positive changes can (and will) successfully transpire, provided a keen awareness of the underlying (and unseen) causes are understood. There also needs to be a committed plan of attack designed to eradicate the culprit(s) once and for all.

In the following chapter we'll delve even deeper into the brain and mind, and learn how we can identify mental infractions regarding our own sexuality and overall health. We'll also learn how we can exchange weak thoughts with strong and virile ones, how some of the Navy Seals condition themselves for "mental toughness," how to incorporate motivational self-help techniques to reprogram your mind and exchange the negative with the positive, and much more ...

Chapter 10

Sex on the Brain

The Effect Orgasm Has On The Brain

Many experts explain why ejaculatory orgasms feel so good — because they are the rewards granted to us from Mother Nature for displaying our procreative ambitions and capabilities. Through a complex process of release (and transfer) of sperm, man can procreate through ejaculation. This is the main mission of man. The universe favors multiplication, and pleasurable orgasm is our reward for doing our parts (men and women alike). The cascade leading up to and throughout ejaculation triggers a psychophysiological cascade of extreme pleasure. Under brain-scan technology known as *positron-emission tomography*, or PET, a specific compartment in the brain illuminates prior to and during ejaculation. This compartment releases powerful hormones into the body, which are both healing and healthy. Interestingly enough, that same brain compartment known as the *ventral tegmental area*, or VTA, also shows heightened activity during memory-related imagery and in vision stimulation. What this means is that we can just *think* about sex and the same biochemical reactions inside the brain are triggered as when we're *physically* active with sex. ("The Orgasmic Mind," Martin Potter, *Scientific American Mind*, April/May 2008.)

Orgasm: Man vs. Woman

(Special thanks to National Geographic for inspiring the following.)

Utilizing advanced positron-emission tomography (PET) brain-scanner technology, Dr. Gert Holstege, (from the University of Groningen, Netherlands) has been undergoing revolutionary sex research that has revealed the exceptional chemistry of the brain during orgasm.

A group of men and women participated in this groundbreaking experiment, which revealed an astonishing difference between brain activity in men and women during sex. Just prior to — and especially *during* — orgasm, the male brain releases huge amounts of the neuro-transmitter *dopamine* that provides a euphoric feeling. Interestingly, blood was seen traveling away from the areas of the brain that store anxious and fearful thoughts, deactivating these cerebral compartments, while other sections of the brain continued to be alert to the man's physical surroundings. Researchers postulate that these *alert* sections of the brain may not necessarily be focusing on the man's partner who was responsible for his orgasm. Helen E. Fisher, Ph.D., believes this is an evolutionary response, as man has had to inseminate females out in the unprotected wild, all while being *on the lookout*. You never knew when a saber-toothed tiger might jump out from behind the bushes, so man couldn't afford to deactivate or shut off his entire brain during orgasim. This may explain (or, between you and me, can be used as a good excuse) why men leave the scene (either physically or mentally) after they've had an orgasm; our evolutionary genetic programming quickly turns our attention away from the sex scene and over to other things much faster than with women. *"Hey honey, if I don't look after the cave, we could lose everything."*

On the other hand, women also experience a surge in *dopamine* during orgasm. But what astonished Holstege during his orgasm experiment was how much of a woman's brain completely shuts down during her sexual climax. Holstege remarks, "In women, there was an enormous deactivation of all the centers of the brain that had to do with anxiety, fear, and alertness. Literally, women 'let it go.'" In fact, Holstege's research has proven that women can actually be rendered unconscious during orgasm whereas men aren't. The phenomenon between male and female brain reactions during orgasm is truly remarkable. What many of you may also make of this is that men don't experience the same or as relaxing an orgasm as women do. (Taken from *The Brain*, History Channel, History.com.)

Psychology of Sex: You Are What You Think You Are

When it pertains to male sexuality, the *big* head strongly influences the performance of the *little* one.

As a former coach for numerous Olympic and professional athletes and teams, I know that when an athlete pessimistically thinks about their weaknesses, failures, fears, or injuries; is intimidated by competitors; or has the slightest doubt about his (or her) performance abilities, chances are that athlete will actually validate what they're thinking about ... and fail. These failures — which I've seen more than I care to admit — prevail even when the athlete has a superior win-loss record and more advanced physical attributes when compared to their opponents. The power of suggestion, or the programming of the conscious and subconscious mind, can drop a Goliath to his knees. (One of the greatest sporting examples was the Ali vs. Foreman *Rumble in the Jungle* where the majority believed, including the Ali camp, that Foreman was the stronger, tougher, superior opponent. Ali, however, had an independent opinion of his comparison to Foreman, regarding himself as the more talented athlete, maintaining a more positive mindset. He had an enormous amount of determination and will to win at all costs, along with the pride not to lose. Ali prevailed.)

One of the most exciting elements of competition is the never-ending list of stories pertaining to victorious outcomes from the so-called *underdog.* Man's desire to recognize, then actualize, accomplishment. Does the body succeed, or is the credit given to the mind?

Just because an athlete has inferior *physical* abilities in comparison to his competitor doesn't mean that athlete is sure to lose. We see it all the time, especially now with mixed martial arts (MMA), the fastest growing sport in the world. A champion fighter gets into the cage, surging with testosterone, pumped up with rage, sporting a win-loss record that's splattered with a string of KOs; or as a champion, he's fiercely determined to defend his title and win the prize money that will allow him to continue to support his family. But minutes, sometimes even seconds, after the first round's bell rings, he gets clobbered by his underrated (underdog) opponent and is knocked out cold.

When anybody, especially the athletes in these scenarios, strongly believe in themselves, they *are* the superior one. That's because they're 100% confident and primed to succeed. Of course, there are exceptions, but there's nothing like confidence. Confidence, or that *for sure* attitude, is needed in all aspects of life: business, social, academic, and — of course — sexual situations. If you have an inkling of a thought that you are an underdog, then prepare to become (or remain) one. If you desire to change, then the first step is to alter your mind and belief patterns and step up into a higher level of consciousness.

Several polls have indicated that women regard confidence as the #1 sexiest quality a man can possess. This can be a lingering trait driven by the female's evolutionary genetic code that stimulates attraction to a man who can regularly supply her with an indulgence of dinosaur meat to feed on, father a lot of healthy babies, and protect their cave in the midst of being surrounded by fierce competition. So lift your chests, raise your chins, and hold your shoulders up; this body language might just help you attract more sexual opportunities, or certainly enhance the one(s) you already have. And don't worry, you won't have to kill dinosaurs to impress modern-day females!

In sexuality, confidence is especially key when it comes time for the erection to occur. When a man has the slightest doubt that he'll be able to get or remain erect; when a man is scared, stressed, or simply has to work too hard to make his erection happen; when he is shy of his partner, chances are, he will fail. This failure compounds itself over time because the subconscious portion of the brain registers everything we experience and think, especially about ourselves, and those memories come wrapped in the same emotions that caused them. Thoughts of failure unconsciously strengthen the priming of the thinker for more failure.

If a guy thinks his penis is not going to get hard, and has thought about that any number of times in the past, the accumulation of that thought builds up and is stored inside the brain's vast psychological network, which is ultimately connected to and communicates with trillions of cells throughout the body. With this negativity programmed inside the brain, it will respond exactly how it's being commanded to respond, literally paralyzing a man's senses — and his penis. The brain is simply taking orders, and the man is the one who's placing those orders into his mind. The dominating thoughts in a man's *big* head are the ones that control him. But since the subconscious parts of the brain operate mysteriously, separately and silently, men might not even know why or how their failures are occurring. They might be (consciously) thinking to themselves, "It's going to work this time," or maybe they're thinking, "She's so cute it'll be easy to get an erection." However, the more dominating voice wells up from the deep reservoirs of his memories and beliefs that are strongly locked inside his subconscious.

Some guys try to escape these mysterious, confusing, frustrating, and uncontrollable happenings with drugs and alcohol and, of course, the now popular erection pills. Or they simply ignore their challenges and allow themselves to become more and more isolated and depressed (SAD). Today, there are plenty of options available to treat depression and other psychological disorders. The longer depression lingers, the stronger the subconscious holds onto those thoughts ... and the farther away that person will distance himself from normalcy in sexual situations and in life in general.

Suffice it to say, the now popular erection pills have rescued many men from their performance anxiety, but these drugs do not re-program the subconscious mind. Many men who use erection pills know (deep down) that they still have a problem; they're now relying on some artificial means to create what was once a natural occurrence. Erection pills require a degree of planning and timing, so fear of missing out on spontaneous moments of sexual opportunities is another cause for performance anxiety the man with ED has to deal with.

The reliance on erection pills, without concurrent attention to the physical causes of ED and the corresponding psychological implications, can be more harmful in the long run. That is because now the guy (subconsciously) believes he's dependent (addicted) on an exogenous source, and he's no longer *normal*. He also feels (actually, he knows) he has lost his spontaneity and is running away from the cure that's *causing* his problem in the first place. Men like this also believe they are aging more rapidly, as the health and performance of their penises provide feedback to their self-images and status of health. Let's not ignore the fact that if, or when, erection pills lose their efficacy, men ultimately lose a great deal of hope.

In spite of all the brainwashing we received in our schools, churches, and most of society, it's okay to desire pleasure and passionately seek ways to have it. To deprive yourself of pleasure is masochistic. In fact, it's okay to desire to be the best you can be. In my lectures I promote *selfishness* as an essential quality for successful living. I believe the more we can give to ourselves, the better we become — and the more we can give to the world around us. Even though it has a mainstream negative definition, there is a positive way of being selfish. This is because your success benefits not only you, but also your family, business, charities, and everything you are a part of. Give yourself what you *need;* then give yourself what you *want* — there is a difference. You deserve to have both your *needs* and *wants* fulfilled. Sex, I'm sure, is positioned somewhere (high) on your list; otherwise you wouldn't be reading this book.

"In the event of an emergency, an oxygen mask will deploy from the overhead compartment. Please secure that mask on yourself first before assisting others."

Sounds a little selfish to me. But the better you are, the better others around you will be!

Remedying ED

The first step to remedying and curing ED is to admit it. Admit it to yourself, and admit it to your health professional. If you keep saying, "No, I can't be experiencing this," then guess what? *You'll be making it worse.* Ignoring or suppressing *it* only deepens your problem. Each time you deny, avert, hide, avoid, or pretend *it's* not there, you strengthen the negative priming of your thoughts, beliefs, and actions. Despite ducking from it, you actually know the real truth. And this eventually becomes your reality. Sex is supposed to be fun. It's also natural and very healthy. So you must be responsible enough to do what's right for yourself. Remember, the better you are, the better you can contribute to all aspects of your life. The more you give, the more you receive.

Brain Chemistry: Libido, or the thought of sex, kicks an entire cascade of physiological events into action; this includes the secretions of pleasure and sexual hormones like dopamine, serotonin, gonadotropin-releasing hormone (GnRH), oxytocin, lutienizing hormone, follicular stimulating hormone, and testosterone. Nitric oxide and cGMP are also produced. Many men with ED have a disconnect somewhere in their HPTA cascade, which basically means that when they think about sex (a *mental* process), their penises do not respond (a *physical* process). The conflict is maddening. Not having something that's desired is frustrating. And too much frustration, as Freud puts it, leads to various levels of anxiety and unhealthy consequences. The good news is that the disruption between the brain and penis can be corrected when diagnosed and properly treated.

Think Up

Envious is the man who remembers the times when he could just think about sex and his penis became hard, with no sexual stimulation. As a man ages, his *thought-erection response*, or his brain-penis connection, declines. This may be one of the reasons why many women claim older men are better lovers — it takes longer for older men to get aroused and to reach orgasm. And let's not forget about longer refractory periods, which means more time for communicating, fondling, and cuddling; translation: actual foreplay. Ironically, many men put excessive pressure on themselves to be fast at achieving an erection when, in fact, most women enjoy a slower *let's-take-our-time* lover. Knowing this fact can help ease the tension and allow men and couples to explore more options during foreplay and after-play.

Priming and Psychology: Taking a Deeper Peek into the Field of Psychology

If you think or even suspect that you are a certain something, then you *are* that something. So if you think you have ED, you do. The more you negatively think about *it*, the more strength *it* has over you. There's a popular saying in the metaphysical realm: "Change the thought, change the thing." If you think you have *it*, you do; it's that simple. And if you keep thinking about *it* from a pessimistic viewpoint, the more *it* will manifest and persist.

Malcolm Gladwell's excellent book, *Blink*, explains a study that was designed to measure how certain stimuli influence the (mental) process of thought, learning, and action. A group of men and women were led into a large room in a big building. They had to walk a fair distance to enter the room and sit themselves down. The test seemed simple enough. The group was asked to (silently) read several five-word sentences. That was it.

However, what these people didn't know was that these sentences were intended to set them up for a change in behavior. Inside each sentence were *hook* words like *old*, *bingo*, and *Florida*. Unbeknownst to the group, there were hidden cameras that were closely watching them upon their entry into and their exit out of the classroom. Their walking and talking speeds were also timed and measured. Not so surprising to the test conductors was the fact that these people entered the room with more speed and energy than when they exited. The reason was simple. Words like *old*, *bingo*, and *Florida*, known to relate to elderly people, were strategically implanted into these short sentences. Upon reading them, these words traveled beyond the readers' conscious levels of thinking and penetrated into their subconscious minds; hence the reason for the slower exit. They simply felt older and acted older as they became programmed into acting that way.

What the test conductors were doing was a simple technique used in psychology known as *priming*. Priming happens all the time; in fact, all of us are primed in life. Priming is used for better or for worse — to influence, convince, sell, control, brainwash, motivate, promote, manipulate — and it's never stagnant. We are all primed, and in our daily communication with others, we intentionally (and at other times, unconsciously) prime one other.

Advertisers prime their consumers, sales people prime their buyers, coaches prime their athletes, lawyers prime their defendants and juries, politicians prime their voters, authors (oops, I'm admitting it) prime their readers, songwriters prime their listeners, lovers prime their partners, and hypnotists prime their patients. That's just how it goes.

This particular test made these people *feel* older, slowing them down in the process. The same happens to men who dwell on their ED and sexual disorders. This influence doesn't only relate to words we read, see, or hear. In fact, any thought, feeling, or belief, especially one that's repeated over and over, will prime a person into acting out (or becoming) what they're constantly dwelling on. U.S. Anderson, in his great work *Three Magic Words*, refers to the destructive primed beliefs deeply tucked inside many minds as the *negative prompters*. These are the thoughts, feelings, and beliefs a man possesses that are satiated with negative energy; they are responsible for holding a man back from achieving success in his life.

It's not only the negative thoughts that prime the mind. The same principle works in reverse, as confident and motivated thoughts will prime one for success. This is the basis for prayer, affirmations, chants, mantras, forgiveness, and positive thinking — all intended to keep the subconscious, or the ruling mind, in line with our desires and goals. Thoughts of fear, anxiety, failure, embarrassment, frustration, anger, disappointment, and rejection will prime a person for much more of the same. And it often requires a lot of practice and self-control to choose between the two thought forces: positive and negative. For instance, a person who is successful, happy, and content today can fail, becoming insecure as the result of a shift in thoughts or in priming.

The words we think and say, and the meaning we give them; the words we read, hear, and pay attention to — they are all priming our subconscious minds, the mental compartments that actually rule us.

Priming can happen in an instant, and it can also develop slowly, yet exponentially, over long periods.

But there are other ways in which our brains become primed, and that is through *subliminal* influence. Hypnosis is subliminal. Music can be as well. A subliminal message is information that the brain receives; it is often unidentifiable to the conscious mind, but nevertheless penetrates into the subconscious mind. Subliminal messages are everywhere, embedded in media like music, many intentionally designed to trick normal perception as they enter the subconscious mind. Subliminal messages can work for good and bad, success and failure. Audio messages can be layered with one message that is more pronounced, and *heard* by the conscious mind, while a deeper layer has a much lower-toned message that's still *heard*. The only difference is that this deeper layer bypasses consciousness and enters into the subconscious mind.

Mental Muscle: Think of the brain as a muscle. When it doesn't receive proper activity and nourishment, it weakens. However, when it's given adequate exercise and nourishment, it strengthens. Thoughts *are* (intangible) elements of energy that facilitate a potent influence on brain chemistry in extraordinarily profound ways. What and how you think determines the health of the chemistry *in* your brain. It also determines the secretions of hormones that circulate throughout your entire body and into your penis. Think up!

It's Everywhere

What's so interesting is that we're bombarded with subliminal influence from all directions. The conversations we don't particularly pay attention to but overhear in a restaurant. Somebody sitting behind you on a bus who's yapping away on their cell phone. The television or radio playing in the background as you're preparing dinner. We are sensory creatures, and we don't miss a thing.

According to experts — although we may not consciously hear, understand, or even realize what the chatter is all about — the subconscious mind regards *all* information as *fact* because it does not reason like the conscious mind does. If there are hate messages in a song, it doesn't even matter what the volume is — our subconscious mind, as a powerful receptor of information and *vibration*, hears and actually believes those words.

Successful, healthy, and spirited people are different. They, like everybody else, hear all words, but, due to their positive mental habits, have primed themselves to look past the gloom. They have the ability to handle negativity and not be negatively affected by handling it — an impressive quality indeed. And, as you can imagine, negativity fans the flames for all sorts of disorders, including sexual difficulties.

Of course, becoming and staying mentally healthy requires practice and support. This is why all people with sexual challenges must control what they think about, believe, listen to, read, and see. This is one of the major reasons disclosing your challenges (admitting *it*) to somebody you can trust will take the burden off you. It will prevent negative priming from happening in the first place.

Listen Up: The Technique of Exchanging

A psychological technique I refer to as *exchanging* can be implemented immediately to help anybody turn negative into positive. When a negative word, thought, belief, or memory enters your mind, it's your chance to *exchange* it with something positive; to nullify its negative energy and influence over you. Use words, thoughts, and feelings that contain positive energy so that the subconscious mind has the option to exchange the negative thought with a positive one. A great way to practice this is to get out a sheet of paper and write down a long list of positive words. Don't stop until that entire page is filled. Words like *strong, courage, happy, money, sexy, virile, confident, lean, healthy, kind, loving, happy, rich, tolerant, successful, poised, relaxed,* and zillions of others should make up your new (personalized) vocabulary.

If you have nobody to turn to for assistance, then you can start to effectively change the negative, success-blocking language in your mind by yourself with another technique. All you need is an inexpensive audio recording device to record your own *personalized motivational audiotapes* (PMA), just like the ones you'd purchase from a motivational speaker. Instead, this time, *you're* the motivational speaker!

Simply press the *record* button and start talking to yourself. Assume the roles of your own coach, motivator, disciplinarian, and, above all, best friend. Encourage yourself. Defend yourself. Support yourself. Correctly critique yourself. Push yourself to strive more ambitiously toward all your goals. Persuade yourself that you can handle and defeat any challenge and strengthen any weakness. And, above all, respect yourself. If a friend or loved one ever came to you in need of support for an extreme challenge, you'd respond by acting like a motivational powerhouse. You'd share your best (passionately charged) advice and diligently strive to see them relieved of their trepidations. So why not use this same technique on yourself?

After you record your own PMA, it's time to rewind and listen. You can listen attentively, focusing on every word and statement that you recorded; or you can attend to other tasks, not really paying (conscious or focused) attention but nonetheless allowing your (self-recorded) words to subliminally influence your subconscious mind. Either way, a constant influx of these words will reprogram, or re-*prime*, your brain, and you *will* begin to realize a positive shift in that direction. The trick to continuously improving with PMAs is to always speak to yourself from a first-person perspective; you are talking to you — and with an *I have* or an *I am* meaning, rather than an *I want* one. Also, since change happens (periodically for some, frequently for others), you must erase and re-record new PMAs when you reach higher levels of accomplishment. Older recordings will become outdated and can hold you back from progress. I promise you will accomplish great results from this technique. (More listed on my Web site.)

ANALOGY of *exchange:* When we go into a buffet (smorgasbord), we're surrounded by food and have many choices as to what we're actually going to put into our bodies. What and how much we decide to eat, as we all know, will have its consequences. Good food is *good* for us. Junk food (need I say?) has unhealthy consequences. Eating food, however, is made possible largely through a physical gathering process; we actually choose which foods we want to eat (a mental decision), then consume them (a physical act). However, thoughts are all mental. So we have choices about which thoughts to think and which ones we actually decide to believe and act upon. Your thoughts are analogous to the smorgasbord. You decide which thoughts enter, which ones stay, and which ones will create the consequences in your life. Simply, but not often easily, choose the healthy food instead of rushing over to the ice cream counter.

Imagine … it's easy if you try!

John Lennon

Every Thought Counts

Many holistic health practitioners, and certainly many psychologists, understand the power thoughts have on the mind and body. It doesn't even matter whether or not the thing that is thought of is actually true. It largely relates to the placebo effect. The doctor tricks the patient into thinking they are taking a drug or using some treatment that's designed to miraculously cure their ailment. Much to the doctor's surprise, and to the ignorance of the patient, the ailment goes into remission; however, the pill they swallowed had absolutely no ailment-fighting ingredients. So how did the patient get healed? He *thought* it, and by thinking it, he *believed* it; that's the miracle. By consuming that (fake) pill, but trusting and believing what he heard his doctor say, the patient's subconscious mind had become primed with complete faith that this was *the* remedy he needed to allow the healing to manifest.

Carolyn Myss — world-renowned author and intuitive healer — often discusses that *every thought has a physiological consequence in the body*. What Myss is referring to is that memory-based thought, once believed to be stored only in the brain, actually takes residence in the cellular physiology throughout the entire body. Another way of saying this is that our thoughts, feelings, and beliefs become stored, exerting direct influence over all our organs, tissues, and cells (all 75 trillion plus of them).

We've all heard expressions like ... "That person gives me a headache."

"When I think about what happened, it makes me sick to my stomach."

"Breaking up with her has broken my heart."

Our thoughts target various organs in our body, e.g., brain, intestines, heart, sexual and reproductive organs. Myss refers to the organic system of the body as the Chakras — channels of energy in the body, which can be used to incite an ancient philosophy of healing. Originating from Tibet and India, this healing method has been embraced by many, especially Buddhists. That's why Buddhists meditate and chant so often — to engage their own life-force energy and to use it to heal, to regenerate, to renew, to prime themselves.

To expound on the statement that *every thought has a physiological consequence in the body*, let's take a look at the movie *What the Bleep Do We Know?* In the movie, a Japanese scientist named Dr. Masaru Emoto revealed findings from various studies he conducted regarding the influences thoughts have on ordinary water. As we all know, water is one of the most abundant resources on the planet, covering 75% of planet earth. It is also the most abundant resource in *all of us*, comprising (interestingly enough) approximately 75% of the human body —

an identical percentage. Water is also the most conductive source of energy of the four elements: water, air, fire, and earth.

Emoto discovered that thoughts change the molecular structure of water. Under the lens of a microscope, healthy and happy thoughts clearly indicate a fluid and artistic molecular structure. Unhealthy, sad, or evil thoughts crystallized the water molecules and demonstrated erratic inconsistencies. Emoto's mission is to ignite mass consciousness to the awareness of what and how we think regarding all facets of our lives. Emoto believes the thoughts of mankind are exerting negative influences on Planet Earth; many of our native Indian cultures believe in a similar philosophy. It's fair to say that if our bodies are comprised of 75% water, while our brains contain 80% water, our thoughts, as in the Emoto findings, can form negative influences and disrupt body and brain harmony. (Blood also has a high percentage of water at 90%.)

To take this a step further, consider the scientific fact that thoughts create chemicals in the body. We already know that thoughts of fear create adrenaline, cortisol, and other harmful chemicals. The chemicals in tears when somebody is crying out of sadness, compared to the chemicals in tears from joy, are different. The tears may look the same, but under a microscope, the illusion disappears.

So those people with sexual challenges and who succumb to negative thoughts about their conditions can, based on substantial scientific evidence, be destroying their internal (hormonal and sexual) fortitude; their brain, blood, organs, nerves, and tissues receive the brunt of the burden. Psychological trauma (like that experienced with ED) can be the first domino in the chain of events that takes a man down to his knees. But it doesn't have to be.

You become what you think about the most.

So think about what you want to become the most!

Yours Truly

The Attitude of a Navy Seal

Eric Potterat, Command Psychologist for the Navy Seals, together with a team of experts, developed an innovative mental toughness course that included a set of principles designed to boost a man's courage and control his fear. When applied, all of these techniques (positively) influence brain blood chemistry.

The protocol Potterat developed is called the Big Four: 1) goal setting, 2) mental rehearsal, 3) self talk, and 4) arousal control. All these principles condition the thinking mind to focusing on one's goals, providing control over bedlam and keeping the emotional centers of the brain safeguarded.

Regarding self talk, the average person (nonverbally) speaks between 300 and 1,000 words to themselves every minute. When we don't pay attention to what we're saying to ourselves and how we're thinking — especially if these words are negative — then unfavorable consequences are certain to result. However, Navy Seal self-talk techniques override fear signals in the brain by apprehending one's inner chatter, exchanging weak, fearful words and thoughts with strong, courageous ones.

The Brain, History Channel, History.com

Look into My Eyes...

Hypnosis can prime the person who's being hypnotized, all from an outside source. This practice is really about the power of *suggestion*, as hypnotists can assist their hypnotized patients in overcoming obtrusive mental blocks and becoming *what they desire to become*. For instance, if a person desires to lose weight, quit smoking, become more extroverted, overcome a sexual anxiety, or whatever their goal might be, the hypnotherapist will insert certain *hook* words and *hook* phrases into their messages to prime the mind of their hypnotized patient. If everything goes as planned, these hooks will take root inside the subconscious. Hypnotherapists can be very instrumental in priming their patients for success, although there are plenty of self-hypnosis techniques you can learn and apply on your own (including your PMAs).

One way to hypnotize yourself, even if you don't go into a trance, is with *autosuggestion*. This can be accomplished through repetitive thoughts, dwelling on one train of thought, or repetitive listening to your PMAs. By *reciting, confirming, and affirming*, autosuggestions condition your subconscious mind, enabling you to believe and live out what you are listening to and thinking about.

Day-dreaming is a form of autosuggestion — we're just not always aware of it. I ask many of my students to *think about what you're thinking about when you're really not thinking about what you're thinking about*. Yes, I wrote that correctly. Read it again, then try to do it yourself. When you're not really paying attention to your thoughts — like when you're driving in your car for a long distance and you enter into that *zone* — what are you *really* thinking about? What words, feelings, and beliefs are in your mind? When you look into a mirror, or step onto the bathroom scale, what are you *really* thinking about? And if you're like most who are suffering from any discomfort or disorder, you might just be thinking about your shortcomings, which directly harms everything else you do. This is the first step to self-control and positive re-programming. *Change the thought, change the thing.*

Let the (Head) Games Begin: Participant or Spectator?

Although ED is not easy for any man to live with, single guys have a different set of challenges. When a single guy is planning to get to know a potential sexual partner, his most powerful deterrents are his thoughts about what might happen when future intimate opportunities actually present themselves. The anxiety of imagining how the experience will play out, which is a result of fear-based memory, is powerful enough to stop most guys dead in their tracks from pursuing the relationship at all (SAD).

When the opportunities present themselves, all men, not just single guys, often become their own spectator, observing nearly everything they do, judging their actions instead of relaxing and enjoying the spontaneity of the situation. This is known as *spectatoring*, a common problem that can wilt erections once the *spectator* feels he (or she) is not performing up to their expectations or ideals. Spectatoring can even prevent erections from happening in the first place if the spectating is prior to or during foreplay.

Sexual spectators often make it extremely difficult to relax and live in the moment. The added pressure they place on themselves to perform at a certain level of expectation destroys their chances of being successful in the bedroom; rules that beat to a different drum.

Quit Monkeying Around

In Buddhism, references are often made to the ego of (hu)man, which is referred to as the *monkey mind*. Since we all make decisions based on experiences and beliefs, one voice in the mind may say *"yes"* while the other voice says "no." Or a barrage of "what ifs" might possibly fill your head. Spectators, especially those who have specific thoughts of sexual expectations, are *monkeying* around in the bedroom with these mental antics.

The goal to controlling any disorder, and to attaining ultimate sexual performance, is to control the monkey in your mind. The monkey is wild, climbing everywhere and grabbing at everything it sees and hears and thinks. And if it sees failure, or wants to instigate it, performance anxiety becomes so powerful that many men not only quit standing at the plate to swing their bats; they don't even show up at the ballpark to play the game in the first place (another SAD occurrence). Total withdrawal affects millions of people worldwide. It's time to start swinging your bats again, gentlemen.

The monkey mind is especially dominating and destructive in those who have religious guilt or are ashamed about their sexuality. Many religions teach that sex is only for procreation; any act of sex outside of marriage and parenthood — including masturbation and same-sex relationships — is sinful, as all those forms of sex are merely intended for sexual pleasure.

Bad (mental) habits are easy to develop; just do what the monkey says and chances are you'll live a less-than-favorable life. Good habits are often difficult to develop, but once you've developed them, life can be good — really good! You decide what kinds of thoughts and habits you want to develop and which ones you need to reprogram. Tame that monkey!

In his famous book, You Can Work Your Own Miracles, Napoleon Hill states that "mastery over fear is the key to success." Napoleon lists the "Seven Basic Fears" — four of which can pertain, directly or indirectly, to a man's feelings about his sexuality. They are 1) fear of criticism, 2) fear of ill health and physical pain, 3) fear of loss of love, and 4) fear of old age.

Chapter 11

ED: *It's* a "We" Thing

"Couples who have sex frequently are happier."

Oprah Winfrey

Sexpression

Humans are creative beings. In fact, we must create, as (pro)creation is our innate driving force. Our (or any) species would become extinct if this program to reproduce, encoded into our cellular DNA, were ignored, denied, suppressed, or shut off. This driving force is not confined to procreation; it also pertains to sexual expression. The desire for sex consumes the psyche. The pleasure of orgasm is a gift Mother Nature grants to us for expressing ourselves as procreative creatures, proving we're worthy to contribute to the survival and advancement of our human race. Nocturnal erections and nocturnal emissions (wet dreams) are two other natural phenomena that Mother Nature has gifted us with to inspect our systems, and to confirm whether or not we're capable of expressing ourselves procreatively.

Sexual expression is imperative for healthy living and self-betterment, so any deterrents are challenging to live with, if not downright destructive. Suppressed sexual expression is frustrating, even maddening. (Freud knew about all this a very long time ago.) One of the most destructive emotions a person can possess results from suppressed or denied expression of love and/or sexual needs. Just examine the many people who are institutionalized due to mental disturbances, most revealing some history or pathology ranging from slight suppression to complete rejection of love.

In a marital or committed relationship, two people become one. Each person in that dynamic duo complements the expressive needs of the other: "He makes me feel so much like a real woman"; "She makes me feel like I can do anything." Great relationships are those that make two people better, individually and collaboratively.

One of the most destructive elements of a relationship is the suppression, disrespect, and/or rejection of expression: "No matter what I say, he's always ridiculing me"; "She blurts out demeaning remarks about me when we're around our friends, and that makes me shrivel up."

When a man denies a woman of her true expression, or when a woman denies her man, the relationship is at risk of being destroyed.

A man needs a woman who makes him feel like a man, and a woman needs a man who makes her feel like a woman.

For the man with sexual performance challenges, a partner who doesn't understand the reasons for his romantic and intimate withdrawals can worsen his ED. Women who are demeaning and condescending, or who become offensive, can severely damage a man's ego, pride, and confidence, exasperating his (and their) problem.

Admitting any sexual discomfort or difficulty to your partner shows respect. It also demonstrates that you care for and regard this relationship as a *we* thing, instead of a *me* thing.

According to Dr. Ann Marie Tommey, an expert in female and couples sexuality, women produce higher levels of a hormone called *oxytocin*, which is also known as the *touchy-feeling* hormone, or the *hormone of love*. This is why most women want to be cuddled before and definitely after sex. Oxytocin is released in higher amounts after a woman experiences orgasm and remains high in the female for days afterwards. Tommey explains that women are ready for intimacy for 36 hours or longer after one orgasm, a result of oxytocin's influence, combined — of course — with her attraction and respect for her lover.

So here's one explanation of putting that Mars vs. Venus story into perspective. Tommey explains that a man's levels of oxytocin drops quickly after orgasm, versus days in his partner, an obvious divergence between these two planetary objects that could very well explain why (many) women complain their mates aren't intimate enough.

Men produce less oxytocin than women; while their post-orgasm blood oxytocin levels wane after a few hours, women's levels remain high for several days. One explanation points to a man's levels of free testosterone that may negate the action of oxytocin.

Keep in mind that we're discussing evolution here, not only modern day man and woman. Built into our biological genes are innate response systems that have been carried with man since the beginning of human existence. You've got to agree that hunting a dinosaur required a great deal of time, energy, courage, and risk. So as man was evolving, he was performing intercourse on predatory battlefields, all while striving to fulfill his genetic obligation to advance the human race. Immediately after inseminating his mate, off he went to hunt another dinosaur or protect his cave from invaders. Unfortunately, men still have that genetic code programmed into their DNA, as the oxytocin-lowering response may just be an inherent primitive survival mechanism, or a terrific excuse we guys can use the next time we're scolded for leaving the bedroom too early. Wham-bam-thank-you-(cave)-woman.

Okay, we're all mature adults, and we'd be silly to use the caveman story as an excuse for one's lack of intimacy. As you will soon read, supplemental oxytocin is available and can be helpful for couples. But the good news for you ladies reading this, and for you guys who are not as virile as you used to be, is that the lower the testosterone the more oxytocin remains in our system. Older guys do *do it better!*

Oxytocin is now available under several trade names like Pitocin and Syntocinon, or just as generic oxytocin. I have found several sources on the Internet, but at this time, I can only recommend a legitimate version from HealthPlus Pharmacy in San Luis Obispo, California.

Knowing that oxytocin can enhance the intimacy of couples, it will be interesting to learn how this relatively new-to-the-marketplace compound plays itself out. Oxytocin is known to play a key role in enhancing the refractory period in both men and women, shortening the time required to become sexually aroused and to achieve another orgasm (male/female) and seminal ejaculation (male). Becoming conscious of how to elevate oxytocin levels may just keep us guys connected to our partners long after we ejaculate, causing the dinosaur excuse to eventually lose its validity.

Being Realistic

It's a fact that many aging men (and women) won't be performing like they did in their younger days, nor should they expect to, placing an extra burden on themselves with such unrealistic expectations. If you compare your *now* ability with your *then* ability to perform sexually, you could actually be making your ED worse by assuming the position of an overly eager spectator. By doing this, you're creating a negative thought-belief pattern that leads to performance anxiety and frustration when the time for sex presents itself, inhibiting ultimate performance.

With this understood, many men aren't as bad as they believe themselves to be. They just have unrealistic expectations of themselves (or are reminiscing about their wild and crazy college days) and simply need to make some mental adjustments. Instead of understanding and enjoying the experience in the *now*, many men make their sexual experiences more difficult than they really are. They enter the bedroom with a scoreboard bolted above the headboard — one that's outlined with very specific rules of engagement, play patterns, goals, and expectations that must be fulfilled. Above all these things, they also have their "personal records" to beat. When men do this, they're only setting themselves up for more complications and disappointment.

My advice to you? Just relax! Eliminate your game plan, make adjustments, and most importantly, enjoy your partner!

Men need to relax and enjoy the process of lovemaking, rather than expect that *wham-bam-thank-you-ma'am* style most guys remember from their high school and college days.

Keep in mind that many people experiencing sexual disorders, especially men with ED, do not have a problem — physically speaking. Their problem lies in the fact that they have unrealistic expectations or are experiencing performance anxiety. Men have a set idea about the quickness at which erections are supposed to be obtained. They even have expectations regarding the duration and frequency of intercourse.

When dealing with ED in a committed relationship, factors like boredom, financial worries, annoyances and grievances, anger, scheduling issues, and fatigue must be considered. Also, many couples truly *love* one another, but they may not necessarily *like* each other any longer. Love, like, and respect are very important factors that play a role in the attraction one feels toward another. It could be something as simple as not liking the way one snores or tosses in bed, or the length of time it takes her (or him) to get out of the bathroom. Grievances add up, and the accumulation can repel, not attract, two people from becoming sexually intimate in spite of them loving one another. (Couples notoriously prime one another.)

Old Partner Syndrome: Let's face it: some relationships lose their fizzle. Attractiveness wanes — partners become older, more out of shape, less sexy, weaker, or unenthusiastic. Stress and incompatibility issues have crept in, contaminating the relationship. Before you start to seek greener grass, counseling may be useful in repairing a wilting relationship.

New Partner Syndrome: You're now single ... again. It wasn't supposed to be that way, but the marriage just didn't work out. Time to start dating! (What a concept.) But *it's* not like it was before — eager and always up for the occasion. Instead, performance anxiety consumes one's thinking. What makes this anxiety worse is the fact that you are desperate to find and secure a compatible partner that you feel comfortable with. Take it slow, go on a few dates, and accept how things pan out.

Masturbation

Although it has its place on the menu of sexual activities and pleasures, many may just think that masturbation is a quick way to achieve orgasm, and basically ... they're right. But according to studies, self-induced orgasm is far inferior and delivers questionable health benefits (mentally and physically), when compared to orgasm achieved through sexual contact with a person you're attracted to, and even more so, in love with.

Internet pornography can become very damaging because it causes detachment from socializing and meeting partners. This, of course, can also lead to chronic masturbation. Dependency on masturbation is the easy, fast way for sexual relief and the surest way to avoid embarrassment from exposing one's sexual disorders or social fears, but it does nothing to remedy the problems.

Chronic masturbation is often the result of a more troubling sexual disorder resulting from fear of failure, or performance anxiety. This condition prevents people from seeking out a sexual partner due to fear of potential failure, rejection, or embarrassment; and there are those who are just flat-out fed up with relationships. This is often referred to as something I mentioned before — sexual aversion disorder, or SAD. Yes, it's SAD indeed; a habitual trick the emotions play that forces people to avert potentially pleasuring situations in an attempt to avoid the pain of failure, rejection, or disappointment. Over time, and as expressed by Elizabeth Gilbert in her #1 *New York Times* Bestseller, *Eat, Pray, Love*, people with SAD actually begin to believe or, at least, *justify* their reasons for averting sexual encounters, which deepens their (negative) subconscious programming.

Hyper-Sexuality

As a youngster, like most guys around my age, most of my sexual education on female anatomy came from the department store catalogs, specifically, the women's underwear and bathing suit sections. Sex was not taught in school, nor did my parents discuss the topic *ever*. Every now and then, as I got older, I was able to get my hands on *Playboy*, but that was basically it. When Marilyn Monroe's dress blew up or Jane Mansfield bent over to show us her cleavage, the public went crazy. But then, as the 60s and 70s moved on, things really started to change. Miniskirts and bikinis became popular, while free sex, love, and peace were promoted instead of war. The visibility of sex began to show up everywhere. Feeding our curiosities, fantasies, and emotions, sex started to become connected to absolutely everything, everywhere and, seemingly, all the time. This constant barrage of sexual associations had no limits, ranging from the foods we ate to the clothes we wore, the cars we drove, the vacations we decided to go on, and even the shampoos we washed our hair with. Sex was connected to every facet of our lives. And our hormones sat in the sidecar through all of it.

The way sexuality is regarded and understood has changed dramatically over the last half century. The constant influence of sex-connected-to-almost-everything has primed us to think and act differently. Who should be having sex? What's considered normal? How often should we have sex? Questions like these — and a zillion more — exert a great

deal of stress and anxiety on those who are just aspiring to enjoy a satisfying, pleasure-filled act and deem themselves normal.

Since *sexy* is considered norm or vogue, and those advertising it
sensationalize it in unrealistic and overly frequent displays, many men
and women, young and old, are now primed with distorted opinions
and beliefs about their own sexuality — opinions and beliefs that are
not based on who they *really* are or what they're *really* capable of. The
influence of the mass populous is so powerful that far too many
people have lost their sense of self, and true sexual identity, robotically
cloned from perverted external forces.

For instance, according to some studies, a normal guy is satisfied
with sex that delivers orgasm once or twice per week. But many men
don't want to be normal; instead they want to be hyper-normal, or
hypersexual. Craving sex more than one actually gets it, like most other
unfulfilled desires, creates tension, stress, frustration, anger, resentment,
depression, and fatigue. Hypersexuality, then, can wear a man out —
especially those guys who have the responsibilities of a business, family,
community, and personal self-betterment.

I consulted a guy who was the classic A-type in his early thirties.
The subject we discussed pertained to his health and fitness, but the
issue of sexual behavior came up occasionally. Mike (not his real name)
was panicking. He complained that he couldn't have sex with his beautiful girlfriend as often as he wanted. Mike wanted his girlfriend to
share three to four orgasms a night with him — a very ambitious
objective, especially since Mike ran a demanding business. On top of
that, he was borderline obese. He complained that after he ejaculated
the first time of the night, his seminal volume was noticeably lower the
second time … and the third. And by the fourth, he was all dried up.
He explained that he was experiencing a very irritating pressure in his
rectum for days following each of his sexual marathons.

As stated, I was Mike's fitness consultant, not his doctor, but I knew him well enough to know that 1) He had unrealistic expectations for the amount of orgasm-producing sex he was striving for, especially at his age when testosterone and DHEA start to decline more rapidly; 2) According to statistics, Mike's sex drive and frequency of intercourse was perfectly normal. He was able to get erections upon command, but he wanted to speed up his refractory periods, shortening the length of time between orgasms to speeds you could only keep track of with a sprinting coach's stopwatch; and 3) The pressure in his rectum, I assumed, was from the strain he was placing onto his prostate, which was being forced into producing more seminal fluid without sufficient time between orgasms to replenish depleted supplies.

I advised Mike to relax, and to be pleased with what he was getting. He had nothing to complain about in light of what some other guys, with real sexual problems, were complaining about. I encouraged Mike to see his doctor, but he never ended up going. He did, however, become more aware of the imbalance between his desires vs. his actual ability to meet those expectations, and although we didn't discuss it after that, I'm guessing Mike's rectal issues subsided.

Laugh *IT* Off

We're living in an era of epidemic rates of depression, fear, anxiety, sadness, despair, and unhappiness. The millions of people who are suffering from these maladies are living an obscure life. The emotions that arise from these symptoms are deadening, not only to oneself, but also to those in contact with these people. Christianity categorized these conditions under one label: *sloth*. And throughout history, it has been branded as one of the Seven Deadly Sins.

Worried about your health or financial status? Concerned about the well-being of your relationships or your ability (or inability) to perform sexually? Is your self-esteem low? Are you unconfident about your future? You can STOP ALL THAT (temporarily or permanently) by partaking in some laughter.

Throughout this book, I make several references to how the thought centers of the brain influence the mind and body. You can refer to Gladwell, Anderson, Hill, Emoto, Dispenza, and Myss, who all believe, in their own unique ways, that "every thought we have has a physiologic impact on the body and influences the consequences in our lives."

This is profoundly useful data that when understood can serve as yet another tool to coach ourselves on a daily basis. Get a sad thought, and LAUGH it off. Get angry, and LAUGH that off too. Worried about performing (sexually) on your date this Friday evening? HA HA HA!

It is known that what you fear *manifests*. And what you resist *persists*.

If you think laughing at these matters is phony then you're right, depending on what state of mind you want to assume. But you can *fake it until you make it*, a mental trick used by successful people throughout history, as the subconscious mind only knows what it's being told; this is a unique way of priming yourself.

In 1976, the popular self-help guru and business powerhouse, Norman Cousins, set off a medical revolution. Besieged by terrible pain from a particular nasty spinal disease, he published his findings in the *New England Journal of Medicine* that 10 minutes of belly laughter allowed him two hours of sleep. That's right. With Cousins *laughing* at his pain, his pain subsided. Seemingly miraculously. But the hormones and other biochemicals that are released with *laughter* cannot be duplicated synthetically, mostly because they are emotionally charged with *happy* energy, and that's a potent mixture doctors can't whip up.

Due to Cousins' findings, hospitals and universities have launched study after study, each giving modern medicine statistical credence to ancient wisdom that laughter actually heals. The doctors from UCLA's Humor and Medical Recovery Program tell of some AMAZING stories about how the simple act of laughter and listening to comedy helps children and adults heal from disease and depression.

As far back as ancient Greece, hospitals were built next to amphitheaters. Why? Because the "mirth of the audience" was believed to have a physiological healing effect on patients. The book of Proverbs says, "A cheerful heart is as good as medicine, but a downcast spirit dries up the bones."

The fact is that in the last 20 years, study after study has proven that bringing more laughter and humor into your life — or just *surrounding* yourself with more laughter — will physiologically improve your health and immune system. At the same time, it will also increase your chances for advancement, social success, and even love. "Laughter is the best medicine." That's what my (earthly) mother always told me. So let's take a moment now and laugh out loud … Ha … Ha … Ha. Feels good, doesn't it?

Being unhappy drains you of precious energy. However, being happy, even sporadically, boosts your overall energy and equips you with the fuel you need to successfully challenge and endure life. Unhappiness leads to (or worsens) many maladies like obesity, depression, hormonal imbalances, increases in the release of negative hormones, impotence, lower levels of nitric oxide in your body … the list goes on and on!

When people aren't happy they don't take care of themselves. They don't care, period. People must find something every day to be happy about. Laughter makes your life better. You are more confident. You're relaxed. You feel more likable. And you're sexier.

Here's an unpublished personal expert opinion from Dr. Franz Ingelfinger, departing editor of The *New England Journal of Medicine*, who reported that approximately 85% of all human illnesses are curable by the body's own healing system.

Laughter and humor literally boost your immune system, speeding up the body's healing mechanisms. At its root, laughter secretes neurochemicals that generate chemical reactions that flood the body with protein chains called *neuropeptides*, which instantly touch every living cell in your body! (Refer to Dr. Joe Dispenza's documentary entitled *Evolve Your Brain: The Science of Changing Your Mind*.)

Be strong. Be courageous. Be brave. Be prudent. Laugh at your problems and watch them submit to their new boss: YOU! ... Ha ... Ha ... Ha!

(Note: It is not my intent to ignore or deny any of your challenges. I am merely sharing information on proven techniques that can change your methods for dealing with distress. Laughter is at the top of that list, and it's worth implementing into your life ASAP.)

Chapter 12

Natural Sex-Boosters: Complete Guide

Dr. Jonathan V. Wright is the medical director of the Tahoma Clinic, located in Renton, Washington; he is also the author of "Guide to Healing with Nutrition." Dr. Wright proclaims, "We are organic creatures comprised of (natural) elements that originate from Mother Nature. When nourished with natural compounds our bodies are able to obtain, then maintain, optimal health and performance."

According to countless experts, Wright included, trillions of cells make up the structure of our bodies, all of which have been constructed from microscopic particles assimilated from the foods we consume. Each one of these cells has its own lifespan, and when they die off, they undergo a regenerating (or replacement) process. Some cells die on a daily basis; some weekly, monthly, and yearly. This destruction-regeneration process operates during all stages of human aging and pertains to the cellular composition of everything we biologically own; this includes our hair, eyes, bones, skin, brain, heart, genitals, intestines, organs, muscles, and nerves (to name a few).

No matter what age we are, regenerating old cells by replacing them with new *vital* ones seems to be the logical and healthy way to maintain optimal health, right? You wouldn't exchange your 2009 Lamborghini for a used 1985 Yugo (listed in *TIME* Magazine's "50 Worst Cars of All Time"). Since we all experience varying degrees of (micro)trauma on a daily basis, nourishment is imperative on a deep cellular level. Even the couch potato has some level of this wear and tear, while the active person's destruction-regeneration process (obviously) is much more demanding. Nevertheless, both lifestyle examples thrive on healthy nourishment.

Wright is correct when he asserts the notion that properly nourished cells are the ultimate approach to obtaining optimum health. This advice, however, is not limited to muscle shape and low levels of body fat. It primarily pertains to positive influences on all our body organs — the hormone-producing factories that secrete the muscle-building, energy-yielding, sex-promoting chemicals that make us healthy and sexually virile.

There's a high percentage of our population that, in spite of exercising and following a sound nutritional regimen, still fall short of their goals. "What's going on?" I asked myself decades ago, eager to find the answers. Then I stumbled onto the *concept* of blood profiling. Nothing new, but nonetheless something uncommon with most fitness buffs. What I discovered, and what has become an integral incentive for writing this book, is that many people are, unknowingly, living with hormonal deficiencies that are preventing them from living life to its fullest. Without healthy levels of hormones, living a vibrant, productive, and sexually satisfying life is a challenging mission, to say the least.

After blood profiles are analyzed, hormonal imbalances can be corrected, and a new person can be born. They are known to experience an increase in muscle strength and energy and accelerate the loss of excess body fat. Libido shoots through the roof and erection power … well, let's just say: it's very good. Or as some ladies like to say: *A hard man is good to find!*

Needless to say, eating healthy is challenging, even for those who are pros at knowing what and when to eat. The obligation is *knowing* how to make educated choices and, if you fall off track, jumping right back on to continue improving.

The following sections are dedicated to revealing some of the foods, supplements, and drugs that contribute to boosting sexual potency, while revving up your internal engines for overall health as well.

Herbs: These are organic vegetation. They're botanicals that are loaded with nutritional and medicinal properties originating from plants, roots, flowers, seeds, barks, berries, stems, branches, and other natural sources. Most herbs possess an amazing array of positive properties that range from boosting energy to promoting sleep, improving overall health and metabolism — and are especially effective at boosting sexual potency.

Many herbs are amazingly powerful, displaying no side effects other than good ones.

I still sense that a large percentage of people underestimate the potency of herbs, an oversight only experience will resolve. Most herbs are completely safe on their own; however, many taken in combinations offer synergistic benefits. This is called *synergistic efficacy*, which basically means one compound increases (or boosts) the potency of other compounds in your body. This is a bonus benefit if those *other compounds* are nutritive. However, the same *boosting* effect will happen with drugs, so overdosing is potentially possible. Be sure to check in with a skilled doctor or pharmacist.

Even certain foods, like grapefruit, can possess synergistic efficacy with other compounds in the body. A common technique used by athletes, referred to as *stacking*, is to consume grapefruit to boost and prolong the actions of aspirin and caffeine (just to name two). The synergistic properties in grapefruit enhance the potency of other compounds, including many drugs.

Many of the supplements I've listed in this book are available off-the-shelf (OTS). Some people believe that OTS-available products lack potency, especially in comparison to drugs, but in actuality, they are wrong. Those who try these supplements will realize just how effective they are at providing the results I've listed, both for short-term and long-term benefits.

A lot of these supplements are considered *pro-sexual* as they benefit the brain, glands, endocrine system, and genitals. They come in a variety of forms ranging from teas, liquids, sprays, capsules, tablets, sublingual pills, bulk powders, transdermal patches, and many others.

Some supplements are affordable, and others are very costly. But they are often less expensive than the ones advertised on TV and radio. This is because the price of the advertised product factors in the expense of producing the (television or radio) commercial and the cost for the airtime media.

In comparison to the delivery and reaction times of most drugs, some supplements may take longer to influence the body and yield their benefits. The time it requires for the body to store up enough nutrition is often called the *saturation period*. Although many of the items listed will work quickly for most people, some require longer periods to saturate the body and influence it to trigger *cellular receptivity*. Be patient with them; understand that they *are* working on a deep cellular level and that your body, by fact of accessibility, is being nourished on the inside.

The effects of nutrition also depend upon your state of mind, lifestyle, counterreactions to drugs, smoking habits, alcohol intake, and the receptivity of your cells.

Sex-Boosting Natural Supplements and Foods

All of the supplements listed in this section are available without a prescription, while some may have synthetic alterations that are classified as prescription drugs. For example, Yohimbine HCL is the synthetic version made from Yohimbe. You can find many of these OTS supplements at your local health food store and even your local grocery store.

Arginine: "L" version: Known as the amino acid that improves erectile function. L-Arginine is a precursor to nitric oxide (NO), the erection-producing chemical that's directly responsible for dilating (opening up) the tissues of the corpal bodies in the penis to make blood flow possible and cause erection. L-Arginine supplements are very useful for stimulating erections (penis and clitoris). Nitric oxide also serves to enhance a woman's arousal and sensitivity as blood is rushed to the vagina and clitoris. L-Arginine has also been shown to increase sperm counts in men and is a useful supplement for those who exercise and want to support muscle-building. According to the Life Extension Foundation, L-Arginine supplementation is an essential part of a longevity plan. It helps to stimulate the production of HGH by influencing the pituitary to secrete healthier levels of growth hormone, the most important antiaging hormone in the body.

Used alone, L-Arginine has been known to exacerbate the herpes simplex virus, causing outbreaks or cold sores. Experts claim that herpes may benefit from high dosages of another amino acid named Lysine; so L-Arginine and Lysine may be a wise combination.

L-Arginine is mostly available in capsule, tablet, and powder forms. Here is a partial list of food sources containing Arginine: dairy products, whey protein drinks, beef, pork, chicken, turkey, wild game (like quail and pheasant), seafood, carob, chocolate (the natural kind), popcorn, brown rice, oatmeal, and whole-wheat bread. Others on the list include seeds and nuts — sunflower, pumpkin, pecans, walnuts, almonds, Brazil, hazel, pine, peanuts, and buckwheat.

Ashwagandha: This herb strengthens the reproductive system, helping to increase male fertility while also boosting libido. Promotes heightened sense of well-being, stimulates a healthy mental outlook, boosts mood, and induces better sleep. Ashwagandha has been known to reverse the harm associated with nervous tension and is considered to be an anti-aging herb. It also serves as an anti-anxiety aid. This is a recommended herb for combating stress, as your adrenal glands respond by producing cortisol in excess. Cortisol is highly toxic to the organs and muscles. Very useful for addressing overall health and to remedy nervous disorders, low libido, intestinal infections, and impotency. Physicians in India regard this herb as a powerful aphrodisiac. This herb is available in dried form (bulk, tea bags, or encapsulated) and also in a liquid version. It can be used as a tea by itself or mixed with other herbs.

Aspirin: This is a synthetic derived from the natural plant White Willow Bark. This chemical agent is used for a variety of purposes. It acts as an anti-inflammatory agent, relieving minor aches and pains, and improves circulation. Many men with ED experience inflammation of the genital tract. Aspirin may be helpful to reduce inflammation in the genital region and assist in improving blood flow into the penis. It's also known to boost the potency of other compounds in the body as it has a synergistic effect, so using Aspirin in conjunction with other medications and supplements must be closely monitored to prevent overdosing.

Avena Sativa: Antiestrogen, aromatase inhibitor. Also known as Wild Oats, this natural herbal wonder has been used medicinally since the Middle Ages. Avena Sativa is known to be an effective libido booster and sexual enhancer. This herb works by freeing up bound (or unusable) testosterone and increasing free or bioavailable levels, making this male sexual hormone more active and equally as effective for men and women. Avena Sativa is great to use with other herbs as it may have synergistic properties that boost its potency. For instance, combining this herb with Stinging Nettles is known to free up bound testosterone in the bloodstream and enhance sexual function. Bound testosterone often turns into radical dihydrotestosterone (DHT). This herb is available in dried form (bulk, tea bags, or encapsulated) and also in a liquid version. It can be used as tea by itself or mixed with other herbs.

Boron: This is a trace mineral that has been shown to serve as a sex booster, increasing the hormone testosterone. Boron helps to maintain higher levels of testosterone in the blood, assisting in muscle building, fat loss, and sexual functioning. It may be connected to alleviating arthritis and improving memory in men and women. Some boron-rich foods include almonds, apples, avocados, dates, red kidney beans, and cashews. Available in capsule, tablet, and powder form.

Catuaba (*Anemopaegma Arvense*): Catuaba is an herb that possesses amazing potency effects in males. Extremely popular in Brazil, this natural wonder has been praised by the indigenous tribe known as the Tupi Indians. Used for its libido-boosting properties, Catuaba is also beneficial for increasing circulation to the genitals, combating fatigue, enhancing memory, calming the nerves, and relieving depression. Many regard Catuaba as a natural aphrodisiac. It's available by itself and can also be mixed with other herbs and nutrients.

Chrysin: This is an antiestrogen, aromatase inhibitor. It's another natural product that helps to maintain healthy levels of free testosterone in the blood and can actually lower an (unhealthy) estrogen ratio. Available in tablet or capsule form.

Cnidium: Also known as *Osthole*. If you try to pronounce this name, *osthole*, it sounds like a drunken way of saying "asshole." Funny as it might sound, this herbal product possesses libido-stimulating effects and also has the ability to help with erections by assisting in the production of NO, which dilates the corpal bodies for an influx of blood flow into the penis. The same benefits may occur in women who are also dependent on NO stimulation for the vagina and clitoris to function sexually. Available in seeds, powder, and capsules.

Damiana: This herb is a very popular natural product in herbology and is known for its benefits as a virility compound. It contains natural hormonal-like properties that assist in testosterone and sperm production, libido, and erection. It may also be useful for maintaining a healthy prostate in men and clitoral health in women. Damiana is popular in Central and Latin America, the West Indies, and Africa, where it's established as a potent aphrodisiac. Some people report that smoking the dried leaves of this herb gives them a marijuana-like effect. This herb is available in dried form (bulk, tea bags, or encapsulated) and also supplied in a liquid version. It can be used as tea by itself or mixed with other herbs.

Dihydroepiandrosterone (DHEA): This is the most plentiful steroid hormone in the body that's mostly manufactured in the adrenal glands. DHEA is popular as a testosterone-like agent that was once available by prescription only. Age, stress, and unhealthy lifestyle habits accelerate the decline of natural DHEA. DHEA is identified for helping the body burn fat, strengthen and tone muscle (with a proper exercise program), and boost libido and genital (penile/clitorial) sensitivity during sex. It is often touted as an antiaging hormone suggested by longevity specialists for overall health, increased cognitive benefits, and cardiovascular health. Medical examinations with complete blood profiles should be obtained prior to using DHEA to ensure safety for correct dosage and duration. Proper cycles of using DHEA will help to keep blood levels within normal ranges.

After its saturation period, your doctor may recommend lowering your dosages; or you might have to switch to an every other day routine, in addition to taking some layoffs before another cycle begins. Too much DHEA, or staying on this hormone for excessive periods, can be counterproductive, as it is known to aromatize testosterone into more estrogen, creating an overload of free radicals. It's wise to eat very well and consume antioxidants to combat these free radicals and to keep your system clean. Excess DHEA can also hamper the adrenals' testosterone-making ability, ultimately depleting the amount of testosterone produced in the gonads (testicles in men, ovaries in women).

DHEA, although one of the more popular hormones used for hormonal balancing and restoration, can be a double-edged sword if used incorrectly. It's available in powder, capsule, tablet, and liquid form.

When consumed properly, DHEA can be very beneficial to the heart and immune system; it can also help with increasing metabolism, improving libido and erections, and combating depression.

DIM (Diindolylmethane): Considered to be an anti-estrogen, aromatase inhibitor. This substance is a naturally occurring phytonutrient (*phyto* refers to plants) that's useful for controlling excess estrogen in both men and women while stimulating higher levels of testosterone. DIM may also be useful for maintaining prostate health and offering benefits for sexual performance. It's available in capsules by itself, or mixed with other ingredients. (Another version is called I3C, or Indole-3-Carbinol, which has double the potency of DIM.)

Dioscorea Villosa (Diosgenin): Traditionally used in females. This is a natural compound that's extracted from Wild Yam and provides a natural source of DHEA. It's available in dried form (bulk or encapsulated) and may also be supplied in a liquid version. It can be used as tea by itself or mixed with other herbs.

Dong Quai: Also referred to as *Angelica.* Regarded as an overall female tonic in Oriental medicine. This herb is used to ease the cramps linked with menstruation and menopausal symptoms (such as hot flashes). Dong Quai helps to nourish the blood that circulates into the female genital region, remedying vaginal dryness and serving as an overall sexual health-enhancer for women. The herbs Black Cohosh and Licorice are also used for these purposes and can either be taken by themselves or in combination with Dong Quai. It's available in capsules or tea. Quick herbal recipe: equal parts of Dong Quai, Black Cohosh, and Licorice.

Enzyte: This used to be a popular TV-branded male enhancement formula that claimed to increase the size and frequency of erections. It had a large following of users, including Smiling Bob. Individual results do vary.

Epimedium: See Horny Goat Weed.

ExtenZe: This is another popular TV-branded male enhancement product. All of the ingredients in this formula can be obtained individually OTS. The claim that a natural pill can increase penis size has raised a lot of skepticism, but you cannot deny the popularity, and consumer repeatability, of this product's success.

Fo-Ti: Also known as *Ho Shu Wo, He Shou Wu.* According to a Chinese legend, *He Shou Wu* means "black-haired Mr. He." Fo-Ti has been recognized in Chinese medicine as a universal health tonic. It's known to possess remarkable benefits in preventing hair from graying (you don't see many gray-haired Chinese), while it is also used to prevent premature aging. This herb is also very helpful for increasing sperm (semen) volume; nourishing the blood, liver, and kidneys; and supporting vaginal integrity in females. It's available in dried form (bulk or encapsulated) and is also supplied in a liquid version. It can be used as tea by itself or mixed with other herbs.

GABA (*Gamma-Aminobutyric Acid*): This is a major neurotransmitter that offers benefits to the pituitary gland of the brain. GABA also plays a role in cardiovascular health and hormonal production. It has a calming effect on the nervous system. GABA's calming benefits may be useful in controlling mood swings, insomnia, stress, and anxiety. It can help to assuage disturbances associated with sexual disorders. It's available in powder, capsule, tablet, and liquid form.

Ginkgo Biloba: Ginkgo has been used for thousands of years. It's an herbal wonder popular for its ability to nourish the brain. Brain tissues are very selective about what chemicals they permit inside their cells. However, Ginkgo has the powerful ability to cross the blood-brain barrier and nourish the cells of the brain, useful for addressing depression, anxiety, and cognitive disorders. Ginkgo improves mental functions that include learning and memory, and since the brain is considered the largest sex organ in the body, Ginkgo is used to increase sexual performance. Ginkgo's benefits aren't isolated to the brain. It also has the ability to improve the circulation of blood to other cells throughout the body, especially to smaller blood vessels, like those located in the genitals. When blood gets into the penis, it becomes erect. Women, especially, can benefit from using Ginkgo. It improves blood flow into the vagina and clitoris, increasing vaginal lubrication and sensitivity, which in turn increases the pleasure in lovemaking. The Chinese believe the seeds offer the most potency while it's also available in powder, capsule, tablet, and liquid form.

Ginseng: An adaptogenic herb. Perhaps known as the "king of herbs" in Oriental medicine, Ginseng has been used for centuries as a staple tonic for the overall reinforcement of health. Ginseng has a reputation for enhancing energy and strength and is known to be very useful as a sexual rejuvenator. It helps to improve testosterone while boosting semen and sperm production. It also nourishes the prostate and testicles. Ginseng has equal benefits for women, helping with female-specific endocrinological needs. It's available in powder, capsule, tablet, and liquid form. It makes a healthy tea by itself, or it can also be mixed with other herbs. (American versions of Ginseng may now be more potent than Asian sources, possibly due to the mineral and nutrient depletion of the soil in which Asian Ginseng has been growing in for centuries.)

Horny Goat Weed (*Epimedium, Yin Yang Huo*): You might feel a little embarrassed walking into a health food store and asking the clerk for that "horny-something-or-other." But get used to it, because this herb is the real deal. Epimedium is often called *natural Viagra*, and for good reason; it acts in similar ways for producing erections as it inhibits the activity of the enzyme PDE-5. PDE-5 both binds and blocks a chemical in the body called *cyclic guanosine monophosphate* (cGMP). cGMP is necessary to dilate blood vessels (vasodilation) and relax vascular tissues that allow blood to flow into the corpal bodies of the penis, making it hard. And for women, this herb can help to increase the circulation to the vagina and clitoris, which stimulates natural (vaginal) lubrication, bringing about a heightened level of sexual sensitivity. Epimedium also demonstrates testosterone-like effects that help to increase sperm count, and acts as a natural aphrodisiac that increases libido in both men and women. Herbologists in China and Japan have known about this herb's special medicinal and nutritional properties for hundreds of years. Available in powder, capsule, tablet, and liquid form.

L-Carnitine: This is an amino acid that has become popular as a fat-burner. L-Carnitine helps to mobilize fat inside the body, which facilitates the transport of fat into the *mitochondria* — the fat-burning compartments inside muscle cells that act as little (yet powerful) fuel-burning furnaces. (This is best accomplished with concurrent exercise.) L-Carnitine is also instrumental for nourishing the brain, bones, muscles, heart, and organs. It also helps to boost sperm count. Recommended as a supplement for those striving to lose body fat. Available in powder, capsule, tablet, and liquid form.

Levodopa (*L-Dopa, Mucuna Pruriens, Velvet Bean*): Levodopa is a drug that is also available in natural forms. This product helps to increase dopamine levels. Dopamine is a hormone that influences brain function, stimulating the hypothalamus and pituitary glands. Dopamine is also useful for inhibiting the effects of *prolactin*, a radical hormone that depletes FSH and GnRH and can potentially lead to hypogonadism. Often used as a treatment for depression, this substance is also recommended for boosting libido and may stimulate the secretion of growth hormone from the pituitary. Available in powder, capsule, tablet, and liquid form. (Note: There's other synthetic versions available.)

Licorice: We've all eaten licorice candy as kids; maybe some of you still eat it as adults. Quite simply, this herb tastes absolutely delicious, and its sweet taste is all-natural. This organic substance is great by itself but is also a terrific synergist as it helps many systems of the body function better. Hormones are nourished when Licorice is present. According to Life Extension Magazine, August 2008, Licorice is also helpful in stress reduction through a series of actions that reduces the damaging effects of excessive cortisol. Promoted as an aphrodisiac, drinking Licorice tea before lovemaking can help to spice things up. Available in powder, capsule, tablet, and liquid form. It can also be made into candy and snacks. A delicious-tasting tea by itself, it can also be used to enhance the flavor and nutritional content of herbal combinations.

LJ, Long Jack: See Tongkat Ali.

L-Lysine: This amino acid is commonly used to treat and prevent many cancers, especially prostate cancer. L-Lysine is also known to stimulate the production of testosterone and increase semen and sperm volume. It is often recommended for those who are infected with the *herpes simplex* virus and for those who need to prevent outbreaks from consuming high amounts of L-Arginine. Available in powder, capsule, and tablet form.

Lycopene: All men, especially those with low levels of testosterone, need to be concerned about the possibilities of prostate enlargement (BPH). Lycopene is a supplement rich in nutrition that supports the tissues of the prostate, which is also critical for making semen and sperm. Lycopene also nourishes the heart, liver, testicles, and adrenal glands. It's available in capsules and tablets. Prevalent food sources include tomatoes (and tomato-based products), watermelon, pink grapefruit, red bell pepper, and wolfberries (also referred to as Goji berries).

Maca (*Lepidium Meyenii*): Known as Peru's (natural) Viagra. Like Horny Goat Weed, Tribulus, Velvet Antler, and many of the other natural supplements you'll find in this book, Maca is a natural wonder for boosting sexual health. Dating as far back as the Inca Indians, Maca has been used as an aphrodisiac for increasing libido, muscle strength, energy, sperm production, and erectile function. Maca's power is effective for both men and women, and it's widely used to remedy fertility problems. Available in dried form (bulk or encapsulated). Can be used by itself or mixed with other herbs in a formula.

Melatonin: This is a hormone that naturally (endogenously) secretes from the pineal gland located inside the brain. Its function is to regulate our daily cycle, known as the *circadian rhythm*, or *biorhythm*. However, ample supplies diminish with age, stress, drugs, sleep deprivation, and other unhealthy culprits. Melatonin secretes out of the pineal gland when light is inhibited; this is the reason why the majority of us (naturally) get sleepy at night, when it's dark. Better sleep equates to better health and, according to many studies, improved sexuality and quality of life. Since sleep is one of the major periods when human growth hormone is (endogenously) secreted from the pituitary, melatonin supplementation may help to improve muscle tone, nerve strength, tissue recuperation, and sexual function, which are all direct benefits from healthy HGH production. Available in capsule, tablet, powder, and liquid form, it can be used by itself and also combined with other relaxing agents.

Milk Thistle (*Silybum Marianum, Silymarin*): This is a natural powerhouse that is known to offer protective benefits for the liver, spleen, and kidneys. Those using an excessive amount of drugs, alcohol, and steroids can use this herb as a defense against organ and tissue damage. It's also helpful for hepatitis. Available in capsules, tea bags, and formulated with other nutritional items.

Minoxidil (*Rogaine, Regaine*): An OTS liquid medication that was originally intended for high blood pressure; however, it was found to re-grow hair in balding patients (male and female). It's rubbed onto the scalp to treat male-pattern baldness (MPB). There are versions for men and women. Some side effects have been reported, such as itching and irritation on the application area. Available in liquid and foam.

Mucuna Pruriens: See Levodopa.

Muira Puama: Also known as *Potency Wood* in its native Brazil. This rainforest botanical has been proven in clinical studies to be an overall libido booster. Some regard it as the "Viagra of the Amazon." In a study at the Institute of Sexology in Paris, France, patients who were experiencing lack of sexual desire were given the herb. After only two weeks, nearly two-thirds of the subjects who complained about their loss of libido reported improvements, believing the herb had helped. This herb appears to enhance both the psychological and physical aspects of sex, affecting the endocrine and nervous systems that stimulate the sex organs to receive blood, increasing excitement and sensitivity. It also eases menstrual cramps and PMS, treats fatigue, helps with gastrointestinal and reproductive disorders, and combats stress. The short-term effects of Muira Puama include increasing blood flow to the pelvic area, aiding erections in men, and increasing vaginal sensation and orgasm in women. Longer-term use is applied for stress management, overall health, and the production of sex hormones in both sexes. It has no noted side effects; however it can slightly raise blood pressure. Can be useful for increasing testosterone levels. Available in capsules and liquid. Can be used by itself or mixed with other herbs in a formula.

Nettles (*Stinging Nettles; Urtica Dioica*): This herb has a long medicinal history as a remedy for joint and muscle disorders. Europeans have used Nettles as an herbal option to treat *benign prostatic hyperplasia,* or BPH. According to laboratory studies, the effects of Nettles were found to be comparable to the (synthetic) chemical *finasteride* (brand name: Propecia) in slowing growth of certain prostate cells — without side effects. This herb can be used by itself, while it's known to work well when combined with Avena Sativa and Saw Palmetto. Nettles exists in both leaf and root versions, while the root version offers the best potency. Available in capsule and liquid form. Can be used by itself or mixed with other herbs in a formula.

Phenylalanine: This is an essential amino acid that the body converts into dopamine. Phenylalanine can be helpful for boosting sexual desire in both men and women. (Do not confuse this with DL-phenylalanine, which reduces pain and therefore sensitivity.) This amino acid is found in all high-protein foods, which include nuts, seeds, beans, cottage cheese, and soy products. It is also available in capsule or tablet form.

Pregnenolone: This is a natural hormone our body produces that plays a role in a process called *steroidogenesis;* the transforming of one steroid molecule into another (better) one. Some of these (better) hormones include androgens, progesterone, and estrogens. Many experts are now suggesting Pregnenolone in place of DHEA, as it acts similarly playing a role in many vital body functions, including those directly responsible for sexual function. It could be useful as a brain enhancer that improves memory, vision, libido, and sexual sensitivity. Available in powder, capsule, and tablet form.

Pygeum (*Pygeum Africanum*): This herb is often prescribed in holistic medicine as a preventative measure against benign prostatic hyperplasia (BPH) and to maintain the health of the prostate gland itself. It's also used to treat urinary tract symptoms that are caused by BPH. This herb is used by itself or combined with Saw Palmetto for added benefits.

Quebracho Bark: Chemically similar to Yohimbe, and often used in combination, this herb has been used throughout South America as an aphrodisiac with no known side effects — other than creating powerful sexual excitement. Not easy to find. Available in capsules and tablets.

Rooibos: Also known as *Red Tea* or *Red Bush Tea*. This natural caffeine-free herbal plant originated in South Africa and is popularly used as a tea. It is known to assist in digestion and prevent or remedy allergies, and it can reduce anxiety and nervous tension. Men with performance anxiety may benefit from using this herb. Available in capsules and tea.

Sarsaparilla: This is an herbal product that's been used by the indigenous peoples of Central and South America for centuries.

Sarsaparilla is known for remedying sexual impotence and skin ailments. It also helps with physical weakness. Sarsaparilla is now available in a variety of tablets, capsules, and liquid extracts, and can be found as a component ingredient in an assortment of herbal remedies formulated for libido enhancement, hormone balancing, skin disorders, and the boosting of athletic performance.

Saw Palmetto: As a man ages, or as his testosterone plummets to dangerously low levels, his chances of obtaining a condition known as BPH (benign prostatic hypertrophy, or enlargement of the prostate gland) increases making him prone to a potentially sex-ending life-threatening condition. This herb helps to block estrogen receptors in the prostate, therefore minimizing the threat of tissue growth, or *hypertrophy*, also called *hyperplasia*. Saw Palmetto helps the body maintain a healthy level of the sex hormone testosterone, preventing it from converting into the radical dihydrotestosterone (DHT). Supplementing with Saw Palmetto is a prudent choice for a man who wishes to maintain a healthy prostate. This herb is used by itself or combined with Lycopene and/or Pygeum for added benefits. Available in capsule, tablet, and liquid form.

Schizandra: Known in Chinese medicine as a potent adaptogenic natural wonder that helps the body fight stress and maintain a healthy nervous system. It helps to promote mental function, boost immunity, and stimulate the nerves without jittery excitation. Used in China, Russia, Europe, Scandinavia, and the United States, this herb is also regarded as an overall body tonic that strengthens the sex organs. Available in capsule, tablet, and liquid form. Can be used by itself or mixed into formulas.

Tongkat Ali (*LJ, Longjack*): Tongkat Ali improves sexual ability by raising testosterone levels, or more specifically, the levels of free testosterone available to the tissues. A large portion of the testosterone that circulates in the body is bound (or locked up) by a protein called *sex hormone binding globulin* (SHBG). When testosterone is bound by

SHBG it's rendered ineffective. Only free testosterone is effective. How exactly Tongkat Ali extract increases free testosterone may be explained by its ability to bind itself to SHBG, rendering SHBG inactive. Tongkat Ali is also known to stimulate the secretion of luteinizing hormone, which ultimately stimulates the testes to produce more testosterone. An elevated level of free testosterone will demonstrate a positive effect on libido. Available in tablets and capsules.

Tribulus Terrestris: This herbal sensation became enormously popular when strength athletes and bodybuilders discovered its ability to boost natural testosterone levels without the side effects associated with anabolic steroids. Steroid abusers or, for that matter, anybody who's experiencing sexual inadequacies, can use this product to help in restoring sexual functions, and for boosting libido and erectile ability. Tribulus improves libido through an elevation of free testosterone made possible by an increase in luteinizing hormone (LH), which is a direct result of the hypothalamus and pituitary glands — an integral part of the HPTA. These functions help to reactivate the (dis)connection between sexual thought (libido) and erection of the penis. Tribulus is useful as a post-steroid cycle therapy to help bring down-regulated hormonal functioning back to normal.

I was introduced to Tribulus in the mid-90s by a Bulgarian weightlifter who claimed he had exclusive distribution rights in the USA. Within a short time, Tribulus products appeared everywhere; apparently this guy didn't have it exclusively.

Tribulus consumption can be tricky. It works, and then it doesn't work. So, in spite of this being a potent and efficacious natural substance, *cycling* is necessary to prevent the possibility of down-regulation, or negative feedback, of the HPTA. After a certain period of use, the body reaches its peak in tissue saturation, followed by a slowing down or reversal of actions. This seems to be temporary, so it's best to cycle this product, using it for several weeks at a time and then laying off, as opposed to relying upon it on a day in/day out basis.

The actions of this product are also extremely potent in women, helping them to gain muscle strength, boost metabolism, increase libido, and enhance sexual sensitivity and orgasmic pleasure. Used by itself or now combined in many sexual-enhancement formulas. Available in tablets and capsules. I've even found a bulk version at an Asian herbal market.

Tryptohpan: This is an amino acid that plays a role in serotonin production. Serotonin is an important neurotransmitter that promotes relaxation and a heightened sense of well-being. Low levels of Tryptophan have been linked to sleep disturbances, binge eating, and even depression. Tryptophan is often known as the *sleepy protein* that most of us experience every year shortly after Thanksgiving dinner. (Turkey is loaded with this protein.) Due to its serotonin-boosting benefits, and as supported by the clinical research gathered at the Life Extension Foundation, Tryptophan is an effective sleep aid that may play a role in influencing the pineal gland, similar (or complementary) to Melatonin. In 1991, Tryptophan was banned in the USA when a tainted Japanese supply came into the country, and ruining a great thing for a lot of people. Fortunately, it's back on the market and available in liquids, tablets, capsules, and powders. Food sources include, oats, dates, bananas, milk, yogurt, cottage cheese, red meat, eggs, fish, sunflower seeds, pumpkin seeds, and peanuts.

Tyrosine: This is another amino acid that may play a role in boosting libido. Since the brain is known as the *true* sex organ, arousing mental function may lead to sexual benefits. Tyrosine's properties act as a neurotransmitter that allows the cells of the brain to better communicate with one another. It's also used to address depression and to increase mental alertness. Many people experience headaches when using this product, so start with a low dose. Available in tablet, capsule, and powder form.

Velvet Antler (*Antler, Deer Horn, Elk Horn, Pantocrine, Lu Rong, Velvet*): Antler is Asia's elite natural health product, even prized over

Ginseng. Its first use was recorded in a document recovered from a Han Dynasty tomb in 206 B.C., listing the use of Antler for a variety of nutritional and medicinal purposes. Throughout the centuries, Antler has gained widespread approval for its health-enhancing benefits. Antler is processed from the seasonal harvest of antlers that grow and naturally discard from deer and elk. The nutrients contained in the antlers originate from the natural plants and herbs these animals consume in the wild. During the mating season, or *rut*, deer and elk undergo dramatic hormonal upswings that eventually lead to the production of new antlers. This cyclic event is a marvel to molecular science, as the development of the antler is a result of a highly sophisticated hormonal/receptor mechanism. (According to the suppliers, harvesting antler in no way harms these animals. Unlike the illegal and unethical poaching for rhino horns and elephant tusks that destroys these animals, the deer and elk continue to live on.)

In humans, Antler is known to stimulate endogenous hormonal secretions that produce vitality, strength, and energy. Its benefits are known to relieve the symptoms of menopause and remedy sexual dysfunctions (in both males and females). Antler is also known to increase sperm count, control blood pressure, improve blood flow, repair tissue damage (it has anabolic effects), and alleviate arthritis. In 1989, I learned that Antler was used by Russian athletes to restore imbalances to the HPTA of those who were experiencing negative side effects from steroids. Available in capsules. The best source of Antler is available through the Life Extension Foundation.

Yohimbe: (Please note that *Yohimbine* HCL is the synthetic "prescription" alteration for Yohimbe.) Yohimbe is extracted from the bark of an African tree; it has long been prescribed for men who lack sexual desire and who wish to maintain a high state of arousal, experience a boost in energy, and address erection difficulties. Most studies have focused on the effects of Yohimbine HCL (not Yohimbe, per se, so read the studies closely) regarding its benefits to pelvic-genital circulation and how it targets the penis. Some men become nervous, agitated, and nauseous when using this compound, especially the prescription version under the Yocon label. Both the natural and synthetic versions may cause rises in blood pressure. Clinical evidence suggests that Quebracho Bark has similar effects but without the side effects just mentioned. Quebracho Bark is often recommended for women and men who are seeking to improve their desire and prolong arousal. Available in capsule, tablet, and liquid form. (Also see Quebracho Bark.)

Vitamins and Minerals (Partial List)

Calcium: This is the most abundant mineral in the body. Over 99% of it is stored in our bones and depletes with age, lack of exercise, drug use, excessive drinking, stress, and smoking. It also diminishes in post-menopausal women. People who lack Calcium are at risk for skeletal breakdown as their bones become porous and brittle. This is a condition known as *osteoporosis*, which was once labeled as the *stealth disease* due to the fact that patients and their doctors didn't see it coming. Far too many people are deficient in this mineral because of the consumption of nutritionally-void foods. Calcium supplementation works best when mixed with Vitamin D3 (see below), or when skin is exposed to (at least) 10 minutes of natural sunlight daily. Calcium is found in eggs, fish, milk, cheese, and many vegetables like spinach and broccoli. If you are lactose intolerant then refrain from dairy products — unless you find lactose-free brands. Also available in capsules, tablets, powders, and mixed into formulations.

Cyanocobalamin (Vitamin B12): This vitamin is similar in structure to that of an androgen. Useful for nourishing the blood, it plays a significant role in most body functions for both sexes, including fertility and semen health. Available in capsules, tablets, sublingual caplets, and sprays. Pharmaceutical versions are available and administered through injection (by prescription only).

Niacin (Vitamin B3): This vitamin is often referred to as the *great sex pill*. It produces a flushing effect throughout the body, increasing skin sensitivity. In a sexual context, Niacin stimulates mucous membranes in the mouth and vagina that may rouse up sexual lubrication. Many claim that Niacin enhances orgasm, intensifying pleasure, often called the *orgasmic flush*. Available by itself or used in formulations. Itchiness and skin reddening are known side effects that may be dose related. Lower dosages are recommended at first, which can be elevated according to your reactions. There are nonflush versions of Niacin available that do not cause these reactions. Tablets and capsules are the most common.

Vitamin B Complex: This is an essential family of nutrients that are available individually or together. The B vitamins play vital roles in all body functions including digestion, nervous functions, immunity, libido, orgasm, and sperm production. (Also see Niacin and Cyanocobalamin.) Available in many forms.

Vitamin C: Probably the most popular vitamin, thanks to Dr. Linus Pauling, who is often referred to as the "Father of Vitamin C." Vitamin C possesses extremely potent antioxidant properties that, as Pauling proved, combat free-radical cellular attacks caused by unhealthy eating habits, drug use, stress, anxiety, and other biological villains. Vitamin C plays a critical role in sexuality and reproduction, and it has been known to accelerate healing after injury and boost sperm count. Available in many forms.

Vitamin D: (Also see Sunlight under "More Sex-Boosting Options".) This natural substance comes from the source of all life — the sun. Since all life is contingent on the energy provided from the sun, those who are deprived of direct sunlight should take a Vitamin D supplement; the D3 version is recommended. Vitamin D has a vitalizing effect on the entire body and plays an essential role in all bodily functions that can ultimately boost sex drive. Available in many forms.

Vitamin E: Also known as the *sex vitamin*. Plays an essential role in the production of hormones. Also plays a role in the circulation of blood throughout the body and in keeping body joints healthy. Both our reproductive and sexual health are regulated by hormones; the metabolism of these hormones is dependent upon nutrients, including Vitamin E. Erectile function may be helped by using Vitamin E, while women need this supplement to ensure overall reproductive health. Available in many forms.

Zinc: This is a trace mineral that plays an essential role in many body functions and is essential in regard to sexual maturity. Zinc is necessary for the health of a man's prostate. When the prostate gland is healthy, Zinc is found in high concentrations. It helps to manufacture higher volumes of seminal fluid and sperm. With age, the prostate gland tends to enlarge, which is (partly) caused by Zinc deficiencies. Prostate enlargement places pressure inside the rectum. This pressure is very irritating and can often diminish libido, lowering potency. Zinc is concentrated in semen, so frequent ejaculation will deplete its supplies in the body, which places stress on the prostate. (Remember Mike?) In addition to its benefits on the prostate, Zinc also supports the integrity of muscle tissue and the adrenal glands. It can be a nutritious aid for testosterone synthesis. Since oysters have been reputed to be an aphrodisiac, it is not surprising to find they are an excellent source of Zinc. This trace mineral even plays a role in testicular function by increasing testosterone and sperm count (Abbasi 1980). Zinc supplements are recommended as insurance for preventing prostatitis and also as an aid for men with erectile problems. Since Zinc helps to raise testosterone levels in men, it's likely that it does the same for women. According to Earl Mindell, R.Ph., Ph.D., who is the author of *Vitamin Bible*, "Most zinc in food is lost in processing, or never exists in a substantial amount due to nutrient-poor soil." This underlines the importance of Zinc supplements. Available in many forms by itself or used in combination with other nutrients.

More Sex-Boosting Options

Star Dust: Going from SAD to GLAD

Sunlight: All life on this planet, including you and me, completely relies upon sunlight and the energy it provides. Being deprived of sunlight creates a host of mental and physiological disruptions that include — to name a few — depression, anxiety, muscle weakness, fatigue, low sex drive, and a condition known as *seasonal affective disorder*. (Yes, that's right — SAD! Not to be confused with *sexual aversion disorder* or *sexual arousal disorder*. It's getting tricky keeping track of all these acronyms.) Many people have become dependent upon antidepressant drugs when they simply lacked adequate exposure to sunlight. However, sunlight, like many things, can easily fall into that too-much-of-a-good-thing category. So limit your time in the sun, striving to get (at least) 10–15 minutes of natural sunlight daily.

I'll Drink to That!

Tea Formulas: Many of the herbal supplements suggested in this book are supplied in various forms and often referred to as teas. You have all kinds of options to select from; you can choose to swallow capsules, drink a liquid extract, spray a mist into your mouth, tuck a sublingual tablet under your tongue, or brew up your own nutritional-medicinal-hormone-boosting tea, either hot or chilled.

You can drink teas individually or mixed together in formulas. I really enjoy mixing teas with coffee. Consuming herbs is a wise and healthy practice. Here's a little more history:

Tea: Referred to as any herb (or organic product) that originates from a seed, plant, leaf, bark, root, vine, stem, bud, flower, or branch. Rooted in soil, herbs extract the minerals and other nutrients from the earth, sun, and rain. As they grow, their roots continue to penetrate deeper and wider into the ground, absorbing the minerals and water from the soil. The stems, branches, and leaves grow upward and outward, attracted to and thriving on rain and sunlight to absorb star-energy and Vitamin D3, which is known as *photosynthesis.*

Camping Accident

In ancient China, when mountain ranchers were sitting around a campfire one night after a long day of gathering, they noticed that some leaves had blown into their boiling water. To their surprise, the flavor of the leaves enhanced the flat taste of the water they boiled, so they drank it. However, as sleep time came upon them, the Chinese ranchers found it impossible to fall asleep and soon postulated that the leaves possessed mysterious energy-boosting properties. This was the first documented use of leaves for tea.

Tea is an ancient beverage steeped in history and romance and loved by many (my hand's raised). In fact, after water, tea is the most commonly consumed beverage in the world. Although tea had a modest beginning (remember, it was discovered by accident), its popularity spread from its origins in China to Western Europe, then to the Americas. Throughout history, tea has been believed by many to aid the liver, kill germs, purify the organs, preserve mental equilibrium, and boost sexual function in men and women. Over the past few decades, scientists have taken a closer look at the potential health benefits of tea, discovering that much of the folklore about its healing properties is actually true. These findings are nothing less than extraordinary, and if you're in tune with Mother Nature, I'm sure you completely understand the power teas have.

Other Discoveries: The antioxidant properties of tea play a role in reducing the risk of cardiovascular disease. Tea has the ability to decrease lipid oxidation, reducing instances of heart attack and stroke. It may also beneficially impact blood vessel function, an important indicator of cardiovascular health and genital functionality. Tea may lower the risk of certain cancers by inhibiting the oxidative changes in DNA from free radicals and some carcinogens. Compounds in tea have been shown to support the human immune system. All this is sexy news.

Black tea and green tea have high levels of antioxidants and help to increase circulation. However, due to their energy-yielding levels of caffeine, some potencies of these teas may exasperate performance anxiety and interfere with sleep, so timing their consumption needs to be taken into consideration.

Coffee originated on the plateaus of central Ethiopia in A.D. 1000. During the fifteenth century, traders transplanted wild coffee trees from Africa to southern Arabia. The eastern Arabs, the first to cultivate coffee, soon adopted the Ethiopian's practice of making a hot beverage from its ground-roasted beans. Its caffeine stimulates the brain, improving one's focus and concentration. One of the world's most popular beverages, coffee is also one of the world's most important commodities. Coffee is recently making big headlines for its anti-obesity effects; it can also possibly reduce the risk of the latest disease epidemic, Type II Diabetes. There's even some evidence that coffee may stop headaches, boost mood, and prevent cavities. Coffee is very useful for improving exercise and workout power and athletic performance through an increased excitation of nerve and muscle activity. It can aid fitness buffs in shedding unwanted body fat and toning muscles quicker.

Natural caffeine, as contained in certain teas and coffee, can provide some very beneficial effects. However, caffeine mixed into many of the sugar-loaded energy drinks, like those that are flooding our beverage market these days, cannot be compared to caffeine obtained from a fresh cup of coffee or tea.

Coffee today is not the same as the coffee of yesteryear, especially in light of the popular java cafés that have popped up on almost every street corner. The drinks available today are loaded with creams, sugars, syrups, and plenty of artificial additives that disrupt the body. In its organic form, coffee possesses a plethora of health and satiable benefits, especially when mixed with tea or other herbal compounds. The practice of mixing herbs is common, also known as *formulation;* mixing coffee with tea (both considered to be herbs anyway) has been success-fully practiced by a select number of people. If you feel a little guilty about drinking coffee (or think you're over-caffeinating yourself but simply cannot deprive yourself of that java jolt), go ahead and mix in some herbal tea. That way, you can avoid the artificial additives. This can be a very healthy and rewarding practice for you.

Sex-Boosting Foods

Almonds: Almonds are a wonderful and delicious source of essen-tial fatty acids that, in addition to their great taste, provide the basis for the healthy production of hormones, which has a significant influence on regulating sex drive (amongst other things!). The smell of almonds is found to arouse passion in females.

Apples: An apple a day keeps the doctor away, and it could also prevent ED, female sexual disorders, and a host of other health issues. This popular fruit is loaded with Vitamin C and a powerful mix of antioxidant nutrients and enzymes that help to prevent heart disease and cancer (prostate in men, breast in women). Apples are also useful for controlling cholesterol and weight gain.

Asparagus: This vegetable is known to act as a libido booster. Asparagus also happens to be very high in Vitamin E, which (as I mentioned earlier) has long been promoted as the *sex vitamin.* The Vegetarian Society suggests "eating asparagus for three days for the most powerful effect." The odor from urine after eating asparagus is from the discharge of a sulfur-containing amino acid called *methionine.* It might smell odd but it's not harmful. Asparagus is a super healthy food.

Avocado: The Aztecs called the avocado tree *ahuacatl,* or *testicle tree.* Interesting fact: avocados help to increase libido in both males and females. It contains very high levels of essential oils and folic acid that assist in metabolizing proteins, thus providing more energy. Avocados also contain Vitamin B6 (a nutrient known to improve hormone production) and potassium (which helps to regulate a woman's thyroid gland). For something tasty and diverse, try dipping a chip into some guacamole, or spread some avocado over a piece of toast!

Bananas: This jungle fruit is a great source of B vitamins. They're also commonly known for their high levels of potassium. These nutrients help to increase the body's total energy levels, libido, and sex-hormone production.

Basil: A wonderful herb that's often used as a spice to boost the flavor and nutritional content of salads, sauces, and a host of other dishes. The chemical properties in this plant are known to improve circulation, stimulate the sex drive, and boost fertility. It's also great for enhancing well-being for body and mind. Basil oil was once known to be used by prostitutes as a perfume to attract customers! Personally, the scent of basil makes me want to drive to the nearest Italian restaurant. Rumored to increase the size of the penis. Healthy and tasty.

Blueberries: I can't remember where I heard it, but this tiny tasty fruit is known to help with erections. It's likely that the potent array of nutrients and antioxidants this fruit contains are certain contributors. Now, don't run out and eat blueberry pie; that doesn't count! I'm referring to fresh blueberries. Eating them raw is like munching on candy — at least from Mom's kitchen.

Brazil Nuts: Rich in essential oils and selenium, these nuts contain nutrients that assist in hormonal production and sperm volume.

Cardamom: Cardamom is an aromatic spice. In many cultures, it's used as an aphrodisiac and for treating impotence. It can be mixed with Maca and other herbs for some *interesting* results. It is high in *cineole*, which can increase blood flow in certain *important* body areas!

Carrots: This tasty vegetable is believed to be a sexual stimulant. Its phallus-shaped structure has been associated with stimulation since ancient times and was used by early Middle Eastern royalty to aid with seduction. High in vitamins and beta-carotene.

Celery: Considered an excellent food to ramp up sexual stimulation. It naturally boasts a potent substance known as *androsterone* — a hormone that's released through male perspiration. This kind of sweat, often referred to as a *pheromone*, has a strange effect on women. The same effect might be accomplished with a dozen roses and a bottle of wine as well.

Chilies: This member of the pepper family has the ability to (literally) heat up your sex life. It contains an ingredient named *capsaicin*, which is the substance that gives you that hot sensation when consuming peppers, curries, and other spicy foods. Capsaicin can trigger the release of endorphins; therefore it can be a feel-good substance for your brain! It also stimulates nerve endings while elevating core body temperature (*thermogenesis*) and heart rate. Eating hot peppers can make you perspire excessively and create higher levels of thirst. Many people believe that eating peppers makes them feel more sexy. (It's important to know that if you chop the chilies yourself, make sure you wash your hands very thoroughly — and especially avoid eye contact or rubbing onto your or your partner's genitals.)

Cocoa: (Also see Dark Chocolate.) This is what chocolate is made from, less the artificial sugar additives. High in antioxidants and other nutritional properties, cocoa is known to release dopamine from the brain, which plays a responsibility in sexual arousal and libido. It's fair to say that cocoa is an aphrodisiac. Available in many forms.

Coffee: (See above.)

Dark Chocolate: (Also see Cocoa.) This treat offers a dopamine-releasing effect that stimulates the sexual compartments of the brain, which triggers arousal. In fact, a study of 163 women published in *The Journal of Sexual Medicine* found that those who consumed at least one cube of chocolate daily reported significantly greater desire and better overall sexual function than the individuals who abstained. The reasoning? High-flavonoid chocolate consumption has been linked to improved circulation. Chocolate contains *theobromine* and *phenethy-lamine,* alkaloids that have a physiological impact on the body and have shown to increase serotonin levels in the brain. Be careful not to consume the brands that contain excessive sugar. (I sense you didn't want to hear that last part.)

Figs: Interestingly enough, some sources suggest that figs represent the shape of a man's testicles. Therefore it seems logical that they've been used as an aphrodisiac. Whether this is accurate or not, figs are very high in nutritional sugars, fiber, minerals, and amino acids, all of which are important for increasing libido and sexual stamina.

Garlic: Bad on the breath but good on the sex drive. Garlic contains high levels of a compound known as *allicin,* which has been known to improve blood flow to the sexual organs. Allicin also has been known to demonstrate immune-boosting and antifungal properties.

Grapefruit: As an excellent source of nutrition, including high amounts of Vitamin C, grapefruits need to be eaten with caution for those who are taking drugs of any kind or even using prosexual natural supplements. The chemical ingredients in grapefruit enhance the potency of other compounds in the body, therefore making overdosing possible. Athletes have known of the grapefruit's synergistic effects on everything from aspirin to caffeine to steroids. So be careful about delighting yourself with this tasty fruit if you're taking anything that needs potency control.

Mustard: A useful condiment that's believed to excite the sexual glands and boost desire.

Nutmeg: Chinese women regard this herb as a potent aphrodisiac. In high quantities, nutmeg can create a hallucinogenic effect. A light sprinkling of nutmeg in a cup of tea or coffee can help to *spice* things up.

Nuts: (Listed individually throughout this book.) Most nuts are helpful for maintaining cellular integrity of the muscles and joints, promoting the production of NO, and improving sexual capacity. They contain essential oils that are necessary for the production of hormones and also help to protect the heart and organs.

Omega-3 Fatty Acids: Found in fatty fish like salmon and sardines, omega-3s are known to improve cardiovascular health and lower harmful levels of triglycerides.

Oysters: Probably the most popular food that's ballyhooed as an aphrodisiac. Romans in the second century A.D. recognized the potency of oysters and made them a staple ceremonial item prior to sensuous nights. Some believe the oyster resembles the female genitals, which is the reason for the turn-on. (It's kind of similar to how figs and avocados are testicle look-a-likes.) Oysters are also high in iodine, an essential mineral known to regulate thyroid function. In reality, oysters are very nutritious; they're also loaded with zinc and high in protein.

Pomegranate: A delicious fruit that is extremely high in nutrition and antioxidants. The properties of this fruit are known to be helpful to the heart, immune system, liver, and prostate. It can lower bad cholesterol (LDL) and even boost healthy cholesterol (HDL). According to the Life Extension Foundation's February and May 2007 reports, pomegranate is also known to enhance the production of nitric oxide, which protects cardiovascular health by increasing blood flow through arteries and veins. Nitric oxide reduces injury to the vessel walls, helping to prevent the development of atherosclerosis. NO is also imperative for making erections. Messy to eat but worth the hassle, pomegranates are delicious and now becoming very popular as a juice.

Pumpkin Seeds: Pumpkin seeds contain a high amount of zinc, which is important for sustaining sexual desire and producing testosterone in both men and women. Pumpkin seeds are also rich in the essential fatty acids, which act as a precursor of *prostaglandins* (hormone-like substances that play a key role in sexual health). Due to their zinc content, munching on pumpkin seeds may support the prostate gland and overall hormonal production.

Raspberries and Strawberries: Delicious and highly nutritious. Both are high in Vitamin C, natural sugars, minerals, and antioxidants, and making one heck of a healthy snack.

Shellfish: In addition to oysters, consider abalone, clams, scallops, shrimp, and lobster.

Tomatoes: Packed with lycopene. Known to nourish the prostate. Yes, marinara sauce, salsa, and ketchup are on the list too! However the potency of raw tomatoes might be best.

Wine: Has the ability to stimulate all senses and evoke sensuality. Its tiny molecular structure allows it to quickly pass the blood-brain barrier, so results are rapid. A glass or two of wine can be ideal for enhancing a romantic interlude. However, as with any alcohol, excessive consumption can have an adverse effect and make you sleepy; the excess sugar that enters the body can negatively affect the pancreas gland, insulin production, and levels of body fat. Wine can greatly enhance a romantic interlude while providing you with a degree of free-radical-fighting antioxidants.

Wolfberry: Also known as *Goji Berry.* Renowned in Asia as a highly nutritious food and recently established as a nutritional wonder snack here in the U.S., Wolfberries have been used in Chinese medicine for centuries. They are extremely rich in nutrients and contain high levels of antioxidants that are known for their roles in enhancing the immune system, improving circulation, increasing sperm production, and protecting the organs.

Fruits: Saturated with sweet-tasting natural sugar, vitamins, minerals, fiber, and antioxidants, fruits are known to possess numerous aphrodisiac properties. Many fresh fruits are as sensual as they are nutritious and delicious. Apples, apricots, bananas, cherries, dates, figs, grapes, mangoes, papayas, peaches, pears, plums, pomegranates, raspberries, and strawberries — just to name a few — are all to be appreciated and celebrated.

Protein Power: Positive Nitrogen Balance

Whether you're a hard-training athlete, someone who just wants to live a normal healthy life, or someone wishing to maintain youthful ultimate sexual performance abilities, living without protein is impossible. Protein is needed for the proper growth, maintenance, and repair of the muscles and cells in the body, also playing a crucial role in the production of sexual hormones, nitric oxide, sperm, and much more.

Protein is made up of smaller elements called *amino acids*. In total, some experts claim there are 22 amino acids needed for optimum human health. All of these amino acids must be available to the body if one is to live a healthy productive life. Of these 22 amino acids, 8 are considered *essential* for human health. The term *essential* literally refers to the fact that it's essential one ingest these amino acids on a daily basis from food or supplement sources to maintain proper health. The remaining 14 amino acids are *nonessential* and can be produced by the body in the event they are not made available with food.

When a protein food or supplement contains all of the eight essential amino acids, that food is regarded as a *complete* protein. There are many other foods that contain protein but are classified as *incomplete* because they lack one or several of the essential amino acids. Soy is considered by some to be a high-protein food, but many regard it as an incomplete source of protein; it lacks methionine, one of the eight essential amino acids. If a food source lacks an essential amino acid, simply eating another type of food may supply the missing amino acid and provide the body with all of its essential building blocks. Many health enthusiasts then have resorted to *food combining* to ensure nutritional balance for all nutrients, especially protein.

Proteins are complex molecular structures that are extremely versatile. Most other nutrients contain carbon (C), oxygen (O), and hydrogen (H). Protein also contains COH, but they include a backbone of nitrogen (N). The more N our bodies can retain, the stronger and healthier we become — physically and sexually.

When protein intake is adequate to meet normal daily requirements and no more, a condition known as *nitrogen equilibrium* is experienced. However, when one is deprived of adequate protein, a *negative nitrogen balance* is the known condition. Negative nitrogen balance is bad news because your body is deficient in its essential building blocks. Of course, nitrogen equilibrium is better than *negative nitrogen balance*, but those who eat adequate protein on a regular basis develop a condition known as *positive nitrogen balance*. This should be the goal for every man wanting strong, lean, energetic muscles; for every man who wants to have the sexual power of someone much younger than he is. Positive nitrogen balance often means your tissues are receiving more protein and retaining more N than what's being excreted daily.

Physiologic Dynamics

I've stated that protein must be consumed on a regular basis if one is to maintain optimum health and sexual performance. When one is deprived of protein, their body will fall into a *catabolic* state. That literally means the tissues of the body are atrophying away, or the body is cannibalizing itself. Drops in muscle size and strength, hormone levels, nitric oxide, sperm count, and seminal volume occur as they await their essential amino acid supplies.

Muscle tissue is composed of living organisms, which means it's metabolically active. The muscle maintenance process is made possible by amino acids. Scientists claim that in as little as every six months, all of the muscle tissue in our body is completely replaced by the amino acids we received from the foods we eat. Since muscle tissue is constantly being remodeled, it makes sense to feed the body with adequate protein (from high-quality foods and supplements) on a regular basis. (Note: although bacon, sausage, hot dogs, and lunch meats contain some protein, these foods are loaded with hormone-destroying chemicals that can ultimately affect overall health and sexual function.) Good time to pause with the reading and scramble up a few egg whites!

In addition to boosting nitrogen balance and rebuilding muscle and nerve tissues, protein is *hydrophilic,* meaning it attracts and holds onto water. As stated, 75% of muscle tissue, under normal and healthy circumstances, is water. So the more protein-rich foods and supplements you consume, the more you will attract and hold water. And this is exactly where (inside the muscle cells) you want the water to be held — in the *intercellular* spaces, or inside the tissues and cells. You don't want water stored in the *subcutaneous* spaces, which are over the muscle and under the skin. This is known as *edema.* To the contrary, fat is *hydrophobic,* meaning it doesn't like, nor will it mix with, water. Fat is a solitary entity, and there is a lot of it in any one of our bodies right now. So drink plenty of water, consume sufficient amounts of nitrogen-rich protein, and watch your muscles grow stronger and more energetic.

Protein Supplements

These have become extraordinarily popular supplements that are available in pills, liquids, bars, and bulk powders. They're also available in pudding and tear-and-stir (or blendable) powder packs in the form of mixtures, or better known as *meal replacement formulas* (MRF). You can even find many of the nutrients from MRF in cookies, brownies, and oatmeal. When protein supplements first hit the marketplace they tasted like chalk, but today we have a variety of flavors to choose from that are deliciously satisfying, some more nutritious than others. The mixtures can contain any configuration of protein, vitamins, minerals, enzymes, and antioxidants. Proteins are offered in their single versions, like casein, whey, milk, soy, or plant, or they're mixed together to ensure a better amino acid profile. No matter what your lifestyle involves, protein supplements can play a significant role.

Center of Attention

Protein should then become the staple food category for almost every meal (snacks not included). In fact, when preparing every meal, the source of protein should first be considered. Then everything else should revolve around that. It's almost like Thanksgiving dinner where everything revolves around the turkey!

Nutritional Insurance: Pay Now or Pay Later!

The list of nutritionals listed above is brief. Along with the other suggestions that will follow, this list is a reminder that we thrive on feeding our body and its trillions of cells with proper nourishment. You can boost your overall health and protect yourself from free-radical damage by consuming nutrient-rich foods and taking a variety of nutritional supplements — herbal compounds, antioxidants, vitamins, minerals, and proteins. These nutrients are commonly found in high concentrations in fresh fruits, fresh veggies, high-quality protein sources, and whole-grain foods. Committing to a healthy ratio of nutritional eating ensures that our organs, hormones, genitals, and sexual abilities are properly nourished. Eating healthy is a wise investment that lasts for the remainder of your life.

Chapter 13

Sex-Enhancing Eating Strategies

With literally trillions of cells composing the anatomical makeup of the human body, each cell dependent on adequate nutrition, common reasoning makes it apparent that eating healthy is a prudent habit. That is, if we plan to live a healthy, productive, and sexually satisfying life.

In the last chapter, you read about all the different supplements, herbs, and foods — and the benefits that each one brought along with it. Before I keep going, let me ease your apprehension by stating that you don't need to eat like a runway model ... or separate every yolk from its white ... or count every calorie that sits on your plate. Actually, sensible eating is a very simple process — if you adhere to some basic principles.

Let me remind you that being *selfish* is a good thing. And that means giving yourself everything you need to become the best you can be. This is not limited to looking good only on the *outside* of your body, having a six-pack set of abdominals, or running faster in a 10K race. It's about the way you feel on the *inside* of your body. It's about invigorating the psychophysiological systems that will allow you to obtain ultimate sexual performance.

In addition to being your own coach and motivator, you also need to become your own disciplinarian, especially when making food and meal selections. Commit to making small yet sustainable and significant changes that inevitably lead to healthy consequences now ... and later on. So, as your own Body Boss, increase your awareness of the potential consequences for all your choices, selections, decisions, and actions.

Here's an extremely simple and easy-to-follow success-proven method I designed for developing healthier eating habits.

Do N.O.T. Diet™

The underlying basis of this eating plan originates from my experiences with and understanding of balanced nutrition. Addressing the concerns of health, simplicity, variety, satisfaction, time, and convenience, this diet is the diet you will enjoy because, in reality, it's really not a diet at all. Coincidently, I've named it the **Do N.O.T. Diet.**

N.O.T. represents **N**utritional **O**rganizing **T**echnique™. Unlike other plans that detail exactly what and how much you are supposed to eat (and are impossible to follow 24/7/365), the **Do N.O.T. Diet** places the responsibility in your hands for selecting your own foods and arranging your own meals — mostly from the foods you normally eat. This is a quick plan that helps you eat meals that are more nutritionally balanced, ultimately leading to significant health benefits.

With the **Do N.O.T. Diet** there is no need to weigh your food on scales or count calories.

CONCEPT: Over the years, while contemplating how people consumed the various categories and groups of foods, I discovered that an extremely high percentage of people eat out of balance. I began taking into account a person's total food intake and noticed that most people eat a limited number of foods or, more accurately stated, eat within a specific (limited) category of foods. Not only that but they eat those foods in overabundance. As a result of this excess consumption, imbalances are created, causing deficiencies for the nutrients that are only obtained from the (healthy) foods or food categories they avoid, or eat very little of.

The ratios of *healthy versus unhealthy* foods are grossly uneven, by sheer nutritional mathematics. Let me explain:

As I was ascertaining their total consumption, many of the people I studied (both laypeople and athletes) were eating incorrect types and/or amounts of foods (approximately) 90% of the time. Obviously this means they were eating correctly only 10% of the time, which is not enough nutrition, in my opinion, to maintain health, lose excess body fat, and become a sexual gladiator! My goal was to enhance this ratio. So instead of presenting these people with an absurdly unreasonable eating plan, I thought … if I could persuade them to shift from their 90/10 ratio to, let's say, 70/30, then they'd be consuming healthier foods 30% of the time. That's an increase by a (significant) 20% margin over their previous eating habits. I felt this could be a substantial contribution to their health — and it was!

As time went on, the method was proving itself. Those who became more motivated, obviously after seeing how effective the results were, strove to improve their ratio to 50/50, eating good half the time, which was a remarkable improvement over their former 90/10 figures. And then there were the fanatics who committed to (approximately) a 10/90 ratio, which is where I like to be. That allows correct eating the majority of the time, while treats, goodies, and fun foods can occupy the remaining 10%. Not only did this make sense — it worked. While, I might add, kept us from going insane (depending on whom you ask).

Easy-to-Follow Five-Step Healthy Eating Plan

With the **Do N.O.T. Diet** you can easily change the percentages of your incorrect-to-correct food intake and score a healthier nutritional ratio. All you have to do is learn how to select and place food onto your dinner plate in a unique way. (See Meal Wheel chart below.)

STEP 1: Let's familiarize ourselves with two basic food categories:

1. Protein

2. Carbohydrates

STEP 2: Carbohydrates are divided into three divisions, each distinctly different:

1. Starchy or Complex Carbohydrates

2. Fibrous Carbohydrates

3. Simple Carbohydrates

All three of the carbohydrate categories, provided they come from natural sources, can be very healthy.

Starchy or *complex* carbohydrates (aka *starch*) can be very nutritious. They're high in slow-absorbing *long-chain* sugars, vitamins, minerals, fiber, natural starch, and other essential nutrients. However, when eaten in excess (which is often the case in many people), they can lead to obesity and other health issues.

Fibrous carbohydrate foods (aka *veggies*) are extremely high in nutrition, supplying terrific amounts of natural fiber. They are known to boost energy, help fight off body fat, and maintain healthy hormonal profiles. High in vitamins, minerals, fiber, antioxidants, enzymes, and other essential nutrients.

Meal Wheel

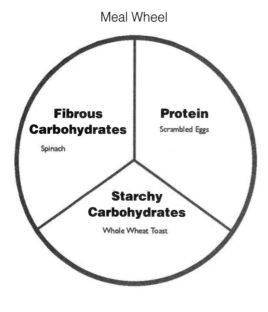

Simple carbohydrates (aka *sweets*) are also very high in nutrition and contain high levels of natural sugars. Due to quick-absorbing *short-chain* sugars, simple carbs can overload the body with an excess in calories, leading to obesity and other health challenges. This even happens when simple carbs are obtained from natural sources.

STEP 3: All of the three carbohydrate categories must be eaten in balance. This means that you should eat them evenly, avoiding the consumption of one category in excess. Example: Pasta is considered a starchy or complex carbohydrate. However, watch most people dine at an Italian restaurant and they're eating the bread before their main course which, of course, makes for two starchy carbohydrates: 1) the bread and 2) the pasta. Now, it's perfectly fine to eat pasta, but in order to provide your body with the nutritional balance it needs, all one has to do is add a protein food, like a chicken breast. And don't forget to add fibrous carbohydrate food(s) like broccoli, asparagus, minestrone soup, or a tossed salad.

STEP 4: The Meal Wheel™: (Refer to Illustration) Regard your (round) dinner plate as a food template. Divide it into three equal parts — 1/3, 1/3, and 1/3. In the first third, place a protein food; in the second third, place a *complex* (starchy) carbohydrate; and for the final third, toss in your fibrous carbohydrates.

Eating healthy balanced meals are that easy to arrange!

Here's a sample of what a balanced meal would look like using my Meal Wheel template (make sure that all foods are equal portions):

1/3 = Scrambled eggs, chicken breast, steak, fish, or any other protein food.

1/3 = Bread, baked potato, brown rice, oatmeal, or any other *starchy* carbohydrate food.

1/3 = Steamed vegetables, tossed salad, or vegetable soup.

STEP 5: EAT! It's that simple!

N.O.T. Guidelines:

- Due to their high sugar content, simple carbohydrates are eaten earlier in the day, typically for breakfast and mid-morning snacks.

- Fats are automatically factored into this plan as many of the protein foods (eggs, chicken, steak, and some kinds of fish) contain varying amounts of fat. Butter, oils, spreads, and sauces are recommended, but they need to be carefully watched — especially when one is attempting to lose excess body fat.

- Condiments and sauces are also suggested but, like fats, must be used moderately as they provide extra calories.

- Severe or extreme dieting can be very dangerous to one's health. In addition to declining levels of healthy hormones, extreme fanatical dieters may experience headaches, chronic fatigue, lethargy, muscle weakness, amenorrhea (cessation of the menstrual cycle in women), complete loss of libido, ED and oligospermia (in men), digestive disorders, elimination disorders, and much more. Eat balanced meals using the **Do N.O.T. Diet** as a baseline format to assist you in supplying your body with adequate nutrition.

  (Please refer to the Web site for more information on the **Do N.O.T. Diet,** recommended foods, meal templates, specific eating plans, and recipes.)

Sugar Blues: Sugar ingestion of any kind, natural or man-made, releases *insulin* into your bloodstream. Produced in the pancreas gland, insulin is a shuttling agent that is responsible for grabbing sugar and carrying it into the cells. The more sugar you eat, the more insulin your body needs to produce…and the more demands are placed onto the pancreas. People who are addicted to sugar condition the pancreas to release insulin more frequently and at greater volumes. What's so ironic is that the brain-pancreas connection becomes so conditioned that people don't even need to consume sugar to produce insulin. The influence from thought, smell, and sight alone are so powerful that the pancreas *knows*, or has become *primed* to know, to turn itself on and secrete insulin; and sometimes it doesn't know when to shut off. I'm sure you've heard the expression, "I get fat just looking at food." Well, there's a lot of truth behind that statement, while some experts refer to this as *maladaptive behavior*, a scientific term for a bad habit. The brain actually prepares the body for what it *senses* is going to happen, because it knows that that person most likely will follow through on the thought of consuming sugar by actually (physically) ingesting it.

Change the thought — Change the thing!

Excessive sugar consumption, along with consequential insulin secretion, will eventually damage cellular integrity by preventing useful blood glucose (or blood sugar) from entering into the tissues of the body to be used as energy. Instead, excess or unused sugar gets converted into fat. This process can ultimately lead to obesity, diabetes, and atherosclerosis — all epidemics that have reached pandemic proportions in our modern high-sugar era. Diabetes can be managed with proper exercise and eating habits.

The Making of a Diabetic (a major "cause" of ED)

- Sugar is actually consumed, or there is a *thought* of consuming sugar.

- The brain reacts and signals the pancreas.

- The pancreas responds by producing excessive amounts of insulin.

- Insulin is released into the blood stream.

- Once in the blood stream, insulin binds with glucose (the sugar in the blood) and serves as a shuttling agent, chaperoning the glucose to the tissues (where it's called *glycogen*) to be used as energy.

- When tissues are depleted of *glycogen* (exercise is great for this), the cells are receptive and accept the entry of more glucose.

- However, when the tissues are already saturated with *glycogen*, like in those who overeat and under-exercise, insulin cannot influence the receptors in the (already saturated) tissues to accept any more glucose. (Remember the doormen at the dance club analogy?)

- The unused glucose, if not eliminated from the body, now has the ability to be converted into fat.

- Fat formed from excess glucose is stored all over the body; under the chin, love handles, abdomen, thighs, buttocks, heart, and other organs. This fat also collects and clogs up the inside linings of the circulatory vessels, including the microscopic ones that feed the genitals and the penis; remember the summer cottage analogy?

- Interior clogging of the circulatory vessels is called *atherosclerosis.*

- When a man's penis is experiencing erectile difficulties this may just be one of the warning signs that indicate diabetes and/or atherosclerosis is developing elsewhere in the body (the canary in the coal mine, as Mark Newell, Ph. D., says).

- To assist insulin, to maintain healthy blood glucose levels, and to prevent diabetes and atherosclerosis, correct eating and exercise are the primary tools for combating excessively high blood-glucose levels.

Sugar and Human Growth Hormone

Sugar-induced insulin secretion can (and will) impede the production of HGH from the pituitary gland. Without adequate HGH, many of the body's natural anabolic processes of rebuilding tissues are destroyed, as insulin often has the power to override pituitary secretions of our youth and longevity hormone.

Many of you are going to abhor this, but I have to tell you that nighttime is one of the worst times to eat sugar. It's especially bad right before retiring. Since HGH is (mainly) produced right after we fall asleep, consuming sugar before bed is notorious for causing insomnia and other irregular sleep patterns. The more sugar/insulin that's in your body when you fall asleep, the more hormonal production is jeopardized, diminishing tissue health and restoration. Consistent hormonal disruption in this manner will destroy overall metabolism, homeostasis, and sexual health through a consistent strain on your endocrine system. Many experts believe it will even shorten lifespan, which is really not too sweet.

Chapter 14

Working *It* Out

Sexual Exercise

Kegels

Even though the penis is not exactly a muscle, nor does it (anatomically) respond like one, it is surrounded by muscles that can be exercised quite effectively.

In addition to penile traction (stretching) and vacuum (suction) devices, other methods exist for working out your *little* buddy or, at least, the muscles that reside in the genital region. (Listen up, ladies, because these same muscles are also present in your genital anatomy and are very healthy for you to exercise as well.)

As an assistant professor of gynecology at the University of Southern California School of Medicine, Arnold H. Kegel, M.D., F.A.C.S., extensively studied a certain muscle structure in the body that we all possess. Dr. Kegel believed this structure was lacking in strength and didn't perform its job correctly. The muscles Dr. Kegel was referring to are located in the lower pelvic region of both sexes. They're the ones responsible for holding up the organs in that area. Kegel discovered that when these muscles are exercised, they increase in strength, enhancing the functioning of sexual organs.

In 1948, Dr. Kegel revealed his technique, adequately titled *Kegel Exercise*, or *Kegels*. The muscles that Kegels target are called the *pubococcygeal muscles*; PC for short. By squeezing your PC muscles — which you can't see, so looking into a mirror won't help — you'll be contracting muscle tissues in and around your lower pelvic region. This includes your genitals. For you guys, it's mostly between your anus and testicles; for the ladies, it's between your anus and vagina. Voluntary squeezes of the PC muscles develop their strength while improving circulation of blood and nerve energy into that region.

In addition to supporting the pelvic organs, the PC muscles also support the uterus (in women), prostate (in men), bladder, lower bowel region, and rectum (in both men and women).

There are many techniques used to exercise the PC muscles. But if you're in a hurry and want to try it right now, literally, I can tell you just what to do! You don't even have to stop reading while you do this exercise … but you'll have to excuse my quick description on how to perform Kegels, as they're actually a lot more scientific than this:

While seated or standing, pretend you're squeezing the muscles that close the opening of your anus, just like you do to prevent gas from leaking out. (I warned you I wouldn't be so eloquent.) You've experienced this many times before, especially after eating too many refried beans. Squeeze the muscles in and around that area over and over again. These are your PC muscles.

One method utilizes a pulsating technique: *squeeze-pause-squeeze-pause*. Repeat the action for 20 seconds to one minute. Each contraction can incorporate a quick *squeeze-and-release*, or you can hold the squeeze, forcing your PC muscles to remain contracted for a full second or two before releasing and pausing.

Another version of the *squeeze-pause-squeeze-pause* method is to *squeeze-and-hold* a full PC contraction for 3–5 seconds (or longer) before releasing. Then you would pause for the same amount of time and repeat another contraction. If you're like most, you'll feel a sensational force of energy flushing out from your pelvic-genital region and spreading throughout your entire body. This is your sexual energy that often becomes blocked or trapped (refer to the section on the *spinal column*) but now has a way of releasing itself and spreading throughout your body.

Kegel exercises do work and they're healthy too!

Here's what the experts claim you can expect to experience by committing to regular Kegel exercise:

- Improvement in blood flow to the genitals (both women and men)
- Improved urinary control (both women and men)
- Stronger erections (penis/men, clitoris/women)
- Assistance helping a woman during pregnancy and childbirth
- Control over ejaculation (men)
- Elevated testicles (men; toned PC muscles may help to lift a drooping scrotum)
- Vaginal tone (women)
- Vaginal sensitivity (women)
- Greater distance semen squirts out of the penis during ejaculation (men)

According to Sue Johanson, RN, host of the popular TV show *Talking Sex*, Kegel exercise can increase the distance at which semen ejects out of the penis's urethra during ejaculation. In other words, you'll squirt farther when your PC muscles are more powerful and contracting more quickly. (Age diminishes the strength of all muscles, PC included. So if your ejaculate droops out of your penis during orgasm, hitting the floor sooner than it did in your younger days, Kegels certainly might help.)

Strengthening your PC muscles for this purpose is known as the *ejaculatory reflex*. Not only will the ejaculate fluid travel farther but, as a result, you will experience more powerful orgasms as these muscles are explosively contracting.

Sexual Fitness

The popularity of physical fitness and exercise has skyrocketed with mass mainstream awareness over the last few decades. There are greater numbers of individuals performing various activities in attempts to enhance their physical appearance, athletic performance, psychological states of well-being, and overall quality of life. Various clinicians, athletic trainers, physical therapists, and body-sculpturing specialists are prescribing the fitness lifestyle as the remedy for obesity, muscular weakness, stress, fatigue, insomnia, hypertension, immune system dysfunctioning, headaches, joint ailments, depression, metabolic disorders, skeletal imbalances, poor circulation, and sexual disorders.

Benefits of Fitness

Those who partake in an active lifestyle develop a greater number of advantages than initially expected. Even though their intentions may be to reshape their bodies and lose some excess body fat, fitness will not confine itself to just these two benefits. The fascinating fact about fitness activity participation is that it produces a positive psychophysiological chain reaction that influences the entire brain and body.

Metabolism

Each of us has a specific rate of metabolism that converts the food we eat into usable energy. This energy fuels all activity, the operational functions of our brain and body, and the repairing of damaged or worn-out tissue*. This conversion-reparation process is always operating

---

* We need to understand that food is fuel, and fuel is energy in the form of calories. So oftentimes when references are made to food, fuel, energy, or calories, they're all basically synonymous.

whether we're active or sedentary (and is intimately related to home-ostasis). The goal of the athlete and fitness enthusiast is to regularly expend the effort to exercise, then allocate ample time to recuperate.

This cyclic process of exertion-recuperation burns energy in two basic ways: 1) it depletes energy during activity, like in exercise, and because exercise is catabolic, which literally means it's (microscopically) tearing down tissue, it 2) also burns calories during post-activity, or during the body's recuperation periods. This entire process is also known as the *anabolic metabolism,* another relative of homeostasis. So those who believe their fat-burning, strength-building, health-promoting benefits of exercise are confined to the actual times they're in the gym pumping it out are in for a big surprise! The benefits of exercise extend well beyond your activity and cool-downs, as your metabolism carries the baton and runs its operation of repairing the worn out tissues. In other words, we can lose fat, build strong energetic muscles, and secrete higher levels of healthy hormones while we're doing nothing at all; this is, of course, after we've done something significant. This is how the *no pain, no gain* slogan came about.

To make things even better, as explained, exercise stimulates a surge in hormones, like human growth hormone, testosterone, and others that peak during exercise; and they remain high during the post-exercise anabolic (recovery) period. Conditioning the body for a healthy *catabolic-anabolic* cycle is not only terrific for building biceps and pecs and six-pack abs; it's also extremely effective at stimulating the sexual system by way of more powerful glandular and hormonal functions.

The Brain and Nerves

The relationship between exercise and brain function is a remarkably sophisticated and extraordinary system that most take for granted but, nonetheless, must truly appreciate. Consistent participation in physical activities develops a harmonious communication between the brain and the body. And with our nervous system headquartered in the brain, this intricate communication relays electrical (mental/nervous) impulses that send messages to the body tissues. When an action is requested or required, the brain will consent to the demand and command an immediate impulse. For those who are unfit, the deliverance of such commands has no assurance for accuracy; they may even become delayed by weak mental signal-sending abilities. Dull reactions can lead to a hazardous or even an ill-fated situation if the person cannot react appropriately, like needing to slam on the brakes to avoid an accident.

This entire psychophysiological process benefits the sexual organs of the body, as libido, erection, pleasurable sensations, and orgasm are all connected to this system.

Muscles and Bones

Our bodies are literally held together by a network of over 600 muscles and their relative tissues (i.e., tendons and ligaments). In addition to all movement, muscles are also responsible for holding our bodies and bones in proper alignment. Weak muscles cannot support our skeleton, forcing the body to shift out of its natural position, which is known as *misalignment*. The stronger and more balanced our muscles become, the better we can move, and the better our skeletal infrastructure is supported and protected. If we had no muscles at all, our skeleton would literally fall right to the floor. (Laboratory skeletons are bolted together, in case you didn't notice.)

The Heart

We're aware that the heart is a muscle. In fact, the heart is a muscular pump that's responsible for the distribution of blood to all areas of the body from the top of your head to the tips of your toes and, yes, into your penis — quite a task. When we're involved in activity, our hearts beat at accelerated rates.

Cardio Economics

At rest, an average heart pumps (approximately) 75 beats per minute (BPM). Let's do the math from that basis to determine the heart's muscle-pumping responsibility:

Average Heartbeats

75 beats per minute

4500 beats per hour

108,000 beats per day

39,420,000 beats per year

Now let's factor in the number of beats for a person's heart who's stressed out, overweight, out of shape, or experiencing hypertension. I'll be conservative and use a BPM at 90, although many people have much higher:

High Heartbeats	Difference from Average Heartbeats
90 beats per minute	15 *extra* beats per minute
5400 beats per hour	900 *extra* beats per hour
129,600 beats per day	21,600 *extra* beats per day
47,304,000 beats per year	7,884,000 *extra* beats per year *

Exercise accelerates the beating of the heart only during activity. However, once exercise is completed, and the heart becomes stronger and in better condition, the heart can beat fewer times per minute, per

---

* Analyzing the math: An extra eight million (rounded figure) heartbeats per year (obviously) places an enormous burden on one of our most vital organs and its cardiovascular system. Eventually, this will devastate all body cells. Don't regard hypertension, or any of its symptoms, lightly. ED is one of them.

hour, per day, and per year. It's much more efficient at its blood, oxygen, and nutrient-distribution responsibilities.

The Lungs

We already know that the heart beats faster while we're active. Our rate of breathing (or respiration) accelerates too. Oxygen is our life-supporting gas that we cannot live without for very long. We can go without food or water for days, but without oxygen we can't last more than a few minutes. As our respiration increases, our lungs expand and contract beyond normal (or resting) capacities. The lungs are two elastic-like sacks that collect the oxygen-filled air we breathe. As we inhale, the lungs absorb usable oxygen; as we exhale, we eliminate toxic gases. Millions of tiny holes, called *alveoli*, are positioned through-out lung tissue to allow the oxygen to seep into our bloodstream, feeding the body with this most precious life source. The more profi-cient the respiratory system becomes, the more oxygen our cells have access to and receive, making them much more energetic and resilient. All cells thrive on oxygen for survival. Limited supplies or complete starvation of oxygen will wilt cellular integrity; it's just like poking a hole into a balloon filled with air.

Your Looks

Looks? Certainly! When you become active in fitness, the benefits extend upward above your chin as your face receives a tremendous number of benefits as well. Since sedentary body muscles become weak and sag, facial muscles are no different. However, when your body's muscles are strong and firm, your facial muscles often follow the same pattern of progression. While you're exercising you'll notice that your facial muscles acquire a great workout — you curl up your nose, squint your eyes, clench your jaws, and flex open your lips. To prove my point, try looking someone straight in the face while they're lifting weights. They don't look very appealing while they're in a state of exertion. But as their faces contort, flex, and wiggle, dozens of facial muscles are toning and firming themselves at the same time. Healthier-looking faces may just help you attract that significant other!

Make Your Workout Count: Keep On Keeping On!

In the gym, most leg, hip, and buttock exercises, along with those that target the abdominals and lower back, are exceptionally useful for their strengthening benefits to the genital region. These benefits can deliver satisfactory rewards for maintaining youthful sexual power.

I encourage you to make fitness more than a short-term plan. It should be a *lifestyle*. Exercise needs to be part of your way of life. Set fitness goals and strive to meet them. Once you meet them, be proud of your accomplishments. Then you can shift over to a maintenance mode, or set new goals and challenges. Whatever you do, KEEP GOING! If you don't belong to a gym, or you're looking for a quick and convenient workout that targets overall muscularity and fat burning, try my *90 Second Quick Total Body Blast* (see chart); or get yourself a DVD copy of my *No Excuses Workout* (NEW) that offers a remarkably easy-to-follow, no-equipment, anywhere-anytime workout that can be completed in only seven minutes. So now there's no excuses for all of you who claim you don't have enough time in the day or can't afford a health club membership!

90 Second Quick Total Body Blast (90-QTB$_2$)

Exercise	Muscle Groups	Duration	Repetitions
1) Squats	Lower Body	30 seconds	As many as possible
2) Pushups	Upper Body	30 seconds	As many as possible
3) Crunches	Middle Body	30 seconds	As many as possible

90-QTB$_2$ Guidelines

- Only three exercises are required, each targeting one of the three major body regions: 1) upper body region, 2) lower body region, and 3) middle body region, also referred to as the *core* or midsection.

- No equipment is needed.

- Perform as many repetitions as you can during each 30-second set.

- After one exercise is completed, immediately transition to the next without delay.

- Change the order of your exercises from workout to workout. For instance, based on the above outline, you can choose to perform 1) Pushups, 2) Crunches and 3) Squats in this order as well.

- If you have more time and energy, repeat the three-exercise circuit as many times as you have the strength for, and/or lengthen the set duration from, for instance, 30 to 45 seconds. You can even perform one full minute per exercise.

- Your exercise speeds will accelerate as you become better conditioned, so repetitions per set will increase indicating progress.

- Of course, working out can be more diverse than this; however, this simple three-exercise routine is a terrific *quick total body blast* that will condition your heart, lungs, nervous system, and muscles. It will activate your *catabolic-anabolic* metabolism. (If you have a gym membership or own your own equipment, by all means, take full advantage of them.)

- Always learn and apply proper technique when performing any exercise.

- Visit my website at www.SexHealthTV.com (members-only section) for free exercise video seminars and specific instruction on fitness and nutritional techniques.

Sexual Religion: An Introduction to Tantra

Although many have been led to believe that help for their sexual disorders can only be addressed by taking pills, there's a culture that has been practicing sexual vitality and healing for centuries. This art is called *Tantra*.

According to an article published by Discovery Health called "Tantric Sex Techniques to Reinvigorate Lovemaking," written by Amy Painter, the practice of Tantra shows us how to reclaim the sexual intimacy that is our birthright.

Tantra is relatively new to the United States and still regarded as a subculture. It was developed over 6,000 years ago in India as a revolt against the constraints of the local religion that denounced sexuality, claiming sexual pleasure was a deterrent from reaching spiritual enlightenment.

Rebelling against the sexual suppression, a section of India's populous developed their own practice. This belief system encouraged people to have as much (quality) sex as possible, while the pleasures they gained were to be regarded as Divine. This form of sex was not motivated by perverted lust. Instead, Tantra was, and still remains, an evolving sexual health practice that's rooted in ethical and spiritual principles, drawing upon the energies of the universe to (sexually) invigorate the mind and body, taking two people and bonding them intimately into one.

The tradition of Tantric sexual practices is known to relax the stress centers between the mind-body-genital connection, enhance lovemaking, prevent premature ejaculation in men, stimulate powerful orgasms, and even train its students to learn how to experience multiple orgasms. Many of those who practice Tantra claim heightened sensations in their genitals and an overall sexy, tingling feeling throughout their entire body. And the benefits don't end there. Tantra calms the emotions, reduces anxiety, and helps to restore youthful essence and vitality.

One thing's for sure, pills cannot award you the results of Tantra. It's definitely worth the try if you're open to something new, something healthy, and something that really does provide an extraordinary experience and result. Tantra is a terrific activity for couples, one that will not only enhance the relationship but prolong it. For you singles reading this, Tantra classes are a terrific way to meet Miss or Mister Right!

Chapter 15

Beating *It*

By now, you've been made clearly aware of a long list of options that either boost normal performance or are intended to prevent and/or remedy sexual inadequacies. To round things up, and to help you focus in on an immediate "action plan" that helps you accomplish these objectives, I've designed the following step-by-step outline. This is a great starting point that can carry you well into the more advanced stages of accomplishment, while many of you may decide to commit to it on a long-term basis. If you have other options you'd like to try, feel free to experiment exchanging or cycling them as recommended. I encourage you to share this plan with your doctor so they can help you define and organize your own specific sexual health plan.

Six-Step Plan for Achieving *Ultimate Sexual Health and Performance*

Step 1: Admit *it*.

If you have a problem acknowledge *it*. Start out by declaring this to yourself; then you can move on to those you trust, especially skilled professionals. Your *big* head must get squared away with all of your challenges, while you remain vigilant for complete restoration of your sexual powers. If you're a younger virile guy, then prepare for the inevitable as your years advance, with resultant declines in hormonal production and sexual capabilities; be sure to invest your time in prevention.

Admitting a challenge is the first step toward improvement, like the athlete who confides in his coach for help in correcting technical flaws to gain him the competitive edge, or the businessman who seeks advice on how to convert his struggling enterprise into a profitable business. Remaining isolated and withdrawn, dwelling on your inadequacies, and averting sexual opportunities only makes things worse. You must get your *big* head in order, especially if you've been experiencing ED for some time. *It* takes its toll on you mentally, and that must be corrected before you confront your physical challenges. Removing disturbing feelings of sexual shortcomings from your mind is very healing. Understand that millions of men (and women) are dealing with sexual challenges. And also know that plenty of help is now readily available in a myriad of options for you to choose from.

Step 2: Learn *it*.

Knowledge is power. Use this book and my Web site to educate yourself about sexual health, and the mental and physical challenges that "cause" sexual disorders. Learn how the mind and body operate and the manner in which hormones respond to various stimuli. Learn about the products, services, and techniques that are available for boosting overall health and sexual performance. Learn about what options are available OTS and administered by prescription. Having a better understanding of this information will help you identify the culprits of your challenges. It will enable you to know when and how to implement these health-promoting sex-boosting techniques. It can also help you develop the ability to communicate more effectively with your doctor.

Step 3: Seek professional advice.

Many of you may not be in need of a doctor at this point. Maybe you're completely satisfied with all the exercise, eating, and supplement suggestions in this book. Maybe you want to make a good thing better and begin to implement ways of super-charging yourselves into experiencing more powerful orgasms, into having firmer, more frequent erections. However, those of you who are experiencing considerable sexual difficulties and consequential health risks need to secure professional supervision. After selecting the right doctor, you will need an initial checkup, then periodic follow-ups. Blood examinations* may be needed to ascertain precise blood hormonal profiles. This biological data provides your doctor with the information required to locate the causes of your condition that will ultimately lead to a successful recovery. Provide this book to your doctor so they can help you design a complete protocol that, in addition to their prescriptions, includes physical exercise, eating, and supplements. If you're emotionally affected by your sexual challenges then seeking counsel from a psychological sexual health expert is a very prudent thing to do. Remember, sexual difficulties often do not isolate themselves to just your *little* head; your *big* head is affected as well.

*Refer to Life Extension Foundation's Male Panel Blood examination.

Step 4: *Primed* for success

By combining your doctor's suggestions with those listed in this book, you now have the information you need to make positive and healthy decisions and changes in your life. This step has three subcategories:

1. **Thinking:** Replace all unhealthy thoughts with positive ones. *Exchange* your negative, frustrated, depressed, stressful, anxious, and confusing thoughts with confident and successful ones. *Prime* yourself for success in all areas of your life. Make the right choices that yield positive consequences in the future. Avoid the easy (unhealthy) choices that result in unfavorable consequences. In other words, tame your monkey.

2. **Nourish yourself:** Eat a higher percentage of healthy foods leaning toward (at least) a 50/50 ratio of unhealthy/healthy foods; after coasting at that ratio for a while, try and see if you can make it to 30/70 or better. Select and consume the natural supplements and foods listed in this book that pertain to your needs. This way, you can be certain you're nourishing the trillions

of cells in your body (and penis) with the nutrition required to maintain full vitality. (Refer to the Do N.O.T. Diet™.)

- **Supplements:** Here's an effective list of OTS supplements that can help you fortify glandular, hormonal, and genital nutrition, while boosting your sexual potency. These items may be taken individually or mixed into a formula.

Product	Benefit
L-Arginine	Nitric Oxide Production
Velvet Antler	Overall Hormonal Fortifier
Tribulus	Strength and Libido
Ginkgo Biloba	Brain Health
Zinc and Saw Palmetto	Prostate and Sperm
Stinging Nettles	Free Testosterone
DHEA	Hormonal Balancing
Epimedium	Libido

3. **Be your own coach:** How good a coach, motivator, and disciplinarian you are to yourself is essential to your success. Nobody is going to help you the way you can (and need) to help yourself. You're your own boss. Regard your body like you would your own business. Invest in it, manage it, take inventory of it, and provide for it. Give it what it needs to consistently improve. Record your own PMAs and update them frequently to keep you aligned with your progress. Knowing this information is one thing; doing it is another. Set your mind, body, and soul toward self-improvement; then DO IT! Do it with a *want to* attitude, not a *have to* one. Stay committed to these principles, and both your *big* and *little* heads will be impressed!

Step 5: Work *it* out.

I've mentioned how important exercise is for stimulating the secretion of healthy hormones in the body. This is triggered by the catabolic-anabolic (no pain-no pain) cycle that exercise provokes. Exercise strengthens much more than muscles and hormones. Its benefits extend into your brain, heart, lungs, bones, circulatory and nervous systems, and — of course — your genitals. Exercise doesn't have to occupy hours per day to be effective. Perform my *90 Second Quick Total Body Blast*, or the *No Excuses Workout* (only seven minutes long), as they're terrific routines that are convenient, effective, and quick. Remember, the penis becomes hard and remains that way when blood fills its chambers. Without proper circulation of blood and the production of key chemicals, like nitric oxide, erectile dysfunction is the inevitable result. Exercise improves all of these body systems. Also remember to occasionally squeeze your PC muscles. (And I hope it's not only after you've chowed down too many refried beans.) Do your Kegels!

Step 6: Love *it*.

Follow the previous five steps and keep your thoughts raised in a higher level of consciousness, or that *Zone of Achievement*. Become as *selfish* as you can to develop the best *you* you can become. Stay the course, no matter what. Laugh at your challenges and develop in you the courage to succeed, no matter what! And enjoy the rewards of your journey. But unlike most journeys, where the treasure is found only after a long, enduring struggle, you'll be able to consistently smell the roses along the path of your own success, and find much more pleasure in life than you ever imagined! Learn *it*. Live *it*. Love *it*!

I'll see you at the top!

As the Doctor Prescribed

The following is a compilation summary of remarks regarding **Male Sexual Dysfunctions** that was generously provided by Laurence A. Levine, M.D., F.A.C.S. (More listed on Web site.)

Erectile dysfunction is a common disorder affecting up to 50% of men who are over 40 years of age. In some cases it may be the earliest indicator of systemic vascular disease, preceding heart disease by four years on average. There are a variety of effective treatments that address ED, from pills to surgical procedures.

Low testosterone, or male hypogonadism, occurs much more frequently than previously thought. In fact, up to 40% of men over 45, and 50% of obese and diabetic men, have suboptimal testosterone levels. This may cause side effects such as low energy, easy fatigability, diminished erections, and libido problems, and over time can affect muscle mass, bone mineral density, and brain function. Topical and implantable testosterone can correct the low levels and oftentimes improve quality of life (equally as beneficial for women as well). A simple set of blood tests is usually all that is needed to make a diagnosis.

Ejaculation disorders: Far and away the most common is rapid, or premature, ejaculation. This problem may affect up to 70% of men at some point in their lives. But it may be a lifelong problem for many men that results in significant distress for both the affected man and his partner. Unfortunately, there is no curative therapy. Certain anti-depressants like Zoloft or Paxil have been shown to delay orgasm and ejaculation. Sometimes this treatment is improved when combined with talk therapy with a qualified sex therapist.

Delayed ejaculation is far less common but appears to be on the rise, particularly in older men, above 60 years age. The cause is unknown, but it is likely in part due to accelerated changes in the *ejaculation reflex* that occurs naturally with aging. Occasional use of an anti-depressant (Wellbutrin) will help.

Retrograde ejaculation describes the situation when ejaculation goes back into the bladder and is usually due to certain medications or surgery that prevents the bladder neck from closing during ejaculation. There is no surgical remedy, but if the offending drugs are stopped, this problem can be reversed.

Peyronie's Disease

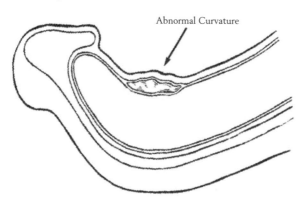

Abnormal Curvature

Peyronie's disease: This penile disorder is a scaring process of the penis that has been shown to affect up to 10% of adult men. Curvature, shortening, indentation, and hinging of the penis are the most common manifestations of this distressing disorder. The cause remains unclear and there is no cure, but several nonsurgical remedies including injection and traction therapy with the FS Extender (Distributed by Fastsize, Aliso Viejo, California) have been demonstrated to be beneficial. Surgery remains the most rapid and reliable treatment to straighten the penis when the scarring process stabilizes. (Author's note: When I began writing this book, I had known of Peyronie's disease and certainly knew what it was — but only from what I had read. It wasn't until I started to gather my research materials that I actually viewed photographs of the penises of men who were suffering from this disorder. So if this sounds like a sales pitch, it is; only because this is a medically proven product that does help men with this disorder. The Fastsize Extender is a remarkably effective product that, according to many experts, provides beneficial results for men with Peyronie's disease.)

Chronic testicular pain is not common, nor is it rare; but it is a devastating problem when it occurs. Currently, no cause can be found, and when conservative treatment, such as anti-inflammatories, anti-depressants, and antibiotics fail, surgical treatment with microdenervation may eliminate the pain while preserving the testicle.

[End Levine]

More Facts to Keep in Mind

Some estimates suggest only 1 in 10 men with ED seek help.

Massachusetts Male Aging Study: Impotence triples between the ages of 40 and 70.

Barbara Marshall, a sociology professor at Trent University in Peterborough, Ontario, argues, "Where I'm critical of the whole (erection pill) enterprise is in what has become a gross over-medicalization of sexuality. It kind of makes sex like going into a fast-food restaurant." Marshall is referring to the bulldozer marketing and oversimplified (and incomplete) understanding of sex that Viagra has become responsible for.

Keep this in mind: The more body fat you gain, the more estrogen your body is likely to produce. The more muscle you gain, the more testosterone your body *will* produce. Fat requires estrogen to maintain itself, while muscle requires testosterone.

The more muscle you gain, the more your body will crave protein foods to maintain its muscle. The trigger for protein cravings is ignited by the teardown, or *catabolic*, effects induced by exercise that cause a *negative nitrogen balance*. The body compensates as the brain creates an appetite for protein that, after consumption, elevates nitrogen levels. This prompts the onset of the favorable biological state: a *positive nitrogen balance*.

Chapter 16

Female Sexual Health

Meet Sue: An American Woman

As a popular kid growing up, Sue was always spunky and outgoing. She was raised in a middle-class neighborhood and always received good grades in grammar school and high school. (She never went to college.) Sue wasn't what you'd exactly define as promiscuous; however, she really enjoyed sex, got turned on easily, and never had a problem achieving an orgasm.

Mr. Right came walking into Sue's life one evening when she was 26 years old; his name was Bob. The timing couldn't have been more perfect. Sue was working two jobs to pay her rent and car loan — along with all those other expenses single women spend their money on. She was growing weary of the dating and bar scene and wanted to settle down and have children of her own. Sue felt that if she didn't start planning right away she'd be looking back on her life in later years regretting how she spent her time growing up as a young adult.

Bob and Sue hit it off. In addition to having a lot in common — socially and intellectually — they were made for one another sexually. In fact, they couldn't get enough of each other. They started living together only three months after they met. They made love daily, sometimes more times than you could count on one hand.

Sue was delighted that Bob, like her, wanted to settle down and begin raising a family, so they officially tied the knot. Bob always told Sue, "You're the perfect wife! I just know you'll be the perfect mother too!"

The family of Bob and Sue began.

FIVE YEARS LATER: Bob and Sue are now the parents of two beautiful children, a four-year old and a two-and-a-half year old. Bob's a bit old-fashioned. He never wanted Sue to work, as he believes his kids should be raised by their mother as opposed to being put in a daycare or with a nanny.

Even though their sexual intimacy became less frequent (kids do get in the way), Bob and Sue always enjoyed great pleasure when they did have sex, making up for less *quantity* by ensuring their (alone) time was high *quality*. But one day, for no apparent reason, a slight shift in Sue's energy occurred.

Shortly after the kids were put to sleep, and Bob saw his opportunity to bring his wife into the bedroom for everything *but* sleep, Sue wasn't in the mood. Despite her lackluster passion, she went ahead and had sex with Bob anyway. But this time, the exchange of pleasure was not mutual. In fact, Sue didn't climax. Bob was oblivious while Sue was shocked by her unusual and uncharacteristic mood. Making love to the man she loved didn't interest her, nor did it feel good. Sue didn't sleep well that night.

Sue's unusual feelings persisted, and she began to dwell on it — a lot. The more she thought about *it*, the more she started to trace things backward. Sue was equally as active at initiating sex with Bob as he had always been toward her. But she was shocked to recall that for the better part of the entire year she was not initiating sex with Bob like she used to. As the time progressed, she stopped initiating sex altogether.

Confusing thoughts tossed back and forth in Sue's head like a slow tennis match, while she tried to convince herself that she was simply burnt out and, like most women her age, was merely getting older. Perhaps she was more focused on the kids getting better grades in school, keeping up an organized household, and the fact that both her parents were facing their challenges of aging. But as the months progressed, that slow (mental) tennis match turned into a constant fluttering of disturbing emotions that started resembling an Olympic-level table-tennis competition, consuming Sue's mind and causing the early (and rapidly progressing) stages of depression.

YOU'D NEVER GUESS: In spite of what seemed to be a match-made-in-heaven marriage, Sue's now divorced from Bob, and approaching her mid-thirties. The breakup was painful, while the final stages of their marriage were emotionally traumatizing. When Sue somehow lost interest in having sex with Bob, she did what many women do; she began to believe that she was just getting older. She believed that as a woman ages, she's supposed to decline in sensuality and sexuality. The symptoms of a total loss of sexual desire, lack of vaginal lubrication, painful intercourse, and even complete orgasmic failure became Sue's new identity and, although frustrating and painful, she (reluctantly) regarded these symptoms as normal and natural.

At first, Bob was okay with Sue's lack of desire. He understood she had her hands full with the kids, the house, and her parents. But his gnawing frustration eventually caused an emotional outbreak, and Bob couldn't contain how irritated he had become. At first, and for many months afterward, Bob wasn't saying anything. He didn't need to because his body language was screaming things like, "Where did my wife go?" "I have needs too!" "Can I please get some (sexual) attention here?"

Eventually, the inner chattering silently screaming inside Bob's head escalated into bickering, then all-out verbal abuse that, sad to say, initiated the beginning of the end for Bob and Sue. The couple reluctantly went on living together for as long as they could tolerate. (Kids do hold parents together.) But Sue would tell you that it seemed like there was an invisible concrete wall running down the center of their bedroom that separated them. Even as they slept side by side, that wall ran right down the middle of their bed. The verbal abuse, physical and emotional separation, not to mention their lack of sexual expression, had reached a breaking point. That was not the type of climax they had planned.

Sue didn't have an inkling as to what had turned off her desire and pleasure for sex. But when you examine Sue (psychologically and physiologically), you see two very different people — a sexually invigorated Sue who was excited about her upcoming marriage, then a stressed-out Sue who was struggling to raise her family (a short) five years later. Analyzing the psychophysiological data, and committing to an expertly designed protocol, you see that the changes that *caused* Sue's sexual demise are, according to Dr. Ann Marie Tommey, accurately identifiable and successfully treatable.

Sue's a great person, but she's far from self-respectful. She was gaining weight consistently since her last child, and she started to dress differently to conceal her body. Her *inside* feelings surfaced on the *outside;* she was the one building that concrete wall. Not only wasn't he able to *feel* his wife any longer, Bob was having difficulty *seeing* her, as she was always covered up. Bob's silent desperation started to leak out with subtle yet profound sarcastic remarks about Sue's enlarging hips, thighs, and buttocks. Hearing this only made Sue crawl deeper into her depression, while sticking her hands deeper into the cookie jar to gain (at least) some satisfaction in her life. It was a vicious cycle.

The fact that Sue always smoked wasn't helping the situation either. And let's be honest, her eating habits stunk. (I wasn't exaggerating about the cookie jar.) Her diet was totally devoid of even the minimum of nutritional requirements she needed — she was a 90/10, easily. Taking care of the kids and the house consumed her time while she was always deprived of sleep. And to top it all off, while she was parenting her own young family, she also had to care for her parents. Sue was burnt out, stressed out, worn out, confused, depressed, and broken. And, as mentioned earlier, when you're under stress, hormonal deficiencies (inevitably) ensue.

According to statistics, there are millions of Sues in America — and millions more around the world. As reported in *Obstetrics & Gynecology*, 44.2% of 40,000 women surveyed reported having either low sexual desire or orgasm difficulties. According to a report by The American College of Obstetricians and Gynecologists, 43.1% of 31,581 females also reported sexual problems pertaining to desire, arousal, and orgasm.

I'm not a mathematical genius, but *70 plus* thousand women is a lot of women to study. And that's just one of the hundreds of other studies being conducted independently.

In addition to her ever-increasing depression, the mindset Sue relied upon to determine the cause of her problem was old-school; she just figured that aging women inevitably lost their sensuality and sexuality. She assumed that her happy, healthy, sexy days were left to memory. But, according to Dr. Tommey, nothing could be further from the truth as revealed by the mountains of research and successful treatments now available. "Modern sexual science has become extremely effective at diagnosing, treating, and even curing sexual disorders in women, no matter what their age," states Tommey. (Refer to Web site for more from Dr. Tommey.)

Female Sexual Disorders: Labels and Definitions

Women, obviously, don't have the mechanical requirements that are necessary for intercourse when compared to men. What may seem to her partner to be a successful sexual experience might not have been so great for her after all. Maybe her libido was low or maybe intercourse was uncomfortable, even painful. There are plenty of reasons for each symptom and cause. Doctors are assigning new names, labels, acronyms, and titles to identify, define, and categorize these disorders.

Here are some of them:

- Female Sexual Disorder (FSD)

- Female Sexual Arousal Disorder (FSAD)

- Female Orgasmic Disorder (FOD)

- Hypoactive Sexual Desire Disorder (HSDD) (low sexual arousal, or desire)

- Inhibited Sexual Desire (ISD)

- Post-Menopausal Sexual Disorder (PMSD)

- Polycystic Ovarian Syndrome (PCOS) (irregularities with menstrual cycle, infertility)

- Persistent Sexual Arousal Disorder (PSAD): Just the opposite of FSAD. The female with this disorder experiences extended periods of arousal that don't diminish, even after achieving orgasm. Although the term *nymphomaniac* comes to mind when you think of a female with an insatiable sexual appetite, urologists don't use that word synonymously.

- Female Androgen Insufficiency (FAI)

- Postpartum Depression (PPD)

- Sexual Arousal Disorder (SAD)

- Sexual Aversion Disorder (SAD)

More Names, Acronyms, and Definitions

- Fear of Ugliness Disorder (FUD): Also known as *cacophobia*. It affects many women and men alike.

- Body Dysmorphic Disorder (BDD): A psychologically moti-vated sexual disorder that's affecting millions of men and women. These people are simply ashamed of their bodies and, especially, do not want to be seen naked or even touched.

- Premenstrual Syndrome (PMS): The most popular acronym that's connected to women, often causing fluctuations in sexual arousal and sensitivity.

- Female-Pattern Baldness (FPB): May relate to the effects of stress and high levels of DHT, just like in balding men.

- Irritable Bowel Syndrome (IBS): Impedes, or blocks, normal digestion and assimilation of food, ultimately causing sexual disturbances.

- Auto-Immune Thyroid Disease (ATD): Disrupts overall body metabolism, mental energy, and recuperation.

- *Anorgasmia*, also known as *clitoral phimosis*, is a condition where the tissue covering the clitoris does not allow for the clitoris to extend outward from the body and become exposed for touch.

- *Endometriosis* is a severe immunological disorder that targets the female reproductive system. According to Uzzi Reiss, M.D., Ob-Gyn, between 7 and 11 million American women obtain this disorder each year. Natural remedies include Black Cohosh, Evening Primrose Oil (EPO), Milk Thistle, Dong Quai, Wild Yam, and Zinc.

A University of Chicago survey found that the most common sexual problem in American women (ages 18–59) is hypoactive sexual desire disorder (HSDD), more commonly referred to as low sex drive, diminished arousal, or declining libido. The survey concluded that 33.4% of the women had this disorder while 24.1% of the women had orgasmic difficulty; 14.4% experience pain during intercourse.

The American Psychiatric Association (APA) defines HSDD as a deficiency relating to sexual desire.

According to the July 2008 issue of Life Extension Magazine, *just one cup of green tea daily halves ovarian cancer risks.* Women who drank one or more cups per day experienced a 54% reduction in ovarian cancer risk compared with those who did not drink green tea.

Recent studies reveal that nearly 40% of women of all ages report having sexual problems. The term "sex" is not limited to intercourse. Sexual activities such as touching, fondling, cuddling, self-stimulation (masturbation), and oral sex are on that list. Challenges occur through all phases of physical contact.

Female sexual dysfunction is not regarded as an age-related disorder any longer. It can happen to women at any age but is more predictable after menopause, when hormone production and circulatory health declines. Lifestyle habits play a critical role as well (source, American Association for Marriage and Family Therapy).

Common Culprits for Female Sexual Dysfunctions

Menopause is often the one holding the smoking gun for causing FSDs. But there are many other causes, some acting alone and others in combination:

Smoking

Alcohol

Anxiety

Stress

Birth control pills

Depression

Financial worries

Emotional problems

Poor eating habits

Lack of exercise

Sexual abuse in the past

Obesity

Abortion (emotional ramifications)

Illnesses

Low self-esteem

Sleep disturbances

Negative body perception

Post-traumatic stress syndrome (PTSS)

Jealousy

Drugs and medications

Back and/or spinal injury

Hysterectomy*

Bike riding

Atherosclerosis; hardening of the arteries

Vaginal atrophy

Relationship problems: boredom, lack of love and respect, etc.

Emotional, social, or psychological disorders require counseling with a professionally trained sexual health medical practitioner like Dr. Tommey.

---

* Hysterectomy: According to Nick Delgado, Ph.D., head of the Ultimate Medical Research Clinic in Newport Beach, California: In addition to removing the uterus, some physicians remove a woman's ovaries during a hysterectomy. The ovaries are the female *gonads* and the major location in the female body that produces testosterone. Women who have this surgery must follow specific lifestyle measures that restore testosterone; otherwise there will be a decline in sexual arousal, pleasure during intercourse, and orgasm. Low levels of testosterone also increase depression and body fat. Muscle weakness and bone loss might also occur.

Some of the sexual symptoms relating to FSD:

✓ Lack of libido; low arousal or loss of sex drive

✓ Vaginal dryness and irritation

✓ Clitoral insensitivity

✓ Orgasmic failure

✓ Painful intercourse

Sexual disorders are more prevalent in women than in men: 43% vs. 31%.

Journal of the American Medical Association (JAMA)

High risk factors that contribute to the onset of FSD include depression, certain antidepressant medications, birth control pills, and post-menopausal hormonal imbalances.

Boston Sexual Health Clinic

Absolutely! Birth control pills can lower sex drive in women.

Dr. Drew Pinsky, from his *Strictly Sex* TV Show

Chapter 17

Female Sexual Disorders Causes & Remedies

After reading the last chapter, you might feel personally connected with some (or all) of Sue's characteristics. Learning about the long list of female health challenges that exist today, along with their modern-day acronyms, and becoming more aware of the options for prevention and remedy, you may now be feeling a whole lot better equipped to improve your own sex life and health. But before you lay this book down, this upcoming chapter reveals yet another list of sexual spoilers, while delving deeper into female anatomy, psychology, nutrition, drugs, blood tests, and female sexual enhancement products.

Body Weight

Overweight and obese women place enormous physical pressures onto their muscles, nerves, circulatory vessels, organs, bones, joints, and spinal columns. When the spine and its vertebra become compressed or misaligned, the nerves feeding the genitalia and reproductive system can become impeded or completely blocked. This is another possible cause of reproductive and sexual disturbances.

Being excessively overweight is not the only cause for spinal deformities. Another is being out of shape, as weak muscles lack sufficient strength and energy to support and move the bones. Pregnancy can also raise many back complaints from women due to extreme torso/abdominal/spinal changes. These changes can place enormous stress upon the spine, pelvis, nervous system, reproductive organs, and genitalia. Exercise that improves muscle flexibility and strength is essential. Yoga, Pilates, weight training, Kegels and low-impact aerobics can all help; the list of activities available today is long and diverse.

Bike Riding

Bike riding is equally as harmful for women as it is for men. The nerves that nourish the female genitalia run through an area known as the *Alcock's Canal*, which is located inches above the location of the bicycle seat. When it's damaged, this condition is called *perineal compression injury* (PCI). So if you're into bike riding — stationary or outdoors — make sure you have a well-padded seat or purchase bike shorts with built-in crotch pads. (Also refer to "The Hot Seat" in Chapter 4.)

Artificial Sweeteners

The artificial sweetener known as *aspartame* (aka *NutraSweet*), and most of the look-alike products on the market, create severe disruptions in the hormonal system by negatively affecting the pancreas gland, located in the abdominal region. Artificial sweeteners also disrupt the hypothalamus and pituitary glands located in the brain. The synthetic chemicals found in these artificial agents even disrupt the gonads (ovaries in women, testicles in men) located in the genital region, also placing excess strain on the adrenals. With sugar consumption reaching an all-time high and increasing every year, this toxic product is destroying more and more lives. Women might be able to fix their loss of sexual desire and orgasmic disorders by controlling the amount of artificial sweeteners they consume.

Partum Me

Many women, while pregnant, find that their cravings for certain foods are more challenging ... and often uncontrollable. This, in large part, can be attributed to a spectacular shift in hormones and a corresponding necessity (natural craving) for more nutrition; two bodies, instead of one, now need to be fed. For instance, blood levels of the mineral *chromium** may often become depleted during pregnancy because the other organism; the baby's body, needs its own supplies. To put it another way, the second body is withdrawing from (and depleting) the pregnant mother's nutritional supply bank.

Other than the need to feed a second body, nutritional deficiencies are also created by poor (nutritionally void) food choices. Hunger persists and, unfortunately, many pregnant women overindulge themselves with the wrong foods. (Remember: you need to consume extra nutrition to nourish yourself and another body.)

Another mineral in great demand during pregnancy is sodium. When sodium is low the mother often craves salty foods. These cravings are healthy and natural, but what's unhealthy and unnatural is what the mother decides to eat. Fish, vegetables, and many low-fat dairy products, just to name three food categories, are healthy foods containing high levels of natural sodium. Bacon bits, potato chips, pickles, and processed lunchmeats are also high in sodium, but — need I say? — they're unhealthy.

Pregnancy is a time in a woman's life that requires special attention and a higher degree of self-respect. Complete nutritional awareness for you and your unborn baby is imperative. As a soon-to-be mother, this is an investment for the rest of your life — and your

---

* What about those sweet cravings? *Chromium* deficiencies have been linked to excessive sugar binging. The healthy choices include fruit, yams, dates, figs, raisins, honey, and many others. Donuts, candy bars, ice cream, and syrup-spiked coffee drinks are not healthy choices.

child's. Now is the time to become very *selfish* and provide the best you can for yourself and your baby. The better you are, the better your child will be. Nine months of commitment to a healthy lifestyle is sufficient time to condition yourself to good eating habits that can be easily maintained afterward.

Speak with your pediatrician, or obtain a referral to a nutritionist or dietician who's an expert in this area. Find somebody who can help you and your baby become the healthiest possible.

Gaining excessive body weight during pregnancy places an enormous amount of extra burden onto the midsection, distorting the alignment of the hips, pelvis, and spine. This especially impacts the lumbar vertebrae, ball-and-socket hip joints, and the femur bones. Added body weight also exerts pressure on the internal organs, including the pancreas, liver, stomach, intestines, and sexual organs.

Many women are brainwashed into thinking that pregnancy ruins their bodies. This is not true. Fact is, during pregnancy, women are experiencing an incredible upsurge in growth and reproductive hormones, and these are the healthy hormones that make a woman stronger. Unless a pregnant woman succumbs to cravings by eating unhealthy foods, she will avoid excess fat gain and keep her body in shape during her pregnancy, returning to normal measurements quickly postpartum.

What about protein? As stated, all tissues and cells in the body are formed from the amino acids found in protein foods. Like everybody else, mothers need to become and remain strong, and protein is the fuel that makes strength possible. Now, like any other food, you can select hotdogs, salami sandwiches, or bacon double cheeseburgers as your sources of protein. Or, to be on the healthy side, you can select eggs, fish, chicken, and turkey, just to name a few. As stated in the nutrition section of this book, maintaining at least a nitrogen equilibrium is at the lower end of the goal for protein requirements, while a positive nitrogen balance is ideal.

Osteoporosis

As I mentioned before, osteoporosis is known as the *stealth disease* simply because doctors didn't have the technology to see it coming. One day a seemingly normal woman can buckle under a collapsing high-heeled shoe, stumble on a step-stool, or trip over her grandchild's toy; the result is a shattered bone in her femur, pelvis, or ball-and-socket hip joint. Gradual mineral loss — a result of consistant mineral catabolism that targets bone — will make bones less pliable and more brittle. Testosterone replacement therapy is known to dramatically improve a woman's metabolism, building stronger muscles and bones. Better eating practices, adequate physical activity with weight-bearing (or resistance) exercise, and the avoidance of a mineral-depleting lifestyle are also recommended.

DEXA technology, *dual energy X-ray absorptiometry*, is a revolutionary bone-scanning test that measures bone density. It is used to diagnose and treat early (and progressing) signs of osteoporosis.

Menopause

Everybody reading this book has heard of this condition. The name relates to a physiological cessation (*pause*) of menstrual periods that puts an end to a woman's reproductive cycle. The menopausal woman is no longer capable of fertilizing sperm or becoming pregnant. Women naturally lose their reproductive ability in their advancing years, or what many claim, their *midlife crisis*. There's a direct correlation between women who are menopausal and those who are experiencing female sexual disorders. But don't let folklore brainwash you into thinking the pleasure of a healthy sex life has ended too. It's accurate to say that Mother Nature is down-regulating the female's reproductive capabilities after a certain age by turning off certain hormones. But reproductive cessation does not mean sexual down-regulation, so satisfying sexual pleasure can continue on.

One Woman's Journey

In her book *Eat, Pray, Love*, Elizabeth Gilbert goes into how *major* depression, amongst other life casualties, negatively affected her sleep, appetite, and libido. Gilbert's loss of sexual desire was so persistent that it uncharacteristically led her to months of (self-chosen) celibacy. This abstinence of sexual pleasure wasn't conducted while she was cooped up in the confines of her home in the suburbs of New York, but rather in the romantic ambiance of the mystifying city of Rome, Italy, where she ran off to find the *real* meaning in her life.

Gilbert admits that the pressures of dealing with a divorce, followed by a rebounded love affair, combined with the struggle to determine why she was such an emotional wreck, led her to suffer chronic stomachaches, backaches, and emotional despair. All of which destroyed her sexual desires.

Gilbert's journey is inspiring. You have to read her book. I applaud her courageousness. Her story gives me yet another reason to encourage every woman who's in need of overcoming their own shortcomings to know that hope and help are just around the corner, especially when you make mental and lifestyle changes.

According to Christiane Northrup, M.D., author of Women's Bodies, Women's Wisdom, "Sexual energy is one of our most powerful energies for creating health." Northrup goes on to say, "A woman's most powerful sex organ lies between her ears." She even adds that sexual desire and sensation can be "short-circuited by fear, guilt, stress, and a host of other distracting thoughts."

Female sexual disorders can lead to a loss of self-esteem, depression, and alienation with partners. If detected and treated early enough, reversal and even elimination of these disorders is entirely possible and may prevent more invasive treatments later on.

Boston Sexual Health Clinic

The Bigger Picture

When we look at all the facts, it's not surprising to see so many women having sexual problems. We're living in an era smothered with the highest rates of divorce, single parenthood, financial pressures, depression, stress, obesity, osteoporosis, and diabetes. All of these can rob desire from any person, while (some) women are robbed of sexual pleasure and their ability to have children.

More and more women are struggling with the pressures of life (especially single women and single moms). Many are sleep-deprived; others are dealing with emotional trauma. Some lack physical exercise and are weak and out of shape. Many are overly caffeinated and addicted to sugar. Others smoke. The statistics are higher than ever before and increasing at epidemic rates for all ages, especially younger females. What were once *adult* diseases, like diabetes and atherosclerosis, are now affecting teenagers. All of these conditions not only deplete a woman's endocrine system, compromising healthy sexual performance, but they also deplete the immune system, digestive system, cardiovascular system, and reproduction glands.

Hypertension — caused by anxious emotions, drugs, caffeine, stress, and anger — stimulates the adrenals to secrete more adrenaline and cortisol, devastating the entire body, depleting testosterone and creating FSDs.

Female sexual disorders are treatable. And as you have read in this book, many of the remedies and cures that apply to men work for females as well!

Female Sexuality

The clitoris acts very similar to a penis in that it becomes erect, or larger, with excitation. (Yes, it swells and elongates during sexual arousal and stimulation.) And, ironically, the clitoris is often referred to as the *female penis*. This organ has the highest concentration of

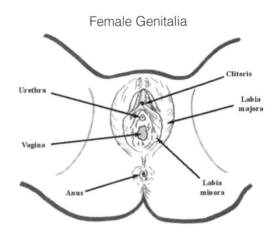

Female Genitalia

nerve endings in the female body. It becomes sensitive in the course of biochemical reactions that originate from arousal; creates nerve stimulation and enhanced circulation of blood that triggers the release of nitric oxide. As with a man's penis, the clitoris becomes erect through the receptivity of these events, all part of the HPGA, and results in the engorgement of blood into the clitoris. The vagina also enlarges and becomes highly sensitive in response to this feedback, getting wider and deeper and wetter (lubricated) as it prepares to accept the entry of a penis. But it doesn't end there. The entire genitalia and vulva, including the labia (outer *lips* of the vagina) swell and spread apart to make penile entry easier and to cause friction. (Hakim; *The couple's disease*)

Erection of the clitoris is the result of arousal.

Vaginal lubrication is the result of increased blood flow. (I regard this as the female equivalent of a man obtaining an erection.)

Blood flow and NO can be increased into the clitoris and vaginal region with prescription *erection pills* like Viagra. However, there are risks to consider.

All of the processes that create the production of nitric oxide are generated through hormones, or *androgens* (much like the arousal and erection ability in men).

Androgens are produced in the adrenal glands and gonads. Stress, as stated, depletes the adrenals and ovaries of their testosterone-making ability, while increasing harmful amounts of adrenaline and cortisol into the body. This is destructive for the sexual experience.

Women, like men, can crush any sexual feelings with anxiety.

Ironically, many of the sexual health supplements used by men (and suggested in this book) are widely recommended and proven to demonstrate varying degrees of efficacy for women. Androgen-boosting is often recommended for women who are experiencing sexual disorders. Testosterone, acting as an androgenic-anabolic agent, is extremely important for females as well; it builds stronger muscles and increases bone density. DHEA, being the most prevalent hormone in the body and a precursor to making testosterone, is a safe and relatively risk-free supplement that can be of tremendous benefit to women. DHEA declines with normal aging and is accelerated by unhealthy lifestyles.

Women who are overweight, stressed out, and depressed, are, no doubt, experiencing androgen deficiency along with concurrent adrenal strain.

Low testosterone (androgen) levels in women can be the *cause* for low libido, vaginal irritations, and orgasmic difficulties.

One of the most popular and controversial off-label sexual boosters and health-enhancers for women is testosterone, which was originally (exclusively) intended as a male hormone. But since testosterone also exists in females, replacement to youthful levels is suggested and proven to be extremely beneficial when levels are low or out of balance.

Since a woman can be more sensitive to upward shifts in testosterone, using many of the so-called *male-enhancement* products may work quicker and more dramatically with females.

For instance, women respond favorably to aromatse inhibitors, testosterone boosters, and prohormones. These compounds lower excessively high estrogen levels, raise excessively low testosterone levels, and may bring the female into a more normal, healthy endocrinological balance. In this state, females experience heightened arousal, sexual sensitivity, and more pleasurable orgasms. And the benefits don't stop there. Total health can be restored, depression ended, obesity corrected, muscles strengthened, and fat reduced. In many cases, female-pattern baldness is ceased. Some stats suggest that there are more bald females than men, which can be partly explained by the overload of radical androgenic hormones in the body, like dihydrotestosterone. A simple drop in (excessive) secretions of radical hormones like DHT and cortisol will bring about an entirely new dimension in a woman's status of health and appearance without any radical lifestyle changes.

The goal is to adjust, then stabilize, all hormones, especially the testosterone-estrogen ratios. Women with higher levels of free testosterone are typically stronger, more energetic, more confident, and more easily aroused, and they enjoy more satisfying, intense orgasms. Like in a man, freeing up bound estrogen and testosterone is critical for these hormones to exert healthy actions upon the female body. Of course, all this is a complex and highly sophisticated science that requires specialized attention. Only a qualified medical professional can really evaluate and address these for you.

Sex: It's Okay!

Sexuality, and the expression thereof, is natural and healthy and should be a part of every woman's life, no matter what age. When you have a healthy desire for sex and can achieve satisfying orgasms, chances are you're healthy elsewhere in your body. However, when women experience mood swings, uncontrollable weight gain, fatigue, insomnia, hot flashes, stress, depression, or hormonal imbalances, sexual disturbances will surface as the symptoms.

Many women (like men) develop a specific sexual identity that is rooted in their emotions and thoughts. These pertain to how the female feels about herself and how she feels about her partner, or potential partner. Her sense of attractiveness, her beliefs and levels of confidence, her trust of her lover, the way she feels about her own looks and her body, her age — all these play important roles in developing sexual and loving relationships. Like men's, women's bodies change with age; so do their emotions, beliefs, and idiosyncrasies.

Modern women are so much different from the old-fashioned female I was raised with. My mother stayed at home, and my parents remained married in spite of plenty of struggles growing up. Today things are much different. Over half of all marriages fail, and if a child has become part of that family, a woman is turned into a single mother. This obviously describes an entirely new stress factor. Men have their fair shares of stress, but women, who start with lower levels of testosterone to begin with, often have a more challenging time rebuilding their lives — and their bodies — after love goes wrong.

As stated in a previous section, stress is the *silent killer,* but it's far from quick. Stress eats away at you one cell at a time, so tomorrow you wake up just a little bit weaker than you did today. And over time, this leads to total devastation of the mind and body. The straws that add up slowly over time eventually break the camel's back.

Though these may sound like scare tactics, that is not my intent. Rather, I regard women in an impressive light. You have a unique ability (and obligation) to raise yourself as you would raise your own child. But you must take charge, accept responsibility, and raise the bar extremely high in regards to your self-respect. Focus on self-betterment; be *selfish*. If you're a younger woman who is living a healthy, stress-free life, then congratulations! Let's slap a high five. You can use this book as a preventative tool while you continue to mature. (Also be sure to share this information to help the people you care about and love.)

All people — men and women — change. They change internally, and they change externally. Levels of self-esteem or confidence, biological integrity, and physical appearance are all factors we live with and are constantly thinking about. When you take care of yourself, your body and mind are in harmony. When there's a disturbance, the harmony between your mind and body is disrupted, inevitably manifesting in symptoms that are difficult to live with, and are certainly robbing you of pleasure.

According to the National Health and Social Life Survey, nearly half of women below the age of 60 experience their own version of ED. The survey also shows that nitric oxide is of help to women, as it stimulates blood to the clitoris.

Drugs That Disrupt Female Sexual Function

These drugs will rob women of their libido and sexual pleasure, de-sensitizing the female genitals (partial listing):

- Prozac
- Paxil
- Zoloft
- Provera
- Depo-Provera
- Premphase
- Prempro
- Wellbutrin (bupropion)
- Elavil (amitriptyline)
- Sinequan (doxepin)
- Tofranil (imipramine)
- Birth-control pills

In a study published by the *New England Journal of Medicine* (September 7, 2000, p. 682–688), transdermal testosterone was able to improve sexual function in women who had undergone total hysterectomies.

Androgens and Sexuality in Women

As stated, the hormone testosterone, commonly associated with masculinity, is actually a hormone all women have, but in much lower amounts in comparison to (normal) men. Testosterone plays a critical role in the sexual health of a woman. Desire, libido, vaginal lubrication, and even orgasm are dependent on testosterone. Women who are peri and postmenopausal are low in testosterone. (During perimenopause and menopause, the best ways to ensure that women stay healthy and maintain a higher level of testosterone are proper nutrition, adequate physical activity, stress control, smoking cessation, and use of many of the supplements that regulate healthy levels of hormones that are suggested in this book.)

Like men, women typically reach their hormonal peaks in natural testosterone and DHEA in their mid-20s. These hormones are referred to as *androgenic hormones* that are produced in the ovaries and adrenal glands.

On average, after the age of 30, the female endocrine (hormonal) system starts to experience a decline in the levels of androgenic hormones, and that decline continues for the rest of a woman's life. Most women often complain about feeling old when they approach the age of 30. Much of this is cultural priming, more like brainwashing, and can be regarded as a figment of their imaginations. However, according to scientific studies, after the age of 30, women experience drops in androgenic hormones. So women then are honestly accurate when they make this complaint. Often labeled as female androgen insufficiency (FAI), the androgenic hormones are running low in women as they age, while there's also a decline in growth hormone, thyroid hormones, and progesterone (to name a few). The drop in these hormones is often met with an increase of *sex hormone-binding globulin* (SHBG) and cortisol. No wonder women claim they feel older when 30 is quite a young age.

Testosterone and Estrogen Replacement for Women

Many unique doctors are now prescribing natural OTS testosterone-boosting agents to their female patients who lack muscle strength, bone integrity, and genital sensitivity. Loss of sexual desire is another reason certain skilled doctors boost testosterone levels in their female patients, in addition to its health-promoting benefits. Many off-the-shelf nutritional supplements are also very effective at boosting testosterone in women. When natural products and therapies fail to meet expectations, more aggressive methods can be administered, like testosterone creams, patches, or injections.

According to the book *The Hormone of Desire: The Truth About Sexuality, Menopause and Testosterone*, written by Dr. Susan Rako, testosterone therapy is a major breakthrough for midlife women. Rako believes that a testosterone deficiency may be to blame for a loss of interest in sex, and therapy could prevent much unnecessary anguish (taken from Discovery Health: Testosterone: A Major Breakthrough for Menopausal Women).

Estrogen will always be an important hormone for women; however, its ratio to other hormones is a concern as a woman ages. Estrogen maintains the health of the vagina, keeping its lining flexible and lubricated. A condition known as female orgasmic disorder (FOD) can be caused by lack of sensation, while it's also caused by vaginal dryness that creates irritation and pain as a penis is aggressively rubbing against the vaginal lining. Women who have estrogen deficiencies or imbalances benefit from taking estrogen, which nourishes the vagina, making it possible to become lubricated and elastic, allowing for plea-surable penetration of an erect (hard) penis.

Tests for Women

Refer to the Female Panel blood exam by the Life Extension Foundation

- Complete blood panel: testosterone, estradiol, DHEA, FSH, LH, prolactin, SHBG
- Thyroid test
- Pelvic exam
- Liver function
- Spinal exam
- Genital exam, including PAP smear for the cervix
- Comprehensive physical exam
- Vaginal pH testing: Determines arousal sensation inside the vagina.
- Duplex doppler ultrasonography: Determines blood flow and nerve stimulation in the vagina and clitoris.
- Vibration biothesiometry: Tests the sensitivity of the genital and spinal nerve receptors.

Female Sexual Enhancement Products

Women can be pleased to know that advances in medically approved technological aids that treat, and even cure, sexual disorders are becoming more readily available. Some are used purely for self-pleasuring, others for maintaining the health of the genitalia. And for those of you who might imagine an upgraded space-age version of the vibrating dildo, you're in for quite a surprise.

Joining the lineup of female pleasuring gadgets, as well as sexual restorative devices, are a myriad of new products and treatments that are slowly entering into the marketplace, while others are still in development. According to an article in *URO Today*, analysts project that the products being manufactured for female sexual dysfunctions could exceed $1 billion annually! These are not only the well-known artificial penises. Rather, many of these are medical-grade, doctor-tested devices that offer state-of-the-art technology and are approved by credentialed professionals.

The Female Enhancer

A newly designed product about to hit the marketplace (not available as of this writing) is called the FS Female Enhancer, another great product from the Fastsize Corporation. It is through the usage of this new and unique product that women, for the first time, can actually treat and prevent the onset of FSD problems. That's quite a claim made by company representatives and, if proven accurate, a real advantage for many women.

The FS Female Enhancer is designed to help improve genital blood flow to stimulate and increase vaginal lubrication and clitoral sensitivity. Similar to the Enhancer for men, this device's mechanism includes a vacuum and vibrating motion. There's also a multifunctional systematic LED (light-emitting diode) that helps to stimulate the release of nitric oxide (necessary for clitoral erection) and safely warms and stimulates the female genitalia at the same time.

Transdermal Testosterone

Also on the horizon is a new transdermal testosterone patch that is being developed to boost a woman's sex drive. This product is made by Noven Pharmaceuticals Inc. and is said to be licensed to Procter & Gamble. As of this writing, no name is given for the product, and there's no word on when it will be available on the marketplace. Transdermal delivery is also more convenient and less expensive as compared to most testosterone replacement therapies that are administered by injection or implants. Transdermal means it's delivered *through the skin* as a testosterone-soaked patch is placed on the body — usually on the shoulder, abdomen, or hip. The patch remains in place for any length of time — usually a week — while the testosterone passes from the patch through the skin and into the body. (Please check Web site for any updates.)

So Where Do I Stand Now?

I want to make an admission here: Whether you read into it or not, I believe I made it very obvious that while researching this book — and even as I started to write it — I felt a great deal of frustration and disappointment. As a man, I felt cheated because, historically, medical professionals gave most of the attention to female sexual needs, leaving us guys completely on our own. I'm referring to all of us guys — our dads, brothers, uncles, granddads. However, after repeatedly scanning the list of studies and statistics that have been revealed in recent years regarding the FSDs that are affecting, astonishingly, millions of women today, it's obvious that yesteryear's medical attention to women was either incomplete or simply (unwittingly) devoid of the proper focus on female sexuality altogether. The medical communities, obviously, allocated their emphasis toward reproductive and menopausal issues. I'm taken aback that none of us (male or female) were regarded holistically, as limited approaches have created much of the (preventable) disorders tens of millions of people are faced with today. I now know better, and so do you. What a relief it is! And since later is better than never, I'm relieved to announce that many sections of our medical communities have (finally) recognized this disparity and are now focusing on female sexual health separate from, and in addition to, menopausal, reproductive, and fertility concerns.

Although it's accepted that women will lose their ability to mother a child with advancing years, their ability to enjoy pleasurable sex can continue on for as long as they abide by healthy lifestyle principles. I believe the information compiled in this book will shed light and raise the levels of confidence for all my female readers, empowering them to overcome any hurdles and experience ultimate pleasure and health!

Glossary of Drugs

The following items are available by prescription, and are either complete synthetic (fabricated) chemical formulations or alterations derived from natural substances.

Many drugs are used for purposes other than the ones listed on their labels. This is known as *off-label* use. Some, but not all, doctors understand the off-label benefits of many drugs and will prescribe them to their patients. For instance, a drug like Arimidex, developed to treat breast cancer in women, is often prescribed for its off-label benefits to men who have low testosterone and high estrogen ratios. Be informed however that certain pharmacists are committed to issuing prescriptions based on *labeled* purposes, and may reject fulfilling off-label prescriptions. The following glossary is for educational purposes only. Do not experiment with any prescription drugs unless they are prescribed by a licensed medical professional.

ACTH (Corticotrophin): This is a steroid that's naturally secreted from the pituitary gland. It is administered to stimulate secretion of the adrenal hormones. Animal studies have shown enhanced erection ability in males and arousal improvement in both sexes.

Amyl Nitrate: On the street this chemical is known as "poppers." Inhaled from a spray, the chemical is known to be very dangerous, working as a powerful vasodilator that relaxes muscle and increases blood supply; it can potentially cause fainting. Reports are inconsistent, as some claim that taking this drug prior to orgasm increases the pleasure of the climax, while other reports are negative. The effects last only 30–40 seconds. Leave it alone.

Anabolic Steroids: I will not get into any details about this category of drugs here as I've already given plenty of attention to them elsewhere in this book. Instead, I'll provide a brief explanation. This is a classification of pharmaceutical drugs that contain a synthetic version of testosterone, or a similar acting compound, and are also referred to as *androgenic anabolic steroids* (AAS). Labeled and off-label uses for athletes include speeding up muscle growth, speeding recovery from injury and training, building muscle size and strength, boosting hormonal profiles, and enhancing athletic performance. But please note that all of these drugs are banned, illegal substances policed by the International Olympic Committee and other amateur and professional sports organizations (like the UFC, NFL, NBA, NHL, and MLB). Off-label use is against the law without a prescription. The term *anabolic* refers to the metabolic process that increases protein synthesis and other body functions, which are responsible for repairing the body from normal wear and tear while building lean muscle mass. Synthetic drugs that mimic this action are called *anabolic steroids*. Don't let the word *anabolic* shy you away; it's the steroid drugs that are harmful.

Arimidex (*Anastrozole*): This is a drug that acts as an aromatase inhibitor and is antiestrogenic. It's typically prescribed to treat breast cancer in women; however, its off-label use is widespread with male athletes and bodybuilders who use anabolic steroids, as well as some obese men, to treat testosterone-estrogen imbalances. Many steroids *aromatize* inside the body, which means they convert into estrogen. Steroid users and obese men can use antiestrogenic compounds to keep estrogen low and testosterone high. Excessive estrogen for men produces femininizing effects that include gynecomastia (enlarged nipples, also called *gyno*). Other side effects from high estrogen include water retention, benign prostatic hyperplasia (BPH), fat gain, lower testosterone levels (*hypogonadism*), ED, and acne. Other aromatase-inhibiting drugs are Aromasin and Femara. Very helpful for restoring the HPTA after it has been down-regulated.

Aromasin: Antiestrogen, aromatase inhibitor. This drug provides a similar action to Arimidex listed above. It was developed to fight breast cancer in postmenopausal women, but as an off-label prescription it's a very effective agent for bodybuilders and for obese men wanting to avoid estrogen-related side effects that include gyno, acne, and water retention; these side effects are all caused by aromatizing testosterone.

Avodart (*Dutasteride*): This is a medication that has been developed to prevent the conversion of testosterone into dihydrotestosterone. High levels of DHT are known to cause male-pattern baldness and an enlarged prostate, also known as *benign prostatic hyperplasia*, or BPH. Although professionally prescribed for these symptoms, this drug is known to produce many undesirable side effects that include decreases in libido and semen volume, and can also cause erectile dysfunction. (Refer to "Prostate Medications" in this section.)

Bremelanotide: This drug is currently experimental. It's designed to enhance sexual desire in men and women. It also works to treat sexual arousal disorders (SAD) and ED. The drug is administered as a nasal spray. As of the completion of this writing, this drug was not yet available. Preliminary trials show some encouraging results.

Bromocriptine (*Parlodel*): As a prolactin-inhibiting drug, this chemical is used to lower blood prolactin levels. It's also used to release dopamine from the brain. Men and women with sexual disorders may see improvement by using this drug. It may also be helpful for boosting libido.

Cabergoline (*Dostinex*): Enhances dopamine levels in the brain while decreasing prolactin. Cabergoline is known to increase libido, orgasm, and ejaculation volume.

Cannabis (*Marijuana*): Known for its mind-relaxing effects and often used as an aphrodisiac. However, many feel this drug diminishes their sexual desire and libido, while reducing sperm count. Others find it helpful for boosts in arousal and genital sensation. Men who have high levels of performance anxiety may find this drug to be unsuccessful at helping them with their erectile ability. All smoking reduces sperm count and quality, so men who are trying to impregnate their wives should avoid this drug. Marijuana is legally prescribed in certain states for medical purposes.

Cialis (*Tadalafil*): An extremely effective erection pill that can produce erections for up to 36 hours, while some reports state as long as 100 hours. Due to its long-lasting duration, Cialis has been labeled the *weekend drug*. If you're a sexual marathoner, then this might be a drug you can benefit from. But if you only plan on having one sexual encounter, reduce the dosage or select another drug. As a result of Cialis' long-duration effects on erection, multiple orgasms with enhanced refractory period may be possible. Cialis is not affected by food. Available in 10 and 20 mgs. There are side effects, so use with caution. (As I was completing the writing of this book, the makers of Cialis began promoting a low-dose version of this drug that was designed for daily use.)

Clomid (*Clomiphene Citrate*): This drug targets the hypothalamus gland, tricking it into producing more gonadotropin-releasing hormone (GnRH). Then the pituitary gland is stimulated to produce follicular stimulating hormone (FSH) and lutienizing hormone (LH), both of which go on to stimulate the gonads. When FSH and LH are low, like in steroid users and hypogonadic men, so is libido and erection-producing ability. Men with low levels of FSH and LH may also have low levels of testosterone and high levels of estrogen, with some degree of testicular shrinkage (atrophy). Clomid is used to address these symptoms as an off-label prescription. Men who use this drug notice that their (atrophied) testicles enlarge, sperm content increases, libido improves, and erectile function becomes more reliable. This is not a causal drug that should be self-administered. A knowledgeable licensed authority (like the ones who are referenced in this book) must monitor your blood hormone profiles, then prescribe the dose and duration of this drug. Clomid can be used by itself or in combination with other drugs. Should be used for a short period, as extended use can cause adverse effects. Very helpful for restoring the HPTA after it has been down-regulated.

Cocaine: I won't go there, but it's a dopamine-releasing drug that creates a sexual feeling.

Dapoxetine: An experimental drug being developed to treat premature ejaculation. It is currently awaiting approval from the Food and Drug Administration.

Deprenyl: Enhances levels of dopamine. This drug has shown to have a strong libido-enhancing effect for men. It is popular in the antiaging communities for both men and women.

Estrogen (The synthetic version of the female hormone): For women, it's wise to obtain periodic blood profiles to measure hormonal levels. If you show signs of an imbalance, your levels of estrogen can be improved with replacement therapy. Healthy levels of estrogen are needed to maintain a woman's health and sexuality, and to protect the integrity of the vagina.

Femara (*Letrozole*): This drug is an antiestrogen and aromatase inhibitor. Letrozole is used to raise testosterone levels with a concurrent reduction in estrogen. It may also increase LH and FSH. Off-label use of antiestrogens and aromatase inhibitors are popular with steroid users. It's also popular with men who have hypogonadism and are trying to prevent the feminizing effects of high levels of estrogen. Excessively high levels of estrogen in men, or an unhealthy testosterone-estrogen ratio, can cause water retention (bloating), fat gain, gynecomastia, lowered sperm counts, loss of libido, and even erectile difficulties. Other drugs that fall within this classification include Clomid, Aromasin, Arimidex, and Tamoxifen. Letrozole is very helpful for restoring the HPTA after it has been down-regulated.

Finasteride (Marketed as Proscar and many other names): This drug is mainly used to treat and/or prevent prostate enlargement or benign prostatic hyperplasia (BPH). It is also used to treat male-pattern baldness. Its mechanism acts as an inhibiting enzyme that blocks the conversion of testosterone into dihydrotestosterone (DHT). Unfortunately, a host of side effects are reported in men who use this drug. These side effects include loss of libido, oligospermia (changes in semen quality and volume), depression, gynecomastia, and erectile dysfunction. This drug might help grow your hair, but chances are it won't grow your penis or libido. Many doctors believe it's better to address the prostate by reducing sex hormone-binding globulin (SHBG), increasing free testosterone levels and reducing estradiol levels.

Flomax (*Tamsulosin*): This drug was developed to relax the tissues, veins, and arteries of the penis to allow adequate blood flow. It also relaxes the bladder and prostate muscles, which may make urination easier, especially for men who have benign prostatic hyperplasia (BPH). Side effects include insomnia, dizziness, irregular ejaculations, and drop-offs in libido. (Refer to "Prostate Medications" in this section.)

GHB (*Gamma-Hydroxy-Butyrate*): Very potent and unpredictable. Made notorious by criminally minded men who attempt to have un-consensual sex with females, hence the name *date rape drug*. Was once available OTS. This drug is impossible to monitor and very dangerous, especially when combined with alcohol or other drugs, as in the case of actor-singer-songwriter River Phoenix, who died while combining GHB with other chemicals. Stay away from this stuff.

HCG (*Human Chorionic Gonadotrophin*): This drug is becoming more and more popular because it has now been exposed to the mainstream. Men with hypogonadism and steroid-using athletes — who are suffering from HPTA damage, testicular atrophy, oligospermia, and ED — use this drug to directly and quickly stimulate (some say *trick*) the Leydig cells in the testicles to jump-start production of endogenous testosterone when levels drop below normal. As a synergist, many use Clomid along with HCG, which helps to complete the entire hypo-thalamus-pituitary-testicular axis. Also known to boost libido levels. Used off-label quite extensively for these purposes by those who understand the science of these chemicals. Very helpful for restoring the HPTA after it has been down-regulated, but dosage and duration of use are tricky.

Human Growth Hormone (HGH): A hormone that is naturally secreted by the pituitary gland located in the brain. HGH is also available in synthetic forms that can be injected into the body when natural levels drop below normal. Some of the newer delivery systems are administered orally. HGH is reported to have age-reversing benefits, is touted as the *fountain of youth* by many longevity experts, and is proven to restore youthful hormonal levels caused by age-related decline. Some brands include Genotropin, Humatrope, Nutropin, Protropin, Saizen, Serostim and Somatotropin. Athletes use this drug for its anabolic benefits in muscle-building, increasing strength, and accelerating fat burning. HGH also helps to boost libido, stimulate overall mental alertness, and improve erectile ability. Excessive amounts of this hormone can create hyper-enlargement of the tissues and bones, also known as *gigantism*, or *acromeglia*, like in the famous wrestler Andre The Giant. Recommended (natural) HGH boosters include exercise and a high protein diet with supplemental L-Arginine. Possession of HGH without a prescription is prohibited by law and may be punishable by imprisonment of up to five years or more. Some states have classified HGH as a *controlled substance*.

Levitra (*Vardenafil*): A powerful prescription erection pill that works within 10 minutes — quicker than most other erection pills. It offers greater spontaneity when sexual opportunities suddenly present themselves. The erection-producing benefits of this drug can last up to 12 hours. The mechanism of Levitra is very similar to Viagra as it acts as an inhibitor of PDE-5, an enzyme that prevents erections. Levitra can be taken along with food, which won't interfere with its absorption. Currently available in 10 mg and 20 mg potencies. There are side effects, so please check with your doctor.

Levodopa (*L-DOPA, Mucuna Pruriens, Velvet Bean*): Both the natural and synthetic versions of this chemical are used as a sexual stimulator by improving the body's level of natural testosterone. Levadopa is related to the dopamine that the brain releases as a sexual stimulator. It increases arousal and libido, and even enhances erection for some men.

Melanotan II: An experimental drug being designed to increase libido. Not yet available as of this writing. (NOTE: The development of libido-triggering and enhancing drugs is a relatively new science.

According to my research, it sounds like some strides are being made in the labs. I'm curious to see what comes out of all this experimentation. We could see a drug that gives us a slight boost in sexual desire or, flipping the coin, we could see a drug that turns us into raving nymphomaniacs. We'll just have to wait and see. I'll post any new info on the Web site once it's available.)

Menotropins (*Pergonal*): This drug helps to stimulate the growth of ovarian tissues in females. In men, it can be useful for sperm production.

Nolvadex (*Tamoxifen Citrate*): This is a popular drug used off-label to treat gynecomastia. This drug is effective at reducing a man's estrogen levels while (concurrently) boosting his free testosterone, creating a more favorable estrogen-testosterone ratio. Tamoxifen is better known (face-label) as a preventive therapy and treatment for breast cancer in women.

Oxytocin: Known as *the hormone of love*. This hormone is produced in the hypothalamus and is released into the bloodstream from the pituitary gland. Foreplay (which includes any cuddling, hugging, and touching) will stimulate this biochemical action. It is released in higher amounts after orgasm in both sexes. Oxytocin is known to be involved in social bonding, along with the establishment of trust between people. That may explain one of the reasons for the powerful bonding effect that is created between a mother and her child. Certain doctors are prescribing this hormone as a remedy for low sexual interest, to boost libido, to enhance orgasmic pleasure, and to shorten refractory periods. According to Dr. Ann Marie Tommey, Oxytocin is released at higher amounts in women. After orgasm, Oxytocin levels rise in men, then drop after only a few hours, while women's levels can last for days. According to Tommey, this may explain why women fall in love (or think they're in love) after they've had orgasmic sex with a man. The orgasm-producing Oxytocin effect makes the emotional compartment of that person's brain believe she has found true love. Studies reveal that blood concentrations of Oxytocin are higher among people who claim to be falling in love. Synthetic Oxytocin is relatively safe when used at recommended doses. It is available in sublingual tablets and nasal sprays. A certified compound pharmacist can help you. In addition to Oxytocin, the drug *Vasopressin* has been demonstrated to have a similar effect in males.

Papaverine (Sold under various brand names): This drug is a vasodilator that is injected with a syringe into the corpal tissues of the penis to open up (dilate) the vessels for an influx of blood that will create an erection. It can be used by itself, while some doctors might compound a mixture.

Permixon: A pharmaceutical (synthetic) alteration of the natural herb Saw Palmetto that can maintain the health of prostate tissues. It also prevents male-pattern baldness.

Phenoxybenzamine (*Dibenzyline*): This is an antihypertensive drug that is also used as a penile injection to create an erection.

Propecia (*Finasteride*): An FDA-approved oral treatment for certain types of hair loss. This drug works by reducing dihydrotestosterone (DHT), the radical hormone that's known to cause male-pattern baldness and prostate hyperplasia. Many men have experienced sexual side effects from this drug including reduced libido, difficulty in achieving an erection, and/or decreases in seminal volume. (Refer to "Prostate Medications" right below.)

Prostate Medications: There's a long list of medications doctors may prescribe to men who are experiencing an enlarged prostate, or any type of prostatic irregularity. The following is a list of some drugs that are commonly prescribed for the prostate. Some are used to manipulate hormones, others are designed to decrease swelling or inflammation, and even others are used to fight infection. Please be aware that most, if not all, of these drugs have been known to have negative interactions with other medications; side effects include loss of libido, erectile dysfunction, and oligospermia.

Avodart, Bactrim, Cardura XL, Casodex, Cipro, Doryx, Erythromycin, Eulexin, Flomax, Floxin, Hytrin, Lupron Depot IM,

Macrodantin, Minipress, Nilandron, Penicillin V Potassium, Prednisone, Premarin, Proscar, Striant Bucl, Tetracycline, Uroxatral, and Zoladex.

Tamoxifen: (See Nolvadex.)

Testosterone: Available in creams, gels, injections, transdermal patches, and implantable (under the skin) pellets. According to hormone specialist Fouad I. Ghaly, M.D., *testosterone is responsible for one's productivity and success in life and plays a critical role in overall well-being and healthy sexual functioning.* Replacement therapy is becoming increasingly popular for boosting libido, muscle mass, strength, and energy. It offers cognitive benefits and can cure sexual disorders. Used extensively by many in-the-know specialists for both men and women.

Testosterone Cypionate: There are many forms of synthetic testosterone, but the *cypionate* version is the one most doctors believe is the safest and nearest to being bio-identical. Cypionate is an oil-based injectable preparation that offers a long-acting effect, keeping testosterone levels elevated for several weeks. Typically, administration is applied weekly or monthly, depending on dosage. Commonly available in 10ml vials, all forms of testosterone are federally controlled substances, so a prescription is needed. Testosterone replacement therapy (TRT) has traditionally received a bad rap by the majority, mostly due to ignorance and the fact that our culture accepts hypogonadism as a normal event of aging. TRT has also been under attack because its anabolic properties have been mistakenly connected with the negative reports associated with steroid-using athletes. However, the man using exogenous testosterone to treat hypogonadism cannot be compared to the (healthy) athlete who's using exogenous testosterone merely to gain the competitive edge and, like Kevin, strives to develop an ultra-realistic physique. Elevating free testosterone levels will demonstrate a significant boost in libido, confidence, muscle strength, and erection ability. Extremely useful for women with abnormally low testosterone levels or who just want a boost in overall health and to regain their sexuality and youthfulness.

Thyroid: There are various natural thyroid supplements as well as synthetic medications available that treat either a slow or hypoactive thyroid (*hypothyroidism*), and a fast or hyperactive thyroid (*hyperthyroidism*). Sold under many brand names — like *Armour* and *Synthroid* — synthetic versions are intended to balance the production of thyroid hormones, which play a major role in sexual function, metabolism, and regulation of bodyweight.

Uprima (*Apomorphine*): This is an erection-producing drug that offers a dopamine-releasing effect to improve erectile function in men and sexual function in women. When this chemical gets into the bloodstream, it signals the central nervous system to release dopamine, a neurotransmitter in the brain that will ultimately play a role in the formation of an erection. This drug hasn't become popular due to its nauseating side effects. (Most, if not all, prescription erection pills can have nauseating effects as well.) Unlike the erection pills, Uprima is not swallowed; instead, it is dissolved under the tongue. Current erection pills on the market do not influence libido; Uprima may. As of this writing, this drug has not been approved for sale in the U.S. or Canada. However, it has been available in Europe since 2000. The drug's co-inventor, Dr. Jeremy Heaton, acknowledges that very few people have heard of Uprima due to the over-popularity of Viagra.

Vasopressin: This hormone is produced in the hypothalamus and stored in the pituitary gland; then it is released into the bloodstream. It plays a role in the regulation of the body's water balance and has been shown to improve cognitive functions. This drug is supplied as a nasal spray that's squirted into the nostrils to improve short-term memory and concentration. Vasopressin has a similar amino acid molecular design as Oxytocin, therefore explaining the boosts in sexual expression, social behavior, and bonding this drug often offers.

Viagra: (*Sildenafil*): Erection pill that was discovered by Pfizer during experimentation to find a new drug treatment for hypertension and angina. Although Viagra is a laboratory accident, it has become the drug of choice for millions of men suffering from ED. Viagra's erection-producing capabilities work through the inhibition of an erection-destroying enzyme called PDE-5. When PDE-5 is blocked, blood can now enter into a dilated penis, and this drug's effects can last up to four hours. Available in various potencies that your doctor can prescribe and monitor. There are side effects that include blurry vision, dryness in mouth, stuffy nose, headache, dizziness, and possibly priapism. (Did I hear you giggle when you read the word *priapism?* Who'd ever think having an erection last longer than a certain period of time would be classified as a disorder?)

Yohimbine (Sold under the brand names *Yocon, Yohimex, Aphrodyne, Viritab*): Derived from the yohimbe plant, the pharmaceutical (synthetic) preparation is called *Yohimbine HCL.* This is reported to be the first FDA-approved drug in the U.S. for the treatment of impotence. Yohimbine is shown to increase genital blood flow that results in sexual sensitivity. It is also known to be an aphrodisiac. Side effects can include rapid heart rate, uncontrollable sweating, and anxiety. Many fitness buffs and athletes use Yohimbe (or Yohimbine, which is more potent) to boost their nerve and muscle power for anaerobic workouts and to burn off abdominal fat quicker. Preparations of yohimbe bark are available over the counter.

SIDE EFFECTS: Please know that there is a long list of side effects associated with using all prescription medications. In spite of the pleasure many can (temporarily) provide, erection pills and other sex-boosting (synthetic) drugs also come with their own directory of risks. Your doctor or pharmacist should spell out those risks before administration.

Also use caution when purchasing any drug or product over the Internet, or from one of Kevin's workout partners. You must feel secure in the source's credibility and the quality control of the products they're selling.

Epilogue

To Be Continued ... I want to thank you for reading my book. Finding and compiling this information was propagated by an extremely adverse situation that I was confronted with but determined to defeat. As stated, one day, a very long time ago, I suddenly discovered that my life wasn't mine any longer — it became something else, and not by choice. But somewhere along my path I was convinced this could become my *greatest virtue*. All I had to do was look for the meaning in the lesson, persistently strive to defeat *it*, and go on to share it with others.

I had to write this book. I did it by investing over three and a half decades into research and practice. And now that this book is finally written, my life is changing once again. And that is because I now have the opportunity to *give back*. I found something that saved my life. I was healed from something so upsetting and demoralizing. I know my demise was (ignorantly) self-inflicted at such a young age. (Remember, I was still a teen.) But the same changes that happened to me will inevitably, according to sheer statistical data and the scores of guys I hear from, occur in millions of men, whether they're a result of genetics, lifestyle changes, or merely getting older.

I feel personally, professionally, and ethically obligated to share this information with you. Now, I'm eager for you to take the information and resources in this book and apply them to your life, so that you can beat *it* too, becoming a healthier, happier, and more productive person in the process.

So let's not say good-bye, because this program does not end here. Now it's time for you to get to work and remain active with your own self-improvement. Use this information wisely. Implement it. Live it.

And realize a lot of extra sexual satisfaction in your life as a result of it! And hey, don't think this is a solo effort. I encourage you to write in and let me know how you're doing, and I'll keep updating the Web site and online newsletters to answer your questions. I'll always be recording and posting new audio and video seminars. And you'll also be able to read about the latest products, supplements, and advances.

So even though the words and pages of this book have come to a completion, we're just beginning our expedition to find that big treasure that's waiting for you on the next horizon. As you begin, let out a big, loud laugh to fuel your success and to inspire in you the courage and determination that you need for every step along the way. Maintain that *I can do anything* attitude. Stay focused, be *selfish* — and keep on keeping on!

Wishing you the Ultimate of Success!

John Abdo

Acknowledgements & References:

www.SexHealthTV.com

Acknowledgements

Dr. Laurence A. Levine, Urology Specialists, Chicago, IL, www.urologyspecialists.net

Dr. Nick Delgado, The Delgado Protocol, Newport Beach, CA, www.ultimatemedicalresearch.com

Dr. Fouad I. Ghaly, Torrance, CA, www.prolongyouth.com

Dr. Ann Marie Tommey, San Luis Obispo, CA, www.annmarietommeymd.com

Dr. Jonathan V. Wright, Tahoma Clinic, Renton, WA, www.TahomaClinic.com

Dana Nelson, R.Ph., Pharm. M.S., F.A.S.C.P., F.A.C.P., San Luis Obispo, CA, HealthPlus Pharmacy, Inc.

Life Extension Foundation, http://www.lef.org/ja, 888-463-0309

Mark Newell, Ph.D., R.P.A.

Prostate Cancer Foundation, Santa Monica, CA, www.pcf.org

American Academy of Anti-Aging Medicine (A4M) http://www.worldhealth.net

John Abdo is available for consultations, workshops, seminars, and speaking engagements. www.JohnAbdo.com

American Academy of Anti-Aging Medicine (A4M)
American Association for Marriage and Family Therapy

American Cancer Society
American Heart Association
American Lung Association
American Medical Association (AMA)
American Psychiatric Association
American Psychological Association
American Urological Association (AUA)
Centers for Disease Control and Prevention
The Endocrine Society
The Hormone Foundation

Male Enhancement Products

(Unfortunately, Fastsize is out of business as of this printing)

<u>Vacuum Pumps, Constriction Rings, and More</u>:

Dr. Joel Kaplan's FDA-Approved Patented Product Line

Androzene®: Popular Male Sexual Health Formula
www.SexHealthTV.com

Recommended Readings

- *Sex, Drugs and Aphrodisiacs*, Adam Gottlieb
- *Erectile Dysfunction? It's Time to Straighten Up*, Bob Bryan
- *Overcoming Impotence*, J. Stephen Jones, M.D.
- *Boosting Male Libido Naturally*, Zoltan Rona, M.D.
- *The Hardness Factor*, Steven Lamm, M.D.
- *Maximize Your Vitality & Potency for Men Over 40*, Jonathan V. Wright, M.D., and Lane Lenard, Ph.D.
- *Super "T"*, Karlis Ullis, M.D.
- *Man and His Penis*, Scott Hays
- *Make Your Body a Fat-Burning Machine*, John Abdo
- *Disease Prevention & Treatment*, 1,500 pages of concise information about therapies that are documented in the scientific literature compiled

by the editors at the Life Extension Foundation. Discounts available for members at http://www.lef.org/ja, or by calling 888-463-0309.

- *You Can Work Your Own Miracles*, Napoleon Hill
- *Think and Grow Rich*, Napoleon Hill (distributed by Nightingale-Conant)
- *Understanding Peyronie's Disease*, Laurence A. Levine, M.D.
- *Peyronie's Disease; A Guide to Clinical Management*, Laurence A. Levine, M.D.
- *The All-Natural Penis Enlargement Manual*, Fastsize
- *Three Magic Words*, U.S. Anderson
- *Vital Living From the Inside-Out*, John Abdo (audio series)
- *The Magic in Your Mind*, U.S. Anderson
- *Body Engineering*, John Abdo
- *Blink*, Malcolm Gladwell
- *Feel the Fear, And Do It Anyway:* Susan Jeffers
- *The Sexy Years*, Suzanne Somers
- *Your Miracle Brain*, Jean Carper
- *Eat, Pray, Love*, Elizabeth Gilbert
- *Nutrition & Healing*, Jonathan V. Wright, M.D. (newsletter)
- *The Sexual Male—Problems & Solutions*, Richard Milsten, M.D., and Julian Slowinski, Psy. D.
- *The Couple's Disease*, Lawrence S. Hakim, M.D., F.A.C.S.
- *Anatomy of the Spirit*, Carolyn Myss
- *Why People Don't Heal*, Carolyn Myss
- *Gray's Anatomy*, Henry Gray, F.R.S.
- *Testosterone for Life*, Harvard Medical School (distributed by the Life Extension Foundation)
- *Iron Man* Magazine
- *Planet Muscle* Magazine

Movies, TV Shows, DVD's and Documentaries

- *Jose Canseco: The Last Shot*
- *Oprah Winfrey*, especially health episodes with Dr. Oz
- *Dr. Phil*, for psychological techniques to overcome fear, anxiety, and depression
- *The Man Whose Arms Exploded*
- *Talking Sex*, Sue Johanson, R.N.

- *Strictly Sex*, Dr. Drew Pinsky
- *Evolve Your Brain, The Science of Changing Your Mind*, Dr. Joe Dispenza
- *No Excuses Workout* (The 7-Minute Workout), John Abdo
- *Fitness Done Quickly™*, John Abdo
- *Walk-Aerobics™*, John Abdo

Exercise Equipment

- The AB-DOer®, invented by John Abdo
- Contour-Weights®, invented by John Abdo

References

Int J Sport Nutr Exerc Metab. 2000 Jun;10(2):208–15. "The effects of Tribulus Terrestris on body composition and exercise performance in resistance-trained males." Antonio, J., Uelmen, J., Rodriguez, R., Earnest, C.

Life Sci. 2002 Aug 9;71(12):1385–96. "Aphrodisiac properties of Tribulus Terrestris extract (Protodioscin) in normal and castrated rats." Gauthaman, K., Adaikan, P.G., Prasad, R.N.

Aphale, A.A., A.D. Chhibba, N.R. Kumbhakarna, M. Mateenuddin, and S.H. Dahat. 1998. "Subacute toxicity study of the combination of ginseng (Panax ginseng) and ashwagandha (Withania somnifera) in rats: a safety assessment." *Indian J Physiol Pharmacol* Apr; 42(2):299–302.

Frawley, David and Vasant Lad. 1986. *The Yoga Of Herbs: An Ayurvedic Guide to Herbal Medicine*. Santa Fe: Lotus Press.

Kirtikar, K.R. and B.D. Basu. 1993. *Indian Medicinal Plants*. 2nd ed. Vol. 1–4. 1935. Reprint. Delhi: Periodical Experts.

Ziauddin, M., N. Phansalkar, P. Patki, S. Diwanay, B. Patwardhan. 1996. "Studies on the immunomodulatory effects of Ashwagandha." *J Ethnopharmacol*. Feb; 50(2):69–76.

Plastic Wrap Toxins. Author/s: Jule Klotter. Issue: Jan 2000.

"Carcinogens — At 10,000,000 Times FDA Limits," *Options* May 2000. Published by People Against Cancer, 515-972-4444. On Channel 2 (Huntsville, AL).

Antidepressant-like effects of Trichilia catigua (Catuaba) extract: evidence for dopaminergic-mediated mechanisms.

Ernst, E., and M.H. Pittler, "Yohimbine for erectile dysfunction: a systematic review and meta-analysis of randomized clinical trials," *J Urol* (1998), 159(2):433–36.

Mann, K., et al., "Effects of yohimbine on sexual experiences and nocturnal penile tumescence and rigidity in erectile dysfunction," Archives of *Sexual Behavior* (1996), 25:1–16.

Rowland, D.L., "Yohimbine, erectile capacity, and sexual response in men," *Arch Sex Behav* (1997), 26(1):49–62.

Susset, J.G., et al., "Effect of yohimbine hydrochloride on erectile impotence: A double-blind study," *Journal of Urology* (1989), 141(6):1360–63.

The Deer Farmer's Magazine, Wellington, NZ, 9/1992, "Deer Antler Velvet: The ultimate natural medicine?"

Conference on "Health Problems Related to the Chinese in America," U of C. School of Medicine, San Francisco, CA, 5/82.

Velvet Antlers for Medicine, University of Edmonton, Edmonton, Alberta, Canada, 6/90.

Chemical Characteristics and Processing Technology of Alberta Wapiti Velvet Antlers, Wildlife Production Conservation and Sustainable Development, University of Edmonton, Edmonton, Alberta, Canada.

International Symposium on Cervi Parvum Cornu, 10-7-94, Seoul, Korea, Hotel Lotte, "The Korean Society of Pharmacognosy, the Velvet Antler Industry: Background and Research Findings," J.M. Suttie, P.F. Fennessy, S.R. Haines, M. Sadighi, D.R. Kerr, and C. Isaacs, AgResearch, Invermay Agricultural Centre, New Zealand.

Invermay Research Center, located in Otago, New Zealand, Dr. Peter Fennessy, ANTLER

Fennessy, P.F. and Suttie, J.M. (1985) "Antler growth: nutritional and endocrine factors." *Biology of Deer Production*, P.F. Fennessy and K.R. Drew (eds). Royal Soc of NZ Bull, #22, Wellington, 239–250.

Sadighi, M., Haines, S.R., Skottner, A., Harris, A.J., and Suttie, J.M. (1994). "Effects of insulin-like growth factor I (IGF 1) and IGF 11 on the growth of antler cells in vitro." *J. Endocrinol.* (In Press).

The Life Extension Foundation, 2000

Dr. Mauro G. Di Pasquale, M.D., Warkworth, Ontario, Canada, February 1993, *Drugs In Sports.*

Chinese Herbal Medicine Materia Medica, Dan Bensky, Andrew Gamble, Ted Kaptchuk, Eastland Press, Inc., 1986.

Rowland, D.L., et al. "A review of plant-derived and herbal approaches to the treatment of sexual dysfunctions." *J. Sex. Marital Ther.* 2003 May–Jun; 29(3):185–205.

New England Journal of Medicine, 2/2006

Wilt T.J., et al (1998). "Saw palmetto extracts for treatment of benign prostatic hyperplasia: a systematic review." *JAMA* 280:1604–1609.

Bent, S., et al (2006). "Saw palmetto for benign prostatic hyperplasia." *NEJM* 354:557–566.

McPartland, J.M., Pruitt P.L. (2000). "Benign prostatic hyperplasia treated with saw palmetto: a literature search and an experimental case study." *JAOA* 100(2):89–96.

Di Silverio, F., et. al (1998). "Effects of long-term treatment with Serenoa repens (Permixon) on the concentrations and regional distribution of androgens, and epidermal growth factor in benign prostatic hyperplasia." *Prostate* 37(2):77–83.

Plosker, G.L., Brogden, R.N. (1996). "Serenoa repens (Permixon). A review of its pharmacology and therapeutic efficacy in benign prostatic hyperplasia." *Drugs Aging* 9(5):379–95.

David Winston (1999). *Saw Palmetto for Men & Women: Herbal Healing for the Prostate, Urinary Tract, Immune System and More* (Medicinal Herb Guide). Storey Publishing, LLC. ISBN 978-1580172066.

Saw palmetto. Natural Medicines Comprehensive Database Web Site. Accessed March 30, 2006.

Saw palmetto (Serenoa repens [Bartran] Small). Natural Standard Database Web Site. Accessed March 30, 2006.

Saw palmetto (Serenoa repens). Coates, P., Blackman, M., Cragg, G., et al, eds. *Encyclopedia of Dietary Supplements.* New York, NY: Marcel Dekker, 2005; 635–644.

De Smet, P.A., "Herbal remedies." *New England Journal of Medicine.* 2002; 347(25):2046–2056

National Cancer Institute. "The Prostate-Specific Antigen (PSA) Test: Questions and Answers."

Bent, S., Kane, C., Shinohara, K., et al. "Saw palmetto for benign prostatic hyperplasia." *New England Journal of Medicine.* 2006; 354(6):557–566.

Barlet, A., Albrecht, J., Aubert, A., et al. "Efficacy of Pygeum africanum extract in the medical therapy of urination disorders due to benign prostatic hyperplasia: evaluation of objective and subjective parameters. A placebo-controlled double-blind multicenter study." *Wien Klin Wochenschr* 11-23-1990; 102(22):667–673.

Bassi, P., Artibani, W., De Luca, V., et al. "Standardized extract of Pygeum africanum in the treatment of benign prostatic hypertrophy. Controlled clinical study versus placebo." *Minerva Urol. Nefrol.* 1987; 39(1):45–50.

Berges, R.R., Windeler, J., Trampisch, H.J., et al. Randomised, placebo-controlled, double-blind clinical trial of beta-sitosterol in patients with benign prostatic hyperplasia. "Beta-sitosterol Study Group. *Lancet* 6-17-1995; 345(8964):1529–1532.

Brackman, F., Autet, W. "Once and twice daily dosage regimens of Pygeum africanum extract (PA): a double-blind study in patients with benign prostatic hyperplasia (BPH) [abstract]. *J Urology* 1999; 161(4S):361.

Breza, J., Dzurny, O., Borowka, A., et al. "Efficacy and acceptability of tadenan (Pygeum africanum extract) in the treatment of benign prostatic hyperplasia (BPH): a multicentre trial in central Europe." *Curr Med Res Opin* 1998; 14(3):127–139.

Liu, C.X., Xiao, P.G. (1992). "Recent advances on ginseng research in China." *Journal of Ethnopharmacology*, 36(1): 27–38.

Liu, J., Wang, S., Liu, H., Nan, G. (1995). "Stimulatory effect of saponin from Panax ginseng on immune function of lymphocytes in the elderly." *Mechanisms of Aging & Development*, 83(1): 43–53.

Van Schepdael, P. (1993). "Effect of Ginseng G115 on the physical condition of triathletes." *Acta Therapeutica.*

Notes: